RACE

John Howard and
the remaking of Australia

ANDREW MARKUS

Allen & Unwin

First published in 2001

Allen & Unwin
83 Alexander Street
Crows Nest NSW 2065
Australia
Phone: (61 2) 8425 0100
Fax: (61 2) 9906 2218
Email: frontdesk@allen-unwin.com.au
Web: http://www.allenandunwin.com

National Library of Australia
Cataloguing-in-Publication entry:

Markus, Andrew.
    Race: John Howard and the remaking of Australia.

    Bibliography.
    Includes index.

    ISBN 1 86448 866 2

    1. Racism—Australia—History. 2. Australia—Race relations. 3. Australia—
    Emigration and immigration—History. I. Title.

305.800 994.

Set in 11/13 pt Adobe Garamond by Midland Typesetters, Maryborough
Maps drawn by Tony Fankhauser
Printed by SRM Production Services SDN BHD, Malaysia

10 9 8 7 6 5 4 3 2 1

Contents

List of tables and figures vi
Acknowledgements viii
Introduction ix

PART 1 CONTEXT
1 The racial imagination 3
2 Change in post-war Australia 11

PART 2 STYLE
3 The new conservatism and the naturalness of bigotry 49
4 John Howard, Leader of the Opposition, Prime Minister 82
5 The politics of paranoia 113
6 Pauline Hanson's One Nation 143

PART 3 MEANING
7 Interpretations 199
8 The role of chance in national life 222

Appendix 1: Immigration intake 226
Appendix 2: Confederate Action Party and
                One Nation policies compared 228
Appendix 3: The electoral fortunes of One Nation 230
Sources 256
Select bibliography 263
Index 266

List of tables and figures

TABLES

2.1   Federal government objectives, 1945–95   13

2.2   Components of population growth   16

2.3   Galbally Report 1978—cost of recommendations (over three years) incurring extra expenditure   28

2.4   Aboriginal land tenure—States/Territories ranked in order of total population   35

4.1   Content analysis of the use of the phrase 'political correctness' in major daily newspapers   98

6.1   Vote, 1996 federal election—seat of Oxley   152

6.2   Five most talked about people of 1996—New South Wales   159

6.3   What made news, 1997–98—radio and television—Australia   159

6.4   One Nation budget statement   183

6.5   One Nation vote, June 1998–March 1999   184

7.1   Support for Hanson-led party/One Nation—Australia   206

7.2   Attitude to annual immigration intake   208

7.3   Attitude to Asian immigration   209

7.4   'How much are federal and state governments doing for Aborigines?'   210

7.5   'Should Aborigines have different land rights to other Australians?'   211

7.6   'Do you approve of the Mabo case decision?'   212

7.7   Ranking of issues—respondents indicating that the issue is 'very important'   213

7.8 Polls compared—views on government assistance to
    Aborigines, 1981 and One Nation Senate vote, 1998   216
7.9 Queensland elections, 1986 and 1998   217
7.10 Queensland state elections—vote for major parties   218

FIGURES

2.1 Settler arrivals, 1950–97   15
2.2 Levels of immigration and unemployment   24
2.3 Immigration intake, 1972–97—component from
    Asian countries   25
2.4 Immigration program outcomes—key components   32
7.1 Ranking of issues   214

Acknowledgements

I gratefully acknowledge the support of Monash University and a number of individuals without whom this book would not have been completed. I want in particular to thank the research assistance of Fiona Graham, Julie Burbidge and Esther Faye. Ian Jackson provided assistance with statistical analysis of election results. Bain Attwood, Esther Faye, Bob Birrell, John Iremonger and anonymous readers provided invaluable critical comment at various stages of the manuscript's development. Monash University provided research funds and the time to enable completion of the first draft of this book.

Introduction

*I*n Australia in the late 1960s there emerged a willingness to accept a more complex structuring of society and a broader tolerance of diversity, in contrast with the one-dimensional value system which characterised the Cold War. The policy of assimilation, which equated citizenship with adherence to the uniform values of a supposed 'Australian way of life', gave way to the rhetoric of self-determination and multiculturalism. The 'White Australia' policy, one of the founding principles of the commonwealth, was abandoned. Federal legislation to outlaw racial discrimination was passed in 1975 and the first substantive land rights measure in the following year. Throughout this period of change bipartisan agreement on fundamentals characterised the approach to Aboriginal and immigration policy. This approach survived, despite times of considerable tension, until 1996 when it was decisively repudiated by the newly elected Howard government.

Criticism of the policies adopted in the 1970s made its first substantial national impact in 1983, during the mining industry's campaign to defeat proposed land rights legislation. This opposition later broadened to include attacks upon so-called special benefits for minorities, immigration policy that no longer favoured the United Kingdom and Ireland, and multiculturalism. Episodes of fierce public debate erupted in 1984, 1988 and 1993, and for considerable periods of time between 1996 and 2000.

The 1996 election saw the victory of two independents who campaigned heavily on racial issues, Pauline Hanson in Queensland and Graeme Campbell in Western Australia. Hanson soon eclipsed her more experienced colleague and following her maiden speech, parts of which were seen to be endorsed by Prime Minister Howard, she became the second most talked about politician in the land. Month after month the headlines of national newspapers were dominated by discussion of native title and to a lesser extent immigration. Talkback radio, particularly in Sydney and Perth, proved the favoured forum for the voicing of intolerant and bigoted views.

How did this change, in part a return to the political agenda of the pre-war period, come about? It is the argument of this book that the mounting level of disputation over racial issues is in part explained by the willingness of a major political grouping to take advantage of, and accentuate, dissatisfaction with new policies. It is argued that the 1980s witnessed a resurgence of conservatism, significant elements of which aligned themselves with the traditions of Australian race-based nationalism while at the same time advocating the potentially contradictory policies of economic rationalism and globalism.

The conservative campaign sought acceptance for the return to an old ordering of national priorities, an old way of seeing and speaking. Its major themes were concerned with the folly of existing government policy, represented as a betrayal of the national interest and an appeasement of minorities. In opposition to pluralism and multiculturalism there was advocacy of full equality of all citizens before the law. Through such policy the national unity which supposedly characterised the nation's past would be reclaimed, Australia would again become 'one nation'.

The ideal of 'equal rights' has been of great power in Australian politics and was central to the campaign to re-shape the political culture. This book explores the shaping of perceptions, the process whereby some approaches to the problems facing society are defined as 'ideological' and 'sectional' while others come to be accepted as representing the national interest, as 'common sense' and hence not open to question. Effective positioning of arguments is achieved when they are presented—and accepted—as of universal applicability, avoiding identification with 'minority' interests.

There are few better illustrations of the way contestable perception becomes 'common sense' than the use made of the argument that governments should treat all equally, in the slogan adopted by the mining industry that 'land rights should be equal rights'.

In the 1950s and 1960s a liberal value system gained primacy which promised to overcome racial discrimination by according all the same civil and political rights. The 'colour blind' state would free Aboriginal people from the provisions of discriminatory 'protectionist' laws and accord them the same political rights as other Australians; racial criteria would be removed from the operation of immigration laws.

Within this value system there was almost no scope for minority rights. The state could tolerate but not welcome, certainly not foster, separatist development. It was not the role of the state to give consideration in policy to the rights of ethnic or racial groups, just as it supposedly did not accord one religious group privileges denied to others. Programs to benefit a specific group could only be approved, if at all, as temporary expedients, to be terminated at the first opportunity. Its advocates saw this approach to ethnicity as the only viable option, the only chance to overcome the problem of discrimination.

The proposed alternative, the entrenching of minority rights, was seen as a recipe for disaster, a return to the era of racial discrimination with but one difference—some shifting of categories, with groups previously denied rights now on the receiving end of the benefits of discrimination. The long-term impact of such an approach would, it was predicted, lead to the disintegration of the state into warring camps fighting over an ever dwindling national wealth.

The equal rights position is able to marshal powerful arguments, but is not the only tenable position, at its advocates believe. It can be argued that it is based on an understanding of government that is more in the realm of fantasy than reality. Far from treating all as equals government policy invariably favours one section of the population over another, as in, to take one example, the application of a means test to grant or deny welfare benefits. Contrary to political rhetoric, there is now wide recognition that the taxation system provides opportunities for tax minimisation so that some earning over a million dollars pay less income tax than others earning $50 000. All are equal before the law, but those who can afford the best legal representation are more equal than the rest. Similar examples could be taken from the education and health care systems.

Thus 'equal rights' in most spheres of life operates at best at a superficial or formal level rather than being indicative of substantive reality. Far from treating all equally, it is in the nature of government policy to favour minorities. Further, the idea that application of universal laws necessarily produces optimum outcomes is brought into question when it is recognised that the laws are applied to social groups in grossly unequal positions.

A second form of argument is more openly duplicitous: advocates of 'equal rights' not uncommonly engage in a form of 'double-speak' through which they advocate contradictory positions almost in the same breath. 'Equal rights' becomes transformed into 'equal rights' for 'our group'. Consider the issue of Aboriginal land rights. Aboriginal people have the right to pursue claims before the courts, as do all other Australians, and it is in the nature of the legal system that decisions favour some litigants over others, that some win and some lose. But when Aboriginal Australians achieved decisions in their favour in the Mabo and Wik cases, based on the cherished traditions of the common law, there was outrage at what was depicted as the unequal application of the law, the unfair favouring of one group. Fault lay with the umpires, the judges. Foul play had occurred. No recognition was accorded to the plaintiffs and the skill of their advocates, although some of those most outraged had only a few years earlier fêted barristers who used the very same common law to upset received wisdom in a case on the rights of unions and employers.

Similarly, those objecting to 'special' benefits for others seem to be blind to situations in which they themselves are recipients of 'special' benefits. It was a feature of the politics of the late 1990s that those objecting to 'special' benefits for indigenous Australians and funding of the multicultural 'industry' demanded assistance for the group with which they identified, for example assistance for rural communities and manufacturing industries. The demand for 'equal rights' existed alongside a valuation of 'us' as worthy of government attention and 'them' as unworthy, while the advocates of 'equal rights' continued to deny that there were contradictions in their reasoning.

An intrinsic element in political advocacy is a capacity not to see—to misinterpret in the act of interpretation, to delude self, to deny informed understanding of other cultures. Thus the slogan 'land rights should be equal rights', audacious in its socialist radicalism, could be mouthed by millionaire miners and landowners with but few noticing the cut of the emperor's clothes.

The experience of the last decades has demonstrated that policies of 'equal rights' can yield outcomes not significantly different to the racial discrimination of an earlier time: policies to favour 'my group', disallowing gains by Aboriginal people at 'our' expense; if the law or interpretation of the law favours 'them', demanded the advocates of equal rights, change the law, change the judges. Such has been the power of persuasion, of ways of reasoning and speaking, that contradictory positions were placed before a public which in general found itself unable to discern the spurious nature of arguments and was convinced that 'common sense', not greed or prejudice, dictated the logic of the 'equal rights' position.

Like the alchemist who pretends to transform base metal into gold, in Australia's liberal democracy the equal rights advocate transforms questionable arguments into ones of seeming universal validity, with public opinion polls consistently showing that 70 per cent or more favour the ideal of equal rights over specific policies to 'favour minorities'.

––––––––

The subject of this book is 'race politics', a term requiring definition. It is my argument that there is a difference between raising of racial issues and the practice of 'race politics', distinguished by four elements. First, race politics is concerned with difference defined in terms of 'racial' or 'ethnic' attributes, rather than, for example, 'class' or 'gender'. Second, in the ranking of issues, 'race' is accorded major significance, it is a 'first order' issue. Third, racial issues are presented not in isolation but as a critical component of the challenges facing the country, integral to its future development and national identity. Last, practitioners of race politics identify themselves and their parties through the prominence they give to racial issues.

Race politics is practised in varying contexts: attempts by minorities to establish specific rights and a distinct relationship with government can be a form of race politics. The form of race politics which is the particular focus of this book involves attempts by groups to persuade government to resolve racial problems through the elimination of difference, by either exclusion (involving limitation of the right of entry through immigration) and/or absorption of minorities through assimilation, entailing removal of the group's distinguishing characteristics and denial of its claims for a special relationship with government.

This book charts the development of a critical way of reasoning and speaking about Aboriginal and immigration policies from the early 1980s to the present day. It deals in part with developments evident throughout western culture. There are, however, uniquely Australian elements, shaped by national traditions and by the distinctive conjunction of issues (particularly indigenous rights and immigration), the political struggles and agendas of major political parties, and the talents and capacities of individuals who emerged into position of political leadership.

The book aims to explore the nature and impact in Australia of the conservative mobilisation of the late twentieth century. The first part seeks to provide a context by examining developments in racial thought and government policy over the last 50 years. The book's second, substantive part, deals with the New Right, the positioning of the Liberal Party, the political fringe, and the phenomenon of

Hansonism. The last part considers the explanations which have been given for the re-emergence of the politics of race and with the role of chance—the 'what if' of history.

The role of John Howard is central to this study. Howard was at the forefront in mediating the political response to what he and other conservatives defined as the 'remaking' of Australia following the Menzies era; he has exercised a key role in setting Liberal policy since 1985 and, since 1996, in implementing the long-term strategy to remake Australia along different lines. In particular, Howard has been instrumental in determining the role of race politics within the unfolding Liberal agenda.

Race is an individual's attempt to make sense of, and interpret, a complex social reality. It presents an argument and the reading of evidence on which it is based. There is no pretence to be value free, which history—whether in narrative or other form—can never be. Its claims are rather to present the results of years spent researching and grappling with explanation. It is written in recognition that significant problems face Australian society, not least the issues of Aboriginal rights, immigration policy and policing of borders, from the vantage point of one who has yet to find evidence that simplistic, populist attempts to sway public opinion and foster race-based nationalism contribute significantly in the long term to the well-being of a society.

PART 1

CONTEXT

1

The racial imagination

An understanding of the concept of racism—or rather of its range of possible meanings—is an essential first-step for any study of race politics. The following discussion will explore areas treated with little understanding in public discussion: the battle which takes place over definitions and the political significance of their outcomes; the core ideas of racial thought and their varying manifestations; the currently dominant form of culturalist racism to be found in western societies; and the need to distinguish between form and substance in evaluation of political argument.

FROM BIOLOGICAL TO CULTURAL DETERMINISM

It is truly said that racism is a term much used but little understood. In Australian politics it has become an epithet to be thrown at one's opponents. 'This politician is a racist', scream the opponents. 'No, she is a believer in racial equality', affirm the defenders—'it is her opponents who are racist, it is the policies which advantage one group of people over another which are racist'.

In the context of political debate the power to define is a strong weapon: a specific argument may be seen as moderate or extreme, depending on the definition (or filter) that is applied. Neither academics nor politicians are in agreement over the meaning of 'racism': the choice of one definition over another is determined less by some form of abstract, value neutral reasoning and more by political exigencies and the needs of specific social groups. Some definitions are so narrow as to exclude all but the most extreme actions, others so broad as to encompass nearly all forms of human behaviour, including policies both of exclusion and inclusion. An examination of the history of racial thought helps us to understand the meanings which may be given to 'racism'.

The modern form of racial thought was developed in the second half of the nineteenth century. At that time racial beliefs focused on populations supposedly biologically distinct, called 'races', whose genetic inheritance determined both the appearance and behaviour of its members. Race, a genetic attribute, was seen as the most important defining characteristic of a human being. Race shaped the individual's values and the racial group's destiny.

Put at its most basic, this form of racial belief saw culture as a function of biology. It held that 'capacity for civilisation', loyalty to the nation and morality were as inescapably linked to racial origin as skin colour, hair type and eye shape. Thus the behavioural characteristics of a people were passed genetically from one generation to the next. To use the terminology of our own age, the racist believed that the behaviour of humans was 'programmed', imprinted on the mind at birth. The character of a people changed as a consequence of racial admixture which altered the gene pool, not as a result of social processes. Where genetic stock was kept 'pure' the character of the 'race' remained constant from one generation to the next; where it was 'tainted' the race and its way of life died out.

A variant of this belief system, not specifically concerned with 'race' (described by some academics as 'racism without races'), placed its emphasis on the culture of national groups. From the late nineteenth century there developed alongside the genetic conceptualisation of peoplehood a variant best labelled 'culturalism'.

Those adhering to 'culturalist' beliefs concerned themselves with the transmission of distinctive cultural values from one generation to the next. The dominant theme was 'not biological heredity but the insurmountability of cultural differences'.

Each distinctive national group was held to possess its own culture, grounded in history and myth, language and literature, customs and physical environment. Individuals born into a culture supposedly took on its character, partly through socialisation but also through some processes difficult to explain in rational terms but no less significant. It was asserted, in reaction to the spread of logic and reason that not everything could be explained in rational terms: beyond the bounds of rationality there was the soul of a people, 'instinctive' and 'innate' human drives. Through some mysterious process a sense of oneness and belonging was transmitted over time, from generation to generation.

Both genetic and culturalist thought converged in their determinism, the idea that there was a necessary or invariable relationship between inherited characteristics and behaviour. It was held that there was no scope for individuals born into a distinctive racial or cultural group to cross boundaries—to change categories—and become full members of another racial or cultural group. In the past such ideas were almost invariably linked to notions of superiority and inferiority, to the notion that 'my' group was better than 'yours', but the bedrock of the racist or culturalist idea is not the claim of superiority; rather, it is the belief in the existence of distinctive human populations with a timeless character and the impossibility for an individual to become assimilated into a group different from the one into which he or she was born. It is this idea that justifies discrimination.

Both racism and culturalism maintain that: (i) as a result of some (undefined) 'natural' process, national groups (or 'races' or 'cultures') have inborn ('essential') qualities which will never alter; and (ii) there are inherent characteristics in such groups which interpose barriers against harmonious co-existence, not least against inter-breeding of populations. Such ideas give rise to closed forms of nationalism which restrict membership to those qualified by birth or descent, in contrast to open forms which grant citizenship to individuals on the basis of residence and adherence to the governing principles of the nation. They justified European colonial rule; the denial of basic human rights and citizenship; segregation in the workplace, housing and education; and policies of genocide culminating in the 'factories of death' established in the period of Nazi domination of continental Europe.

Rarely challenged in western societies prior to 1940, the idea of biological racial difference lost much of its legitimacy in the aftermath of the Holocaust. The United Nations (UN), established in 1945, enshrined the principle of racial equality in its Declaration of Human Rights. Adopted in 1948, it set forth the principle that:

> All human beings are born free and equal in dignity and rights . . . Everyone is entitled to all the rights and freedoms set forth in this Declaration, without distinction of any kind, such as race, colour, sex, language, religion, political or other opinion, national or social origin, property, birth or other status . . .

Through one of its agencies, the United Nations Educational, Scientific and Cultural Organization (UNESCO), the UN embarked on a program of education to counter racism. Between 1949 and 1951 UNESCO sponsored meetings of academic experts aimed at producing an authoritative statement on race. The first meeting, whose findings were published in 1950, concluded that:

> According to present knowledge there is no proof that the groups of mankind differ in their innate mental characteristics, whether in respect of intelligence or temperament. The scientific evidence indicates that the range of mental capacities in all ethnic groups is much the same . . . All normal human beings

are capable of learning to share a common life, to understand the nature of mutual service and reciprocity, and to respect social obligations and contracts. Such biological differences as exist between members of different ethnic groups have no relevance to problems of social and political organization, moral life and communication between human beings.

Such views became standard within schools and universities and provided the intellectual basis for campaigns against racial discrimination in the late 1950s and 1960s: against, for example, segregationist policies in parts of the United States depriving Afro-Americans of the vote and of equality in education, employment and housing. The movement against institutional racism assumed immediate significance in the context of the Cold War as Soviet Russia sought to use evidence of racial discrimination to discredit American capitalism and democracy. By the mid-1960s much had been achieved in the removal of overt discrimination in the western world, with the major exception of South Africa whose segregationist policies were almost uniformly condemned.

Yet exclusivist ideas continued to be maintained, or to be revived in new forms, particularly in the context of opposition to immigration. In the post-war world exclusivist ideas were almost uniformly presented in their culturalist form, with the exception of neo-Nazi and other extremist movements which continued to avow explicitly racial beliefs, proudly proclaiming their White or Aryan superiority.

Britain in the 1960s saw the development of a culturalist mode of thought and expression which sought to avoid claims of superiority while maintaining that there were 'natural' barriers to the intermingling of different national groups. Advocates of discrimination emphasised the unique culture of peoples and the supposed instinct for self-preservation, an allegedly intrinsic human characteristic to exclude the alien, the outsider who, by his or her entry and presence, threatens a people's 'way of life'. It was held to be a natural, fundamental characteristic of humans to form 'a bounded community, a nation, aware of its differences from other nations'. Xenophobia, the dislike of foreigners, was asserted to be a 'natural' human trait. In speeches in 1968 and 1969 the conservative English politician Enoch Powell, whilst leading the movement against immigration from Pakistan and the Caribbean, the so-called 'new commonwealth', stated that:

An instinct to preserve an identity and defend a territory is one of the deepest and strongest implanted in mankind ... I do not believe it is in human nature that a country, and a country such as ours, should passively watch the transformation of whole areas which lie at the heart of it into alien territory.

In a similar manner, Desmond Morris, author of the bestselling *The Naked Ape* based on the study of similarities in animal and human behaviour, wrote:

Biologically speaking, man has the inborn task of defending three things: himself, his family and his tribe ... The fundamental similarities between any one man and any other are enormous. One of these, paradoxically, is the tendency to form distinct groups and to feel that you are somehow different, really deep-down different, from members of other groups.

Such ideas legitimise the view that it is futile to question the logic or reasonableness of opposition to immigration; it is necessary to accommodate policy to 'natural' and unchangeable human characteristics, the genuine feelings of the common man. The advocacy of such a position is not racism, in the frequently quoted remark of the conservative British politician Ivor Stanbrook it is 'simply human nature'.

This mode of thought is now common to a number of western countries, its keywords the glorification of the nation, calls for unity, opposition to 'minorities', demands for government to listen to the masses, for 'balance' in policy and for all to be treated as 'equals'. The nationalist rhetoric urges pride in history and culture and contrasts sense of self-worth with negative valuation of 'minorities' or 'outsiders'—immigrants, for example, are seen as threatening the host society with overpopulation, unemployment, and their unacceptable cultural practices. Although 'outsiders' are always presented negatively, coded and other forms of indirect denigration take the place of overt racial references. Central to this mode of thought is its intolerance of diversity, its unwillingness to seek understanding of other cultures on their own terms, its insistence on a unitary culture in opposition to pluralism and multiculturalism, and its presentation of complex issues as simple and one-dimensional. Emphasis is placed on a distinction between majorities and minorities, between the people and political elites, between national and sectional interests, between the one path and a multiplicity of paths. In some contexts there is a demand for exclusion of foreign elements, in others, often with a degree of inconsistency given the denigration which is part of this mode of thought, a demand for government policies which are 'balanced', which serve the national good, which do not favour one section over another but treat all as 'equals'.

POPULAR UNDERSTANDINGS

While academic analysis of the development of racial thought enables us to understand its range of meanings and changing character, this knowledge has made little or no impact on popular discussion. The label 'racist' is frequently used in contemporary politics, but its meaning is assumed, little examined.

Racism continues to be understood in terms of acts of violence and hatred, in large part its meaning derived from historical association. The racists in history are identified, enumerated. The prime example is Hitler's policy of genocide, followed by the hooded

Ku Klux Klan and the apartheid regime of South Africa. The imagery of racism is of the concentration camp, of lynchings and burning crosses, of segregated park benches bearing the inscription 'Whites Only', of snarling dogs and shotgun-wielding police. As such, meaning is anchored in acts of physical violence—beatings, random killings, genocide—motivated by bigotry and hatred.

Given this frame of reference, there is resistance to the idea that a person adopting a moderate tone, disclaiming any pretence to superiority and bigotry, and defending 'common sense' propositions, can reasonably be labelled racist, irrespective of the substance of the position adopted. Such understanding confuses demeanour with meaning, tone with substance, and avoids consideration of essential elements at the heart of the racial value system, including emphasis on the 'one truth', 'instinctive' and 'innate' human characteristics, a wilful blindness to other cultures and intolerance of diversity.

2

Change in post-war Australia

There has been significant change, some would argue of revolutionary proportions, in the size and composition of the Australian population over the last half of the twentieth century. Between 1947 and 1999 the total population more than doubled, increasing from 7.59 to 18.97 million. Although of lesser significance than natural increase, immigration has been a major contributor to this growth. In 1997 23 per cent of the population was born overseas (up from 10 per cent in 1947) and an additional 27 per cent had at least one overseas born parent—thus fully one-half of the population at the end of the century was either overseas born or the offspring of at least one first-generation immigrant. By the 1980s Australia had the largest migrant intake per head of population after Israel.

Further, the ethnic composition of the population changed markedly. The population identifying as Aboriginal increased from 87 000 or 1.15 per cent of the total in 1947 to 386 000 or 2.08 per cent in 1996. In the same period among the overseas born the proportion from the main English-speaking countries declined sharply: from 81 per cent in 1947 to 39 per cent in 1997. Successive waves of immigrants, first from southern and eastern Europe, then from various Asian countries, lessened the preponderance from the

United Kingdom and Ireland. In the post-war period there has been an equally significant shift in domestic government policy. Assimilation gave way to policies of 'self-determination' and 'multiculturalism'. From the 1970s onwards a range of policies made available for the first time programs specifically targeted for non-Anglo minority groups. The purpose of this chapter is to chart these developments, which by the early 1980s had produced a reaction from individuals and groups who identified themselves as Australian nationalists. The broad pattern of policy change, necessarily simplified, is summarised in Table 2.1.

At the mid-point of the twentieth century the Australian state unambiguously practised a policy of racial discrimination and exclusivity. Commonwealth and state legislation, differing to some extent on a regional basis, deprived Aboriginal people of basic human freedoms, the right to participate in the political process, and equal education and welfare benefits. Arbitration Court determinations withheld equal pay. A racially based immigration policy favoured the entry of British and other 'Aryan' or 'Nordic' people; immigrants from southern and eastern Europe were regarded as second best, their immigration encouraged only when quotas could not be filled from northern Europe, and non-European and other dark-skinned people were denied entry. Changes occurred in the aftermath of World War II but for twenty or more years after 1945 the dominant view was that Anglo-Australian institutions and values were sacrosanct and unchangeable—the previously excluded who now gained entry to Australian society would assimilate, not modify what was termed the 'Australian way of life'.

In the 1950s there were significant shifts in policy towards some groups regarded as racially undesirable prior to the war: this was evident in the gradual removal of overt racial discrimination against Aborigines and the admission of large numbers of non-Anglo-Celtic peoples.

Table 2.1 Federal government objectives, 1945–95

Period	*Policy Area*		
	Aboriginal	*Immigration*	*Settlement (policy towards immigrants after their arrival in Australia)*
1950s	Assimilation.	Large scale immigration intakes. Racially discriminatory policy.	Assimilation.
1960s	Modified assimilation.	Continuing focus on large scale immigration. Limited racial discrimination.	Modified assimilation.
1970s	To significantly improve health, housing, employment and educational attainment. 'Self-determination' and 'self-management' (described by Aboriginal critics as 'welfarism', little different from assimilation); land rights in the Northern Territory.	Less emphasis on large scale immigration. Formal end to racial discrimination.	'Family of the nation'; 'multiculturalism'. Right of cultural maintenance.
1980s–95	As above. Wider significance of land rights. Goal of reconciliation.	Fluctuation in selection criteria and immigration targets. Substantive end to racial discimination.	'Multiculturalism'— changed meaning of the term over time.'Access and equity'.

THE ERA OF ASSIMILATION

Immigration

The new thinking made its first impact in immigration policy, resulting in the recruitment of large numbers of immigrants from continental Europe. There was no period of gradual transition as the new pattern was established within three years of the war's end. Whereas in the first half of the century close to 80 per cent of immigrants had come from the United Kingdom, in the years 1947–51 immigrants from the United Kingdom constituted under 40 per cent of the total and from 1951–61 they numbered just 30 per cent, below the proportion from southern Europe.

The idea that a much wider group of people could become part of Australian society, could come to share the 'Australian way of life', marked a major shift in Australian history, a break with the ideas of racial determinism and exclusivity. The change to policy regulating immigration from Europe was essentially the product of pragmatism; in the aftermath of World War II it was driven by the need to provide labour for economic development and the perceived need to boost population to increase the country's defence capability. These requirements led to the greatest period of sustained immigration in Australian history (see Figure 2.1), an annual population growth from immigration of over 1 per cent, with a peak in the late 1960s. The post-war decades also witnessed a significant increase in the rate of natural increase, leading to a population growth of over 2 per cent per annum for more than 25 years after the war, almost double the rate of the 1990s (see Table 2.2).

The range of people who were encouraged to enter or who became acceptable was widened, but the notion that this might lead to a major shift in the dominant value system was firmly resisted. The goal of maintaining what was perceived to be a monoculture was pursued with even greater vigour than in the past. While the more favoured groups could be left to make their own way, a more conscious effort was required to ensure the assimilation of the newly

Figure 2.1 Settler arrivals, 1950–97

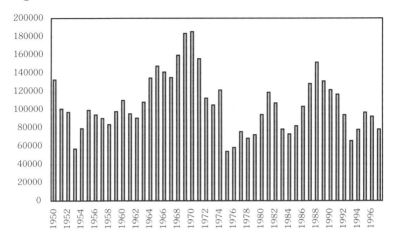

admitted low status groups. Two dangers were perceived: first, that newcomers might form separate communities within the nation— foreign bodies in the flesh of the nation; second, by sheer weight of numbers they might significantly alter the Australian national character and outlook in the course of time.

Assimilationist ideas were based on the notion that the superior Anglo-Australian institutions and values would remain unchanged. All were agreed, according to immigration minister Harold Holt in 1952, 'that Australia must be kept preponderantly British in its institutions and the composition of its people'. Immigrants were 'offered much'; in return they were being asked to 'become Australian'. There would not be a two-way process of adaptation: accommodation would be made by those who were, in the words of Governor-General Sir William McKell, 'deemed worthy to share in our Australian heritage', those given the chance to enter a superior culture and way of life.

There would be no special assistance, no targeted programs to assist immigrants which might act as an impediment to assimilation;

Table 2.2 Components of population growth (annual average)

Period	Natural increase	Net overseas migration	Total increase
1947–60	1.47	1.04	2.34
1960–69	1.23	0.83	1.99
1970–79	1.02	0.51	1.64
1980–89	0.83	0.72	1.49
1990–97	0.76	0.43	1.18

Source: T. Skinner, Australian Demographic Trends 1997, p.1.
Australia Now, Population Growth and Components of Growth, 1999.

it was up to the individual to assimilate and failure to do so indicated individual inadequacy, not failure of policy. A prime requirement was the abandonment of the immigrant's previous culture and language. Migrants (and Aborigines) were discouraged from making their homes in 'enclaves' and forming their own organisations; assimilation required that they merge themselves into the mainstream of Australian life and assume a new identity.

A major shift in policy was, however, to occur in the second half of the 1960s, in response to a range of factors. First, in the context of booming European economies it was becoming more difficult to attract European immigrants to Australia and to ensure that once here they stayed; as a result, governments felt pressure to be more accommodating and less arrogant in their treatment of immigrants. Second, given Australia's international needs and obligations it was realised that discrimination in immigration policy and in the treatment of Aboriginal people was no longer tenable. Of particular significance were Australia's developing trade and other contacts with Asian nations and the role of the United Nations in providing a forum for denunciation of racist practices. Overt racially discriminatory laws were repealed in most countries, including the United States, Canada and New Zealand. In this context, if racially discriminatory policies were maintained

Australia would, like South Africa, become a pariah in the international community.

Critics within Australia lobbied for reform and by the early 1960s opinion polls showed that only a minority continued to support a racially exclusive immigration policy. This time of growing pressure on government coincided with a generational shift in political life: Menzies and Calwell, who had staunchly defended racial discrimination, retired, to be replaced by a new generation of leaders, Holt, Gorton, Whitlam and Dunstan, convinced on the grounds of both principle and expediency of the need for change.

In settlement policy—the policy determining the treatment of immigrants after arrival—the goal of assimilation was replaced with formulations based on 'integration', although in practice change was limited. It was now accepted that complete assimilation might not be achieved in the first generation, but assimilation remained the long-term objective. As late as 1969 Bill Snedden, the minister for immigration, while stating that 'integration implies and requires a willingness on the part of the community to move towards the migrant, just as it requires the migrant to move to the community', was adamant that Australia must remain a monoculture: 'we must have a single culture. Those of different ethnic origin must integrate and unite into our own community so that it will become a single Australian community'. Potential immigrants in the United Kingdom were informed, with more openness than was displayed by immigration officials on the continent, that 'we are essentially a British nation with British ways and traditions, and we want to keep it that way'.

Despite ties to 'British ways and traditions', the government was forced in its quest to meet numerical targets, which in the late 1960s reached the highest levels in Australia's history, to extend its recruitment in southern Europe and to the Middle East and to provide more assisted passages to low status immigrants, to provide better on-arrival housing, more welfare assistance, and to recognise the right of cultural maintenance. The nature of concessions required to be made to attract immigrants is indicated by an agreement signed with Turkey in 1967 which stipulated that the Australian government would work to ensure that children received instruction in the Turkish language and would bring to the attention of employers the need to respect Muslim religious holidays. In 1971 an address by the minister for immigration made clear that in the fiercely competitive market for immigrants it was incumbent upon Australia to 'improve . . . the range and content of what we offer prospective immigrants'.

It was also at this time that the 'White Australia' policy was finally abandoned. While there had been a number of minor modifications to immigration policy over the previous ten years, including the right of entry of spouses irrespective of race and the granting of naturalisation to non-Europeans after fifteen years of residence, it was not until 1966 that substantive changes to the policy were implemented. Within months of the retirement of Prime Minister Menzies non-Europeans became eligible, for the first time since 1901, for permanent settlement, although on discriminatory terms—right of entry was restricted to those with skills in designated occupations, they were narrowly limited in the category of relatives they could nominate for entry and there was practically no chance that they would receive assisted passages. The changes to admission criteria were explained to parliament and discussed without dissent. There was no need for amending legislation; the *Immigration Restriction Act* of 1901 had not specified the groups to be excluded, leaving that decision to the discretion of the minister. In 1966 it was only necessary for the minister to provide new instructions to immigration officials.

Aboriginal policies

In the first half of the twentieth century the dominant assumption in government had been that Aboriginal people would die out, that they had no future in Australian society. In most parts of the country Aboriginal people were excluded from the mainstream and in remote regions polices of calculated neglect did little to alleviate the plight of those designated for extinction. The rationale of such policies began to change in the late 1930s, and after World War II it was accepted that Aboriginal people would survive and in the long term become assimilated. By 1965 assimilation policy for the Aboriginal people was entrenched, as it was in settlement policy. The aim of official policy was that all persons of Aboriginal descent would 'choose to attain a similar manner and standard of living to that of other Australians and live as members of a single Australian community—enjoying the same rights and privileges, accepting the same responsibilities and influenced by the same hopes and loyalties as other Australians'. Although white society was gradually opening the doors to admission, on its own terms, not all Aboriginal people were convinced that this was the path they wished to follow and criticism of assimilation mounted in the second half of the 1960s.

The social welfare legislation enacted in the 1940s by the co-alition and Labor governments no longer imposed a total exclusion on the basis of race; henceforth Aboriginal people could obtain equal rights if they independently supported themselves in the white community. Such measures, however, at first only affected a minority. Entitlement to pensions, unemployment, and mater-nity allowances was granted in 1959 to all Aboriginal people except those classed 'nomadic or primitive', and in 1966 this final dis-crimination was deleted. The discrimination in the right to vote in federal elections was repealed in 1962.

While the commonwealth controlled key welfare entitlements, until the early 1970s in most aspects of their lives Aboriginal people were governed by the laws of the state in which they lived. From the late 1950s discriminatory legislation depriving Aboriginal people of basic human rights such as freedom of movement, freedom to choose place of residence and employment, was gradually repealed.

Victoria and New South Wales removed the last barriers to full citizenship in 1957 and 1963 respectively and South Australia in 1966, although Western Australia and Queensland still retained elements of discrimination at the end of the decade. In 1965 the Arbitration Court granted equal pay to Aboriginal workers in the pastoral industry, to be phased in over three years. In 1967, in one of the most significant referenda in the nation's history (supported by 90.77 per cent of voters) the electorate endorsed greater commonwealth involvement by giving it overriding legislative power in Aboriginal affairs. The referendum also removed a symbolic barrier to full membership of the Australian community, the right to be counted in the census. The first anti-discrimination legislation was enacted by South Australia in 1966 and a very limited form of land rights, restricted to the few remaining Aboriginal reserves, was granted in South Australian and Victoria.

A major reformulation of policy occurred in 1972, at the end of the coalition government's 23-year term of office. While the ideal of a unified 'Australian society with equal access to . . . rights and opportunities . . . and acceptance of responsibilities' was maintained, there was a significant shift with the decision to encourage and assist Aboriginal people 'to preserve and develop their own culture, languages, traditions and arts so that these can become living elements in the diverse culture of the Australian society', and to provide 'effective choice about the degree to which, and the pace at which, they come to identify themselves with that society'.

A NEW POLITICAL CULTURE

Major changes made in the last years of coalition rule were a response to domestic and international pressure rather than the product of conviction and principle. The post-Menzies coalition ministries were being reluctantly dragged into a new world—one much less clearly grounded in British tradition. In contrast, Prime Minister Gough Whitlam and his high profile Minister for Immigration Al Grassby loudly proclaimed that the era of racial discrimination was at an end and in its rhetoric his government placed itself at the forefront of the movement for change.

Aboriginal policies

During the 1972 election campaign Whitlam pledged to give Aboriginal people land rights, 'not just because their case is beyond argument, but because all of us as Australians are diminished while the Aborigines are denied their rightful place in the nation'. The 1970s witnessed a shift in the political culture with a measure of bipartisan support for limited Aboriginal self-determination and cultural maintenance for immigrants.

In the words of Whitlam the objective of his government was to 'restore to the Aboriginal people of Australia their lost power of self-determination in economic, social and political affairs'. There would be consultation, educational opportunities in 'no way inferior' to community norms, the provision of proper housing for all within ten years, a 'health offensive', the grant of land to some Aboriginal groups, notably to those who maintained 'traditional occupancy according to tribal custom', and the teaching of the history and culture of Aborigines as an integral part of school curricula.

A department of Aboriginal affairs was established and using the powers conferred by the 1967 referendum the government assumed responsibility from the states, with the exception of Queensland where there was a refusal to cooperate and the commonwealth had no option but to work alongside the state bureaucracy. Direct spending on Aboriginal programs increased from $30.9 million in 1971/72 to $61.4 million in 1972/73 and $185.8 million in 1975/6. A range of new institutions were funded, including the Aboriginal Medical Service and the Aboriginal Legal Service. A Royal Commission was set up to advise on the implementation of land rights policy in the Northern Territory.

To facilitate consultation the directly elected National Aboriginal Consultative Council was established. Special forms of assistance were made available to Aboriginal people, including financial assistance for parents with children in secondary and tertiary education. In 1975 the last remnants of formal discrimination were outlawed, with the passing of legislation specifically to override Queensland laws and of the 1975 *Racial Discrimination Act* which made it illegal:

> for a person to do any act involving a distinction, exclusion, restriction or preference based on race, colour, descent or national or ethnic origin which has the purpose or effect of nullifying or impairing the recognition, enjoyment or exercise, on an equal footing, of any human right or fundamental freedom in the political, economic, social, cultural or any other field of public life.

This legislation was to assume major importance in the 1990s, limiting the response of federal and state governments to the High Court's decisions on native title.

Despite the bitter political hostility which marked the last year of office of the Whitlam government there was a measure of continuity in the policies pursued by its conservative successor. While the coalition government cut spending from 0.9 per cent of gross domestic product in 1974/5 to 0.6 per cent in 1979/80, it proceeded to enact land rights legislation in the Northern Territory through a revised version of a Bill introduced by Labor prior to its loss of office. Legislation was also passed in South Australia and the New South Wales government set up a fund for the purchase of land for Aboriginal communities. By 1983 Aboriginal people controlled 28.67 per cent of the land mass of the Northern Territory, 10.9 per cent of South Australia and 9 per cent of Western Australia. While the amount of land held as freehold or leasehold was huge in total area, almost all of it was semi-arid and arid, or for other reasons of limited use for European economic activity, with the important exception of mining. In the eastern states—Queensland, New South Wales, Victoria and Tasmania—Aboriginal people gained almost no freehold, a total of less than 200 square kilometres (see Table 2.4 on page 35).

While much was achieved in the ten years after the election of the Whitlam government, the hopes raised that racial discrimination would be overcome were not fulfilled. Increased levels of expenditure did not see a short-term improvement in living conditions, employment, health and education, and it was becoming evident that governments and their bureaucracies were reluctant to transfer real power of self-determination to Aboriginal communities. Aboriginal leaders spoke of the creation of welfare dependency, the neutering of organisations whose existence required continued federal funding, the setting of agendas by bureaucrats rather than the people whose lives were concerned. One of the leading academic commentators on government policy wrote that 'there is the psychological inability of whites to stop talking *about* blacks rather than *with* them, to cease being their protectors and curators, to allow them to act on their own behalf'.

Immigration

In contrast with major developments in Aboriginal policy, immigration fell into the doldrums in the aftermath of the OPEC (Organization of Petroleum Exporting Countries) oil crisis which affected western economies from 1973 onwards. The Whitlam government massively cut the immigration intake, from 156 000 in 1971 to 54 000 in 1975 and placed emphasis on training to increase the skill level of the existing workforce. While settler arrivals increased under the coalition administration, reaching almost 120 000 in 1981, the intake was reduced over the following three years as unemployment mounted, to rise again to high levels in the second half of the decade (see Figure 2.2).

Figure 2.2 Levels of immigration and unemployment

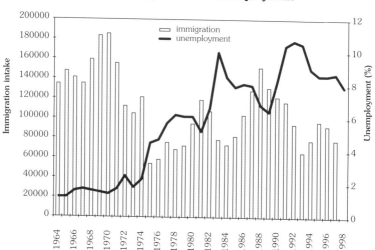

On gaining office Whitlam trumpeted the end of the 'White Australia policy' and in 1973 race was removed from the criteria used to determine immigration selection and the grant of assisted passages. The government ended the collection of demographic data on race, to the chagrin of academics studying population. Such changes did not, however, mean that all national groups were immediately placed on a level of equality. The Minister for Immigration advocated family reunion and 'chain migration', an emphasis which favoured the long established groups. Discriminatory practices continued within the department; for example, relatively strict criteria were applied in the selection of non-Europeans and allocation of personnel to process applications favoured traditional high status regions. A major increase in non-European immigration did not occur until 1977 when the coalition government decided to participate in the resettlement of Indo-Chinese refugees and in the following years when family reunion criteria was eased. As a percentage of the total intake immigrants from Asian countries increased from 16 per cent in 1976 to around 30 per cent by the end of the decade and 43 per cent in 1984 (see Figure 2.3 and Appendix I).

In settlement policy reference to assimilation was formally abandoned. Grassby declared in 1973 that 'the increasing diversity of Australian society has gradually eroded and finally rendered untenable any prospects there might have been twenty years ago of fully assimilating newcomers to the "Australian way of life", to use a phrase common at that time'. Migrants would be encouraged not merely to share in Australia's social and cultural life, but 'to add to it, . . . to enrich our national life and to contribute towards the creation of a new and distinctive Australia'. The Australia of tomorrow would be 'a vital and vibrant nation, . . . a catalyst of progress in our region of the world', its citizens 'heir to all that is best in the culture and heritage of three score nations and ten'. Grassby employed the terminology of the 'family of the nation' to

Figure 2.3   Immigration intake 1972–97—component from Asian countries

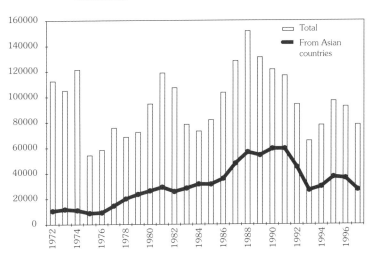

convey the idea of a commitment by all to the common good, without denial of the individuality and distinctiveness of each member. The goal of policy was to provide 'full scope for all to develop their personal potential, no matter how diverse their origins, beliefs, wealth or ability', to overcome disadvantage to provide a true basis for participation in community life.

The Whitlam years were, however, stronger on rhetoric than achievement in the development of multicultural policy, which occurred after the change in government, primarily during the period of office of Michael MacKellar, minister from 1975 to 1979 of the newly named Department of Immigration and Ethnic Affairs. The terminology of 'multiculturalism' dominated discussion in the second half of the 1970s, albeit in a moderate, cultural form compared with some overseas models. Indicative of the changed political culture, a 1977 Australian Ethnic Affairs Council submission to the government argued that:

> our goal in Australia is to create a society in which people of non-Anglo-Australian origin are given the opportunity, as individuals or groups, to choose to preserve and develop their culture, their languages, traditions and arts—so that these can become living elements in the diverse culture of the total society, while at the same time they enjoy effective and respected places within one Australian society.

The landmark Galbally Report of 1978 provided the basis for policy on migrant services until the mid-1980s. The report, published in a number of community languages, concluded that:

> Migrants have the right to maintain their cultural and racial identity and . . . it is clearly in the best interests of our nation that they should be encouraged and assisted to do so if they wish. Provided that ethnic identity is not stressed at the expense of society at large, but is interwoven into the fabric

of our nationhood by the process of multicultural interaction, then the community as a whole will benefit substantially and its democratic nature will be reinforced. The knowledge that people are identified with their cultural background and ethnic group enables them to take their place in their new society with confidence if their ethnicity has been accepted by the community.

Under the new policy, orientation and English language training facilities were improved, spending on welfare services increased and migrant organisations received funding to define their needs and to deliver services to their communities. A network to facilitate consultation was established and Migrant Resource Centres were funded to provide information to individuals and groups. In 1980 the Australian Institute of Multicultural Affairs was established to carry out independent research and through public education provide understanding of the diverse cultures of Australia. The Special Broadcasting Service began to broadcast non-English language programs on radio and television and multiculturalism in the arts was fostered by the Australia Council. Such developments could not have been envisaged during the era of assimilation but the gap between rhetoric and reality was only partially bridged: multiculturalism remained a vague aspiration and funding was, in the words of one commentator, 'parsimonious ... in relation to the breadth of objectives'. Thus the Galbally recommendations, adopted in full by the government, provided only for the spending of $52 million over three years, rising from $8 million in first year to $28 million in the third (see Table 2.3).

LOST IMPETUS

In contrast with the 1970s, there was loss of crusading zeal and consistency of direction in government approach to immigration and Aboriginal issues in the 1980s.

Table 2.3   Galbally Report 1978—cost of recommendations (over three years) incurring extra expenditure

	$million
Initial settlement program	12
Teaching English	13.29
Improved service provision and communication with those not fluent in English	3.54
Improvements in information provision to migrants	0.53
Voluntary and self-help services for migrants	3.46
Ethnic health workers	0.73
Improved child care and support for the elderly	0.77
Multicultural education and establishment of the Institute of Multicultural Affairs	6.80
Development of Special Broadcasting Service	10.77
Co-ordination of programs and consultation	0.60
TOTAL cost over three years	52.49

Source: Migrant Services and Programs, *Appendixes to the Report of the Review of Post-arrival Programs and Services for Migrants*, AGPS, Canberra, 1978, Appendix 1.

After a period of intense public debate over immigration policy in 1984, concerned particularly with the numbers coming from Asian countries, the Hawke government cut settlement programs in the 1986 budget. The funding of English language teaching to migrant children was halved, the Multicultural Education Program terminated, and the Australian Institute of Multicultural Affairs and several regional immigration offices were closed. It was also announced that the Special Broadcasting Service would be merged with the Australian Broadcasting Commission.

The vehemence of protest from migrant communities, sparked

by perception of a deliberate downgrading of ethnic affairs, caught the government by surprise and led to some reversals in policy. The plan to merge the Special Broadcasting Service was abandoned and some proposed budget cuts were rescinded. A new section was established in the Department of Prime Minister and Cabinet, to be called the Office of Multicultural Affairs, with responsibility to liaise with ethnic communities and to provide advice on immigration and multicultural matters. A new research body located within the Department of Immigration, the Bureau of Immigration Research, was established in 1989.

From the mid-1980s the focus of public discussion had shifted from cultural maintenance to 'access and equity', which some advocates hoped would lead to greater concern with 'social justice'—action to lessen the extent of economic disadvantage of some immigrant communities. In this context 'affirmative action' policies, such as ethnic quotas in employment, were advocated but little implemented. James Jupp has written that:

> in essence, multiculturalism as public policy has had limited and pragmatic objectives: ensuring the easy transition of immigrants into Australian society; limiting and reducing prejudice; developing access and equity in the provision of public services; encouraging non-English speaking Australians to maintain their languages and cultures; and advocating tolerance for new religions, cultural groups and languages within the context of acceptance of Australian laws and traditions. All this is designed to alleviate social and personal stress and to avoid the creation of disadvantaged or alienated groups based on ethnic variety.

Access and equity policies had their origin in reports undertaken for the New South Wales (1978) and Victorian (1983) governments. A commonwealth strategy was adopted in 1985 and extended in 1989, with the aim of ensuring that those from non-English speaking background (and Aboriginal and Torres Strait Islander peoples) had full access to government services. Achievement of this goal entailed identification of the needs of disadvantaged groups; provision of information in community languages other than English; provision of interpreter services; training of staff to be aware of cultural needs of clients; hiring staff, where appropriate, with relevant cultural knowledge and language skills; appointment of members of government advisory and decision-making bodies from minority groups; and culturally relevant service delivery (for example, in library collection policy, teaching strategies in preschools and schools, cuisine provided by meals-on-wheels services). Departments were required to develop access and equity programs to ensure compliance, which was monitored by the Office of Multicultural Affairs.

Despite outlandish claims that billions of dollars were spent on settlement programs expenditure was less than $300 million. In 1990/91 the major items were $93 million for the Adult Education Program, $91 million for teaching English as a second language in schools, $61 million for the Special Broadcasting Service, and $16 million in settlement-related grants for ethnic community groups. Other programs operated with small budgets, such as the Migrant Access Project Scheme ($2.6 million) and the Department of Community Services and Health Multicultural Information Strategy ($1.5 million).

A significant new development, evident in government attempts to contain damage from the 1986 budget cuts, was the concern to win and retain what was termed the 'ethnic vote'. The attempt of lobby groups to influence government was not new, but the significance attached to the electoral influence of southern and eastern European nationalities was.

The most influential lobby group in the immediate post-war decades was the growth lobby, represented particularly by secondary industry organisations and the housing industry, which saw immigration as necessary for national development and prosperity. In the 1960s small groups, mainly in the universities, worked for reform of the 'White Australia' policy and from the late 1960s onwards others began to question the need for large scale immigration, particularly of immigrants with low skills and little or no English language competence. Immigration also came to be questioned on environmental grounds.

The first non-British groups to attempt to lobby governments were based in specific communities, notably the Jewish community, which established a central representative body in 1944, and the Italian and Greek communities. In the 1970s, however, a number of additional national groups combined to form state ethnic communities' councils. A peak body, the Federation of Ethnic Communities' Councils, was established in 1979, with its headquarters in Sydney and financial support from the commonwealth. Also influential were the state Ethnic Affairs Commissions and university-based research centres.

In opposition to these groups, increasingly vocal from 1984 onwards, were those who in many cases described themselves as Australian nationalists, rallying around issues of identity, maintenance of Anglo-Australian traditions, opposition to the loss of the favoured place previously accorded to immigrants from the United Kingdom and other policies presented as favouring racial minorities. Although lacking a significant organisational basis beyond the exclusive clubs of some elite elements, its outspoken members included influential newspaper columnists, radio talkback hosts, one prominent Returned Servicemen's League leader, and a few holding senior university appointments.

The perceived significance of the 'ethnic vote' in part motivated the initiatives in settlement policy in the Fraser years and, in the view of some commentators, influenced the determination of immigration policy. It has been argued that lobbyists from the Italian, Greek and Yugoslav communities were particularly influential in winning an extension of eligibility criteria under the family reunion program. Changes between 1980 and 1983 provided for Australian residents to sponsor (on increasingly generous terms) not only members of their immediate family, but also brothers and sisters. By the late 1980s brothers and sisters made up almost half the intake in the family reunion category, which had almost doubled in size between 1983/84 and 1987/88 (see Figure 2.4).

There was a significant unintended consequence of these changes in immigration entry criteria: while it seems that the changes had been adopted as a consequence of the lobbying of southern European groups, recent immigrants from Asian and Middle Eastern countries took most advantage of the concession. The consequence was a significant increase in the proportion of family-reunion immigrants from Asia; many immigrants from Asian countries also gained admission in the independent category on the basis of their skills. Immigrants from Asia rose from 25 per cent of the total intake in 1981 to above 35 per cent in the years 1983–89. In numerical terms, the increase was from between 25 500–29 000 early in the decade to over 56 000 in 1988 (see Figure 2.3 and Appendix I).

The government embraced the arguments of the growth lobby

Figure 2.4 Immigration program outcomes: key components

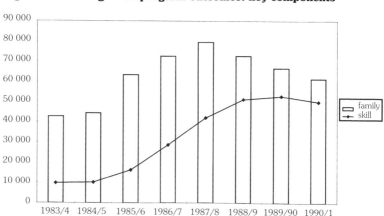

and embarked again on a large scale immigration program from the mid-1980s onwards, despite an unemployment rate of over 7 per cent (see Figure 2.2). At the same time the relative proportion gaining admission under the family reunion category was reduced in favour of skilled immigrants. In 1985 Chris Hurford, the Minister for Immigration, pushed for a program with an increased economic focus. Although he was moved from the portfolio in February 1987 his policy direction was followed, with a fivefold increase in the number of skilled and business immigrants admitted between 1984/85 and 1988/89. A committee to advise on immigration policy, under the chairmanship of former ambassador to China, Dr Stephen FitzGerald, angered leaders of the ethnic communities by calling for a reduction of family reunion numbers and the reintroduction of English language competency in assessing some categories of sponsored immigrants. The Fitz-Gerald committee also recommended an annual immigration intake of 150 000 for the next three years. The targets advocated by FitzGerald were not met although the intake for the years 1987–90 represent the peak for the last 25 years of the century. In the early 1990s, with a steep rise in unemployment, numbers were again cut, most severely in the skill category, with an increase in immigration only in the years 1994 and 1995 (see Figure 2.2). The proportion from Asian countries fell as the focus of the humanitarian program shifted to the former Yugoslavia, Czechoslovakia and the Soviet Union, and as family reunion from these areas increased.

ABORIGINAL ISSUES

While immigration and settlement policies were of major significance in the 1980s and 1990s, Aboriginal issues, particularly land rights and reconciliation, ranked in the forefront of politics.

The policy of the Labor Party committed it to the enactment of uniform national legislation. After the party's victory in the

1983 election Clyde Holding, Minister for Aboriginal Affairs, announced that national legislation would honour five principles: inalienable freehold title, protection of sacred sites, control of mining, payment of royalties and compensation for lost land, with precise terms to be determined. In the same year the Burke Labor government in Western Australia established an inquiry to advise on the enactment of land rights legislation. But in the face of a carefully planned advertising campaign in the west, sponsored by the Western Australian Mining Industry Council, and the threat of its extension to the national media by the Australian Mining Industry Council, both the Western Australian and federal governments modified their legislative proposals, most importantly withdrawing the right to veto mining. Even legislation in this weaker form was unacceptable to the Western Australian upper house, which blocked its passage. Subsequently the Burke government established leases by which Aboriginal people obtained a very limited form of land rights, mostly to former reserves. Federal legislation was abandoned in 1986 as a result of opposition from mining and pastoral lobbyists, as well as from Aboriginal groups which were unwilling to accept the limited rights on offer.

Under existing legislation some further gains in freehold and leasehold were made in the Northern Territory and South Australia granted title to the Pitjantjatjara and Maralinga lands (in 1981 and 1986 respectively). In New South Wales land councils were established in 1983 and gained freehold title to reserves; in addition a fund was established which was to receive 7.5 per cent of gross State Land Tax revenue for fifteen years to purchase land and build up a capital fund for later purchases, but very little land passed to Aboriginal ownership over the following ten years. In Victoria and Tasmania almost no land was gained by Aboriginal communities (see Table 2.4). By 1989 Aboriginal people gained title in various forms to some 13 per cent of the land mass, however there was almost no freehold outside the Northern Territory and South Australia and almost all the land was

Table 2.4   Aboriginal land tenure—States/Territories ranked in order of total population

State/ Territory	1983				1989			
	freehold (km²)	leasehold (km²)	reserve/ mission (km²)	As % of total land	freehold (km²)	leasehold (km²)	reserve/ mission (km²)	As % of total land
New South Wales and Australian Capital Terrtory	171	107		0.0003	507	842		0.16
Victoria	20			0.0001	32			0.01
Queensland	5	12 524	19 671	1.86	5	31 990	95	1.86
Western Australia	30	35 307	190 654	8.95	35	103 227	202 223	12.1
South Australia	106 764	506		10.9	183 649	508		18.71
Tasmania	1			0.002	2			0.003
Northern Territory	366 297	19 604		28.67	453 123	26 009	45	35.59
Australia	473 288	68 048	210 325	9.75	637 353	162 576	202 363	13.05

Source: *Aboriginal Social Indicators 1984*; Department of Aboriginal Affairs, *Annual Report 1989–90*.

unproductive by European standards—desert, semi-desert or swamp land. As one measure of the extent of land held by Aboriginal people, in the mid-1990s the largest corporate leaseholder held 117 000 square kilometres and the largest private leaseholder 47 000 square kilometres.

Although further legislation was abandoned, the issue of Aboriginal rights did not disappear from a central place in the political agenda. For three of the major political parties, Labor, Liberal and Australian Democrat, and within the media, universities and churches, the issue of making peace with the Aboriginal people remained under discussion, underwritten by a belief that until a compact was achieved Australian society would remain mired in the past, unable to celebrate its achievements and plan effectively for its future. The issue of reconciliation was of paramount importance in 1988, the bicentennial anniversary of the European presence, and remained an issue of significance throughout the 1990s in anticipation of the new millennium, the Sydney Olympic Games, and the centenary of Federation.

While the issue of land rights could not be resolved, and the demand made by radical indigenous leaders for return of sovereignty was not seriously discussed, advances were made on other matters of immediate significance.

Three important public inquiries were held: into racist violence (1989–91) and the forced removal of Aboriginal Children (1995–97), both conducted by the Human Rights and Equal Opportunity Commission, and the third, a Royal Commission, into Aboriginal deaths in custody (1987–91). The deaths in custody and 'stolen generations' reports won extensive publicity, provoking shocked reactions, particularly in southern capitals, with their revelations of grossly disproportionate imprisonment rates and the extent and legacy of forced removal of children.

A key initiative achieved in 1990 was the replacement of the department of Aboriginal affairs with a statutory authority headed by elected indigenous representatives, the Aboriginal and Torres Strait Islander Commission (ATSIC), which assumed responsibility for formulation and implementation of programs and provision of advice to the minister. The establishment of the commission was hailed by the government as a major step towards self-determination. In the following year the Council for Aboriginal Reconciliation was established. Comprised of 25 members, twelve Aboriginal, two Torres Strait Islander, and eleven others, it worked for the creation by the end of the century of a 'united Australia which respects this land of ours; values the Aboriginal and Torres Strait Islander heritage; and provides justice and equity for all'.

THE KEATING YEARS

Paul Keating, who became prime minister at the end of 1991, sought to make a significant impact in race relations. In contrast with the consensus approach of Hawke, he saw his role as 'about being right and about being strong'. He was in politics to tackle the big issues, to leave a legacy of achievement that would last long beyond his period in office. Leadership was not 'about being popular'. In an historic speech at the end of 1992 which launched the International Year of Indigenous People, Keating resolutely faced the tragedies of Aboriginal–white relations:

> We took the traditional lands and smashed the traditional way of life. We brought the diseases. The alcohol. We committed the murders. We took the children from their mothers. We practised discrimination and exclusion ... It might help us if we non-Aboriginal Australians imagined ourselves dispossessed of land we had lived on for 50 000 years, and then imagined ourselves told that it had never been ours. Imagine if ours was the oldest culture in the world and we were told it was worthless ...

In a private address on the eve of the 1993 election Keating told his staff that 'I'm more convinced than ever that we've got to make peace with the Aborigines to get the place right'.

Keating worked to give the country a dynamic economy, a sense of identity freed from its British roots, a new flag, and a new orientation towards the Asia-Pacific. He contemptuously described pre-Whitlam Australia as a 'gloomy cave' ruled by a 'semi-hereditary elite'; the Liberals were the enemies of national progress, the 'same old fogies who doffed their lids and tugged the forelock to the British establishment'.

His was an approach that was to make many enemies. His direct, confrontational style and arrogant, combative disposition brooked no public criticism. Responding, for example, to the criticism of Aboriginal policy by Hugh Morgan, the outspoken chief executive officer of Western Mining, he described the comments as 'disgraceful', the mustering of 'prejudice, banality and venality . . . Mr Morgan has always painted himself as a thoughtful thinker on the Right. He has never been thoughtful, and he has never been a thinker. What we have here is just bigotry. It is the voice of ignorance, the voice of hysteria, and the voice of the nineteenth century . . .'.

Early in his term the issue of land rights was revived from a surprising quarter: the issue which the politicians had lacked the will to resolve was thrown back into their realm by the decision of the High Court of Australia in the second Mabo case.

Delivered on 3 June 1992 by a majority of six to one, the Court found, contrary to Australian precedent, that common law could recognise the survival of indigenous property rights following the assumption of British sovereignty. In the determination of the judges a specific act was required to extinguish native title, such as the grant by the Crown of a public or private interest in the land inconsistent with native title, particularly the sale of freehold. Native title survived on vacant Crown land, state forests, national parks, beaches and foreshores, and in other areas yet to be determined. For a native title claim to succeed, however, a most difficult test was imposed: it was necessary to establish continuing connection with the land, according to traditional law or custom, from the time of first European settlement to the present day. Native title could not be bought or sold, but could be surrendered to the government in exchange for a sum of money or other arrangement.

The Mabo ruling, although fiercely criticised by individuals and representatives of mining and pastoral industries and other lobbyist who depicted it as a legal revolution, was a decision consistent with earlier recognition of indigenous people's rights in New Zealand, Canada, the United States and elsewhere.

Following an extensive period of negotiation with state premiers and representatives of various interest groups, not least negotiators acting on behalf of the Aboriginal people, the *Native Title Act* was passed into law on 21 December 1993. The legislation represented a compromise, with Aboriginal representatives agreeing that in the case of freehold, public works and some leases native title was deemed to be extinguished. It established the National Native Title Tribunal for the lodgment and adjudication of claims and criteria to guide its determinations.

As an act of compensation and justice to the great majority of Aboriginal people who had been displaced from their traditional lands and could not make claims under the High Court's narrow definition, the Keating government established a land fund to assist groups to buy land. The *Land Fund and Indigenous Land Corporation Act 1995* allocated the sum of $121 million each year until 2004. Two-thirds of the annual grant was to be invested to build the Fund's capital while the remaining one-third was for acquisition, land management and general administration. It was planned that by 2004, when commonwealth grants would cease, the Land Corporation would have capital of $1.3 billion, the income from which was designed to provide the basis for continuing land purchases.

After the traumas of 1993, the following two years were to be relatively peaceful in Aboriginal affairs.

THE END OF BIPARTISANSHIP

The election of the Howard government in March 1996 marked the end of a long period of consensus by the major parties on aspects of immigration, settlement and Aboriginal issues.

Australia ceased being a country welcoming of immigrants. In some areas, such as the harsh stance towards illegal 'boat people' arriving from Asia and the Middle East and the shift in the balance of the program from family reunion to skill, Labor had led the way but its moves were tentative and subject to reversal when electoral problems beckoned. Labor had also drastically cut the immigration intake in the context of rising unemployment (from 152 000 in 1988 to 66 000 in 1993/94), but then increased the quota as economic conditions improved (97 000 in 1995/96). In contrast, the coalition cut numbers despite continuing improvement in the labour market and pushed ahead with a series of rigorous reforms. Symbolic of the change, in the first Howard government the minister for immigration was excluded from Cabinet.

The first ingredient was a cut in the immigration intake—to 79 000 in 1997/98—and a shift in the balance of the program from family reunion to skill categories. While the size of the humanitarian intake remained largely unchanged at around 12 000 (or 15 per cent of the intake), family reunion was reduced from 56 700 in 1995/96 to 31 300 in 1997/98; this represented a cut from 58 to 40 per cent of the total program while the skill component increased from 25 to 44 per cent. The number of parents admitted as part of family reunion fell from 9000 to 1000 (500 in 1999), all but totally abolishing this element of the program. The points awarded for English language competency were boosted in the selection criteria.

Second, government advocacy of multiculturalism came to an end, with the prime minister studiously avoiding reference to the term. In the first round of budget cuts in 1996 the two major commonwealth research and liaison agencies, the Office of Multicultural Affairs and the Bureau of Immigration, Multicultural and Population Research, were abolished. Policy initiatives were left to the states.

Third, the government severely curtailed assistance to immigrants. It gained Labor support for some of these changes in a political climate hostile to immigrant rights, but there was also significant Senate modification of elements of the government's program. Except for those admitted under the humanitarian program, the waiting period for key social security benefits was extended from six months to two years. The waiting period for the Special Benefit, a welfare payment of last resort previously available to those immigrants who became destitute, was also extended to two years in most cases. An immigrant left destitute through inability to find employment was to receive no government assistance.

In the 1997/98 budget, expenditure on settlement, citizenship and multicultural programs totalled $159 million. The major items of expenditure were the Adult Migrant English Program ($115.6 million, offset by $10.4 million recovered), translating and interpreting service ($18.5 million, $6.5 million recovered), and grants to community organisations to assist with settlement ($23 million). Allocation to core multicultural programs, including access and equity, was $4.1 million. Outside the Immigration and Multicultural Affairs portfolio, the major allocation was $83 million for the Special Broadcasting Service.

There was little publicity and limited public awareness of the extent of these changes, in part due to the complexity of the issues, to a greater extent because Labor decided to limit its opposition. Indeed Kim Beazley, the party's leader, while opposing the shift away from family reunion sought to claim credit for establishing a lower immigration quota when the Labor Party was in office, somewhat misleading given the rise in the intake during the period 1994–1996. While a new bipartisanship was forged on aspects of immigration policy, this was not the case in Aboriginal programs, which dominated public attention.

In the first Howard budget more than $400 million was cut from Aboriginal programs. This represented an average reduction of 10 per cent, but there was considerable variation, with funding levels maintained in health, housing and employment while other areas of spending controlled by the Aboriginal and Torres Strait Islander Commission, such as land acquisition and cultural activities, suffered cuts of up to 30 per cent.

Major public disputation continued over the issue of land rights and native title. In its initial period of office the government resisted pressure to extinguish native title, but at the end of 1996 the High Court again presented politicians with an urgent problem.

On 23 December 1996, in its majority 4:3 decision in the Wik case, the Court ruled that the grant of pastoral lease did not necessarily extinguish native title and did not grant exclusive possession to the pastoralist. Rights of indigenous people (such as the rights to visit sacred sites, hold ceremonies and collect native foods) could continue alongside a pastoral lease, although where conflict of interest arose the pastoralist's needs prevailed. The government asserted that whereas the Mabo ruling had opened some 36 per cent of the continent to native title claim, the Wik decision now added a further 42 per cent. The prime minister appeared on television with a map showing the bulk of the country potentially subject to Aboriginal control. The problem with such an interpretation was that under both rulings it was very difficult to establish native title and the Wik decision specifically upheld the priority of legitimate leaseholder use of land. Nonetheless, vehement public objections were again voiced, often by people with little understanding of the Court's highly complex judgments. Spokespersons for the mining and pastoral groups and conservative politicians refused to accept that Aboriginal people could have rights surviving the British seizure of the continent.

The Howard government's response was to legislate to diminish the rights won by Aboriginal people in the High Court. Within the legal world considerable uncertainty had been created, in part because major issues were yet to be resolved, also because of differences in the terms of leases under the various state laws. A legal minefield beckoned, with the prospect in extreme cases of multiple overlapping claims to one piece of land from different native title claimants. Howard's solution sought to secure the rights of pastoralists by extending the range of economic activities which could be undertaken under a pastoral lease, limit the grounds on which native title claims could be lodged, provide a limited time period for their lodgment and rule out claims on waterways and ocean resources and on land needed for infrastructure such as railways, pipelines, roads and bridges.

Howard encountered great difficulty in selling his package to interest groups and in securing its passage through parliament. In May 1997 addressing a gathering of 2000 angry farmers and their families outside the Australian Stockman's Hall Of Fame at Longreach, in central Queensland, he explained that his policy would guarantee certainty to leaseholders. Answering questions from those fearful for the security of their properties, he sought unsuccessfully to reassure the audience that no pastoral title would be affected or diminished by a native title claim. The president of the United Graziers Association, Mr Larry Acton, stated that 'the message was very clearly that they weren't convinced'.

Howard's immediate problem was that the coalition lacked the numbers to ensure passage of the legislation in the Senate, in which the combined Labor, Democrat and independent vote twice defeated the Native Title Amendment Bill, fuelling the prospect of a double-dissolution election on the issue of indigenous rights. In the course of debates some 400 pages of amendments were passed by the Senate in the longest consideration of a Bill in its history. Critics of the government's legislation charged that it gave to pastoralists greater rights than they enjoyed previous to Mabo and Wik through the change in the definition of 'primary production' and that the list of extinguished tenures which was part of the Bill would result in loss of native title in many tenures where the common law may have allowed their existence.

Almost at the last moment a compromise was brokered with the independent Tasmanian Senator Brian Harradine, previously an opponent of the legislation. Harradine argued that on balance the legislation was less of a problem than the alternative, a justification he had earlier offered when supporting passage of the government's changes to welfare entitlements of immigrants. He saw the country 'heading into a divisive double-dissolution election which would have torn the fabric of our society and put race relations back 40 or 50 years. I wanted to avoid that . . .'. The government made some concessions, including removal of the 'sunset clause' or final date for lodging of native title claims and broadening the basis for registration of a claim, but in the view of Aboriginal leaders, who were shut out from the final stage of negotiations, more was lost than had been gained from Wik. One of the leading negotiators with the Keating government, Noel Pearson of the Cape York land council, argued that Harradine had given away 80 per cent of the Aboriginal people's position. 'Looking at the totality of the Harradine-Howard Bill, it is clear that Howard has managed to rip the heart out of the original native title legislation negotiated by Aborigines with Paul Keating and the Parliament in 1993. No less.'

Following the passage of the legislation in July 1998, shortly after the Queensland election, Prime Minister Howard was exultant. Pastoral and mining groups were pleased with the justice of the final package.

THE EXTENT OF CHANGE: AN OVERVIEW

In less than two decades Australian society had witnessed major change. There had been a shift from a policy of assimilation designed to maintain a monoculture to the rhetoric of multiculturalism and self-determination.

A range of programs designed to provide assistance and benefits specifically to Aboriginal people were introduced and a number of communities in remote regions were able to reclaim significant portions of their traditional lands. While it seemed by the late 1980s that the prospect of further land rights legislation had all but disappeared the situation was transformed by the High Court's Mabo and Wik decisions.

From the 'whites only' immigration policy in force until the mid-1960s the intake changed significantly so that by 1984 over

40 per cent of immigrants came from Asian countries. Asian born residents increased from 258 000 in 1981 to 856 000 in 1996, making up 5 per cent of the total population, unevenly distributed across the country. In 1996 41 per cent lived in Sydney, where they were 10 per cent of the city's population; 27 per cent lived in Melbourne, some 7.6 per cent of the population. In contrast there were almost no Southeast Asian immigrants in many parts of rural Australia: in the region covered by the Maranoa electorate (Queensland) they comprised 0.4 per cent of the population, in Gwydir (New South Wales) 0.2 per cent, in Mallee (Victoria) 0.3 per cent, in Grey (South Australia) 0.4 per cent and in O'Connor (Western Australia) 0.7 per cent. A broader measure of difference, the proportion from non-English speaking back-grounds, shows a similar divide, with less than 5 per cent of the population in these rural electorates compared with over 20 per cent in many parts of urban Australia. The scale of the post-war immigration program had accentuated an important difference between rural and urban Australia.

A reaction to the new policies in Aboriginal affairs and immigration which culminated in the period of the Howard government first became apparent in national debate during 1983 and 1984. It is the purpose of the following chapters to analyse the development of this opposition.

PART 2

STYLE

3

The new conservatism and the naturalness of bigotry

The following four chapters analyse the process by which racial politics re-entered the mainstream of Australian public life. They aim to identify the social groups and individuals who campaigned to change Aboriginal and immigration policy, and the means by which they sought to achieve their ends. The discussion will focus, first, on the group known as the New Right and two of its leading propagandists, Hugh Morgan and Geoffrey Blainey. It directs attention to a central feature of the political process best termed 'naturalisation' (or 're-naturalisation') whereby different political groups manoeuvre to win endorsement for their own positions.

The 'true believers' on the right and the left, the fervent advocates of specific ideological positions, convince themselves that their views are beyond partisan politics. They believe that they represent the 'national interest' and that their policies are in keeping with the 'natural order', 'natural law', 'common sense', 'the truth'. They are armed with 'truth' while they seek to represent their opponents as acting in a 'political' manner, advocating sectional interests rather than those of 'the nation'. Thus Hugh Morgan could present his analysis of the perils facing Australia as 'totally politically neutral. I have no party political purposes'. If the 'true believers' can convince others that their views are 'natural' or 'simply common sense', that their 'definitions' should prevail (as discussed in Chapter 1), they gain a victory of great significance in the political struggle. An example of this form of reasoning is the idea that there are 'natural' roles for men and women ordained by God or nature; hence men are rational, aggressive, competitive; women are intuitive, healing, nurturing. These differences supposedly have a universal validity transcending time and place. Such thinking justifies different gender roles, the proponents convinced that there is no room for disagreement, as the differences between the sexes are ordained by nature. For centuries sexist ideas held sway, with almost no scope to question their validity.

NEW RIGHT VALUES

The New Right represented a conservative mobilisation, focused originally on economic reform. It was concerned with wealth creation rather than wealth distribution and sought a radical reduction of government activity through the freeing of industry and labour markets and the sale of public assets to private corporations—a return to the characteristics of capitalist societies in the early period of industrialisation. The catch-cries were deregulation and privatisation, the domination of market forces and the end of trade union power. The movement gathered strength in the context of the failure of social democratic and communist regimes to transform the position of the working class and the consequent loss of direction and self-confidence by those on the left, signalled by the retreat of intellectuals to the labyrinths of postmodern thought. The most significant figure in the Australian New Right, Hugh Morgan, explained the belief system:

> The common thread which links the New Right is the understanding that government has failed to deliver the great benefits which the Left has claimed, for over a century, that

governments would deliver. Moreover the New Right argues that governments are intrinsically unable to deliver these benefits, and the more they try, the worse the situation becomes ... [F]or a healthier society, for better family life, for greater opportunities for individual creativity and endeavour, and ultimately for the preservation of the State itself, the role of government must be diminished, indeed, must be greatly diminished.

The New Right saw itself as a dynamic, revolutionary force. It attacked with almost religious fervour the orthodoxies of the left which obstructed realisation of their ideal society. Its victories were achieved from the late 1970s, first in the United Kingdom during the prime ministership of Margaret Thatcher and then in the United States during the presidency of Ronald Reagan.

Why such a movement, with its prime focus on economic issues, should involve itself in racial politics is not immediately clear. Part of the answer is that the New Right is philosophically opposed to social engineering, to attempts to redress the position of economically and socially disadvantaged racial or ethnic groups through publicly funded programs of affirmative action. Under New Right policy, market forces are to be the arbiter of society's resources and the first stop to overcoming disadvantage is to recognise the long-term ineffectiveness of special forms of government assistance. Affirmative action is part of the problem, not a step towards overcoming inequality. There is thus an injunction to demolish a wide range of special government programs and to halt the development of new forms.

While there is this common orientation, differences of opinion occur over the role of government. Proponents of radical economic liberalism are concerned almost solely with the unfettered rule of the marketplace, not with attempting to safeguard society from its excesses. In contrast, those influenced by the main currents of conservative thought, far from abrogating social responsibilities, emphasise the need to uphold traditional social institutions and the rule of law. It is this strand within the New Right which has concerned itself with the drawing of racial boundaries—which dovetails with the form of racial thought termed 'culturalism', discussed in Chapter 1.

A core element of conservatism is its pessimistic view of human nature. Thus Morgan could write that 'whilst attitudes change, human nature does not change, and those who ignore our history will, sooner rather than later, come to harm'. Conservatism holds, in the words of one of its leading analysts, that 'we must search for the source of our discontents in defective human nature rather than in a defective social order'. Societies will always be made up of a small number of leaders, the dynamic element, and the great mass destined to comprise the 'army of the rear'. Humans are grossly unequal in most qualities of mind, body and spirit, and can never be made equal.

There is a clear limit to what can be achieved through government action. Governments cannot solve all or even a majority of problems facing society. They can guarantee legal and political equality and equality of opportunity—the right of individuals to exploit their talents to their natural limits. But they can go no further. Such attempts, so the conservative argues, fail because they disregard human nature. In a 'healthy', properly governed society, there is a realistic recognition that while inequality will be a constant feature of the human condition all classes and interest groups depend on each other; each knows its place and serves the interests of the totality; there is balance and unity. A 'healthy' society is characterised by a functional unity, by consensus rather than conflict.

But the conservative, unlike the radical proponent of economic liberalism, does not withdraw to a safe vantage point to observe the battle between the strong and the weak, for there is the likelihood that such a battle will result in the destruction of social order. The great mass of the population, the 'common people', are regarded as potentially violent and destructive, ruled by instinct and passion rather than rational thought. A wise government bases its rule on recognition of instincts and pre-judices. Clinton Rossiter writes that the conservative is 'in his most candid moments, an admirer of instinct, the "innate feeling for the good and the bad", and at least an apologist for prejudice, "the poor man's wisdom" '.

The conservative value system, specifically its regard for the 'innate feelings' and prejudices of the 'common man', traced ulti-mately to a pessimistic view of human nature, provides the second element for understanding the re-emergence of politics concerned with issues of race. While there is no necessary link, the conser-vative is likely to support government policy which in this regard accommodates itself to what are seen as the prejudices of the masses, rather than policy which optimistically—and unrealisti-cally—assumes that such prejudices can be readily overcome or ignored.

The re-emergence of racial politics has also been shaped by a third factor of major importance, the result of the circumstances of the 1980s. In the 1980s key elements within the New Right were of the view that their ends could not be achieved by focusing exclusively on economic issues. For reforms to be fundamental and long-lasting, safe from the whims of electoral fortune, a change in social values and political culture was required. The values which underpinned the welfare state needed to be challenged and defeated. One way to achieve these ends, some believed, was through direct attack on the recipients of affirmative action, on the intellectuals who provided the rationale for policies, and on those bureaucrats whose jobs depended on the administration of government programs. In New Right terminology these intellec-tuals and bureaucrats constituted the 'New Class'. It is in this context that the attacks on what was presented as a romanticisation of Aboriginal culture, on revisionist historians, and on the so-called welfare 'industries', become comprehensible.

THE AUSTRALIAN MOVEMENT

In Australia the New Right was slower to develop and become influential than in the United Kingdom and the United States. According to John Hyde, Liberal Party member for the Western Australian seat of Moore, in 1983 the hardline economic rationalists in the federal parliament could only muster four votes. Hyde found that his arguments were met with scepticism in the party room and the view that they would lead to electoral losses if implemented. Critics from the right believed the conservative government of Malcolm Fraser did little more than mouth the rhetoric of small government. Fraser's successor, Andrew Peacock, has been described by Michelle Grattan as 'entirely non-ideological'. Yet gradual shifts were occurring. One significant event was the election of John Howard, a convert to economic rationalism, to the position of deputy leader of the Liberal party.

The bases of the New Right mobilisation were the so-called 'think-tanks', the most influential located in Melbourne, described by *Bulletin* correspondent Anthony McAdam as 'the traditional home of Australian conservatism and clearly the epicentre of the "neo-conservative" revival'. The major organisations were the Melbourne and Sydney branches of the Institute of Public Affairs, the Centre for Policy Studies (Melbourne), Centre for Independent Studies (Sydney), Centre 2000 (Sydney) and the Australian Institute for Public Policy (Perth). Other organisations included the Australian Lecture Foundation and the H.R. Nicholls Society. In 1985 their operating budgets exceeded $1 million, a large sum by the standards of Australian political lobby groups. Many of the donations, eligible for tax deductibility, came from the business community. To take one example, the Melbourne Institute of Public Affairs' annual budget of around $300 000 was derived from 400 corporate supporters and close to 200 individuals. Industry invested larger sums of money directly in public relations, which in the case of the mining industry involved a successful campaign against federal and state land rights proposals during 1984–85 and expensive legal challenges to union power in the courts. Thus in the mid-1980s the National Farmers' Federation had a 'fighting fund' of over $10 million and the annual budget of its Canberra secretariat was $2.3 million.

Overseas links helped sustain the movement, particularly during its period in the political wilderness. The Australian Lecture Foundation played a major role arranging visits by leading conservative thinkers from the United States and England. In 1985 for example, Peter Grace, chairman of Ronald Reagan's committee on public spending, visited under the auspices of the Institute of Public Affairs; other visitors included the American Norman Podhoretz and the English activist Roger Scruton.

In 1985 Edwin J. Feulner, President of the Heritage Foundation of the United States, was invited to Australia to deliver the 18th Latham Memorial Lecture. Feulner regaled his audience with an account of the strategies and successes of his organisation during the period of the Reagan Presidency, describing how conservatism had become 'the party of ideas'. These successes had been marked in the field of privatisation, defence policy and government support for United Nations agencies. Currently, Feulner explained, his foundation was advocating 'privatising the entire Social Security system' and reform in the housing, education, transport and postal fields. The successes signalled 'a change in the power structure—away from the central government back to the people—away from the "power elites" back to the people'. The great boon of privatisation provided 'greater choice . . . at a reduced cost'.

He explained how victories were achieved. The starting point was the recognition of the power of ideas. Feulner quoted the words of an icon of the opposition, John Maynard Keynes, to the effect that 'it is ideas, not vested interests, which are dangerous for good or evil'. It had been learned that it was not only necessary to inject new ideas into public discussion, but also to ensure that the ideas were appropriately packaged and reached their targets.

Briefing material had to be dispatched to the key staff of sympathetic congressmen at decisive moments in the legislative process and pre-digested material sent to the media. The campaign to 'expose' UNESCO had involved luncheons, seminars, workshops, publications and 'widespread press attention'. The continuing task was to 'build on our ideas, popularise them, and make them available to the people, for them to choose'.

In Australia these ideas reverberated in conservative circles. John Hyde declared that 'ideas have a life of their own and they will, in the end, change the world'. The New Right reached a broad audience initially through *Quadrant*, a monthly magazine of ideas and the arts which traced its origins to the fight against communist totalitarianism. In 1984 its editor Peter Coleman, a Liberal parliamentarian, bewailed that no movement comparable to the strength of American 'neo-conservatism' had emerged. The intellectual hegemony of the 'New Class' was barely dented. In an editorial Coleman called for immediate action:

> ideas matter and the dominant ideas in Australia have become those of the New Class regulators who despise the liberal traditions of the country. There are few more urgent tasks than that of mounting an ideological offensive in support of those traditions and against the cultural and intellectual hegemony of the New Class.

Revisionist historians had attempted to discredit the nation's past, assaulting 'the sources of pride' and values of the ordinary Australian. Instead of celebrating Australian achievements and traditions the 'radical multiculturalists' depicted the years before the early 1970s 'as a contemptible wasteland'. In the education system 'quacks' searched for 'equality of outcomes', 'peace frauds' called for 'defencelessness and appeasement', 'civil libertarians' worked 'to limit civil liberties', the Green movement sought to restrain economic development and feminists were distinguished by hatred of their own gender: 'wherever they gather, in their workshops or health shops, in their demonstrations or drug therapy centres, the Death Wish is high on the agenda'. The task of national destruction was proceeding apace: education standards were in decline, the institution of the family was in decay, foreign policy a shambles.

In the years 1983–85 the Australian conservative mobilisation began to win attention. Key roles in the media breakthrough were played by the versatile Hugh Morgan, executive director of Western Mining Corporation, and Professor Geoffrey Blainey, Ernest Scott Professor of History and Dean of the Faculty of Arts at the University of Melbourne.

Morgan's involvement had begun in the late 1970s. In 1978 he became a member of the Institute of Public Affairs' Executive Committee. Two years later he joined the Centre for Independent Studies as trustee and was a participant in early free market gatherings, including the February 1981 Crossroads Conference. In the mid-1980s he was Honorary Treasurer of the Institute of Public Affairs and chairman of the Australian Lecture Foundation. In 1980 he was elected president of the Australian Mining Industry Council, also serving as its executive director for the first sixteen months of his term before the appointment of James Strong to that position. Morgan had first served the Mining Industry Council in 1976 as chair of its public relations committee, successfully moving the council to accept the need for a public role and leading to its first public relations campaign in 1982. Together with his executive assistant Ray Evans, he was prominent in the establishment of the H.R. Nicholls Society to promote the undermining of trade union power. John Stone, former secretary of the Treasury, was elected inaugural president of the society and Geoffrey Blainey launched the publication of its first conference proceedings.

According to Anthony McAdam, Morgan was the most enthusiastic free enterprise supporter amongst the 'captains of industry'. The *Sydney Morning Herald*'s Paul Sheehan noted in March 1985 that Morgan was 'at the centre of a large and growing network of activists who are seeking to reshape the political agenda in this country'. Another journalist assigned to prepare a feature article on Morgan observed that:

> [he] will turn up at a host of obscure but, for him valuable intellectual discussion groups, ranging from the *conversaziones* run by Professor Claudio Veliz at La Trobe University, to the Friday Club run by journalist Anthony McAdam . . . There is a well-trodden track of academics, polemicists and ideas merchants that leads into Western Mining's lunch room. One industry colleague recalls Roger Scruton, the editor of the aggressively conservative English journal, the *Salisbury Review*, deep in conversation with Morgan and Evans . . .

Morgan articulated the view that 'splinter groups' of the left had gained control of the political agenda. Capitalism and its pursuit of profit was denigrated along with the wealth-making industries of the country. He stated in 1983, in reference to specific mining projects awaiting government approval, that 'our industry is vulnerable to attack by groups which do not employ people, who do not create wealth and who adopt ambush PR tactics'. Indicative of the strength of Morgan's anger is his statement that miners 'have been on the other end of accusations of being heroin peddlers, murderers, guilty of genocide and, quite frankly, as somebody in the mining industry I've had a gutful of a lack of response'. It was time to hit back.

Given the success of the left, Morgan put forward the argument, heard frequently on the New Right, that it was necessary to study the enemy's tactics, to learn from the opposition. The lessons were that lobbying would only achieve limited results—it was necessary to make an impact on the electorate: 'You won't get change through politicians . . . Politicians can only accept what is accepted in the public opinion polls. So you have to change public opinion!'

In this task quiet, moderate discussion of issues would not suffice;

to capture media attention, to 'grab' headlines, a degree of provocation was required. James Strong commented that previously 'people were reluctant to go public for fear of offending government and prejudicing their own enterprise. But Morgan is in the van of the realisation that other interest groups receive greater public attention because industry has sterilised itself. He's seen that you have to be as aggressive and as dramatic as they are . . .'. Further, Morgan argued, to focus on narrow issues would be ineffective. Industries embarking on such campaigns ran the risk of being dismissed as merely seeking to further their own interests. Nothing less than a reorientation of the dominant value system was to be aimed at.

The mining industry, in which Morgan was a major player, may be credited with striking the first blow. In response to proposals by the Western Australian and federal Labor governments to legislate for Aboriginal land rights, the Chamber of Mines of Western Australia hired public relations and market research consultants and provided lavish funding for advertising in the state's print and electronic media, a novel departure for Australian lobbyists. The market research driven advertising campaign would be based on the 'equal rights' argument, its cornerstone the slogan 'Land rights should be equal rights'. One prominently featured Western Australian television advertisement asked of viewers:

> do you think it fair that less than 3 per cent of the population should claim ownership of up to 50 per cent of our land? Do you think it fair that any one group of people should have greater rights that any other group? Do you think it fair that any one group should control the future mineral wealth that belongs to every Western Australian?

BREAKTHROUGH

Nineteen eighty-four marked the turning point in the introduction of racial perspectives in mainstream political debate. Taboos in place for much of the previous post-war decades were broken. In my view Hugh Morgan and Geoffrey Blainey were the first to effectively challenge these taboos, initially in discussion of land rights and immigration policy.

The mining industry's campaign against the proposed extension of Aboriginal land rights, which beckoned in 1983, was first fought in Western Australia. Morgan brought the issue to national prominence with his provocative justification of mining activity. Apparently cautious about embroiling himself in political controversy, he was now persuaded that there was no other way to win public attention. With the help of his executive assistant Ray Evans he developed a justification for mining activity which was discordant in the context of the late twentieth century. It was a justification that would have been more appropriate had it been presented some 100 years earlier, yet it was clearly one deeply felt—and it also provided good newspaper copy.

In a speech to London businessmen on 17 January 1984 he stated, without arousing much media interest, that:

> there now seems to be a competition between the State Labor governments and Federal Labor Government, as to who can give away most land, in the shortest possible time, with the most denigration of the nineteenth century Europeans who settled Australia.

Four months later, in May 1984, he delivered the speech which, in his own words, 'really got things wheeling'; in important respects it prefigured some of the views later expounded by Tim Fischer, Pauline Hanson and David Oldfield, amongst other politicians of the right. At an Australian Mining Industry Council seminar, in the presence of the minister for Aboriginal Affairs, Clyde Holding, he presented a perspective based in part on his understanding of Christian theology. In my interpretation his argument sought to undermine the legitimacy of Aboriginal claims by attacking the moral basis of their society.

Morgan's starting point was the proposition that 'we have to rediscover the religious basis of our own activity'. He argued that it could be demonstrated that capitalism and hence the mining industry was 'part of the divine order'. The authority for this view was St Paul, in his first letter to the Corinthians, 7:20: 'Let every man abide in the same calling wherein he was called'. The 'calling' of miners was an economic one, to be justified in terms of the provision of work and creation of wealth. 'Our task . . . is to be good miners, successful miners, profitable miners.'

In contrast, the claims of Aboriginal people to land were not justifiable in Christian teaching. Morgan argued that recognition of Aboriginal land rights also entailed the recognition of a heathenish and barbaric culture. He challenged the Australian community: after land rights were granted, would there be sanction for 'infanticide, cannibalism, and . . . cruel initiation rites'? He professed himself unable to comprehend how the churches, and Australian society, could sanction action which for a Christian Aborigine entailed 'a symbolic step back to the world of paganism, superstition, fear, and darkness'. Morgan elaborated his position in a subsequent discussion:

if you start off by saying, on the basis of spiritual attachment to land, 'I must allocate this land'; the next phrase is 'I must therefore allocate their law.' Those who have studied and lived with Aborigines for long enough will know the inseparability of Aboriginal spirituality of land from their law and custom. Law and customs that are, in part, operative today. And these refer to initiation rites and a whole set of behaviour patterns that are totally in conflict with the law and custom and the Christian ethic that are the very basis of our law in this country. They are totally incompatible.

He was not content to rest his attack on generalities, invoking such evidence as he could muster to discredit Aboriginal culture. Relying in part on the research of Geoffrey Blainey, Morgan argued that here was a people who in their traditional society engaged in vengeance killing. Such killings exacted a far greater toll than 'any depredations by the Europeans'. On the basis of other sources he presented the view that Aboriginal people were cannibals: nineteenth-century accounts were 'quite explicit concerning the partiality of the Aborigines for the particular flavour of the Chinese, who were killed and eaten in large numbers'.

The notion that white Australians had pursued a policy of genocide represented 'nonsense'. Such charges were 'not used without calculation'—they were levelled 'to incite resentment and animosity within the Aboriginal community', 'to arouse ... white middle-class guilt', and 'to create expectations of compensation payments ... as atonement for past genocide'.

If Aboriginal people were to receive compensation, as advocated by the 'Aboriginal Affairs Industry', how would it be decided who would be the beneficiaries? To allow self-definition would be 'impossible' and he questioned whether the Australian people would embrace the idea of 'a Register of Aborigines, with all of the difficulties connected with racial classification that that implies'.

Such issues, Morgan argued, had not been thought through, the 'full implications of present policies' not realised. 'The Australian people would be appalled' once the issues were 'carefully and simply explained'. There was only one path for the future, that advocated by the mining industry: 'to treat all Australians equally', a position revealed by opinion polls to be 'the predominant good sense of the community'.

———

Geoffrey Blainey's initial foray into the discussion of racial issues predated Morgan's speech by two months. Unlike Morgan, he aroused a controversy that was to continue for the best part of a year, one not matched in ferocity until the 1993 reaction to the High Court's Mabo decision. One survey covering the period 19 March–30 September 1984 found over 350 newspaper articles dealing with Asian immigration. A selection of newspaper headlines from the first month of the controversy gives an indication of its tenor:

Asian entry threatens tolerance: Blainey
Cut Asian intake, warns Blainey
Asianisation of Australia is not 'inevitable', by Geoffrey
    Blainey
Immigration: time for sensible debate
Blainey stirs a sleeping issue
Blainey's spark lights racial fire
The Asian Debate
My critics advocate a surrender-Australia policy, says Blainey
Australia for the Asians, by Geoffrey Blainey

Blainey's views on immigration first won the media spotlight in a now famous speech to Warrnambool Rotarians in March 1984 and in a newspaper article he wrote some days later which introduced into the political lexicon the idea of the 'Asianisation' of Australia, a phrase he attributed to minister of immigration Stuart West.

Blainey sought to highlight a dramatic shift in immigration policy which had led to 'Asians' becoming 'a favoured majority'.

As a people, we seem to move from extreme to extreme. In the past 30 years the Government has moved from the extreme of wanting a white Australia to the extreme of saying that we will have an Asian Australia and that the quicker we move towards it the better ... I do not accept the view, widely held in the Federal Cabinet, that some kind of slow Asian takeover of Australia is inevitable. I do not believe that we are powerless.

This change of policy, according to Blainey, was insufficiently noticed or discussed by the Australian public or media and did not enjoy broad support, particularly in the suburbs and work-places to which many of the recent arrivals went. It was a policy marked by 'arrogance' and 'insensitivity towards a large section of Australian opinion'. Blainey argued that current immigration levels were too high given the high rate of unemployment, for immigration exacerbated competition for jobs. 'The poorer people in the cities' were the 'real sufferers' from this policy, those who had 'the least access to the Press and radio and television. They are the silent ones upon whom Canberra, perhaps unthinkingly, is now trampling'. The pace of Asian immigration was 'now well ahead of public opinion . . .'.

If the situation was allowed to continue serious community discord would ensue; continued immigration from Asia at the 1984 level threatened to 'weaken or explode' the tolerance extended to immigrants over the past 30 years: 'tolerance and understanding are like avocadoes: they grow only in a favourable climate'.

In contrast with the provocative attempts by Morgan to revive the justificatory values of a bygone age, Blainey sought to position himself as the articulator of the views of his contemporaries. He saw himself as the spokesperson of the silent majority, the average Australian, with the task to return balance to political debate.

Blainey sought to avoid the appearance of partisanship, the persona of a propagandist and for the best part of 1984 he was successful in this endeavour. He cultivated the style of the detached, even-handed academic, frequently drawing attention to the different sides of an argument. Some years later he stated: 'All the most interesting issues are really 60–40 per cent issues, aren't they? Yet you take a position and you are forced into a 100–0 debate. The media demand confrontation between people . . .'. Frequently in the early part of his speeches and newspaper articles he would counsel that there were two sides to each argument and both had a measure of validity. Thus, for example, 'the granting of land to Aborigines, and especially specific areas of cultural and religious importance, has much merit'. He did not advocate a return to the 'White Australia' policy. But there was a danger in going too far, in the loss of 'balance'.

Diametrically opposed views were formed of Blainey's public interventions. Some, such as the conservative commentator Frank Devine, saw him as the voice of moderation and reason, almost a decade later writing of his 'calm criticism of multiculturalism as government policy, and of the pace of Asian immigration'. On the other hand his critics, among whom I number myself, saw him as pandering to the basest instincts and inflaming community tension.

During the course of 1984 Blainey hurriedly wrote *All for Australia*, published late in the year. The book used the terminology of invasion and warfare to describe the impact of Asian immigration, prefiguring the politics of resentment and xenophobia which Pauline Hanson was to bring to the national stage in 1996. In a chapter entitled 'The Front Line is the Neighbourhood', he described the attempts of 'poorer Australians' to 'defend their own neighbourhood' from the 'Asian influx'. Areas were 'submerged by newcomers' who 'snatch jobs away'. He presented the views of one of the 'old Australians', a woman whose suburb 'has vanished':

'Can I tell you what we have to put up with? Pavements are now spotted with phlegm and spit because they think it is OK to spit everywhere and spread germs. They are noisy and entertain late, way past midnight. They cook on their verandahs, so the sky here is filled with greasy smoke and the smell of goat's meat.' Everywhere she sees babies and, as a taxpayer, she thinks to herself, I am helping to pay for their child endowment. She sees the new migrants driving big cars: 'I resent seeing Ethnics flying around in flash cars while I have to walk all the time.' She dislikes the strange smells from the cooking and the smell of the garbage, and she names the nationalities who in her view produce the worst garbage . . . And she wonders about her child, a boy of eight. What will become of him. He shares her fears; and one day he remarks that he wishes he could be young for ever because when he grows up all the jobs will probably be taken. An Australian, with an Australian mum, he is the odd boy out; and every day, she says, her son is bullied . . . She privately predicts race riots: 'There will be bloodshed in this country'.

A WAY OF UNDERSTANDING, A WAY OF SPEAKING

In the years following 1984 Morgan developed his ideas primarily through public addresses, Blainey primarily through his journalism. Blainey became a syndicated columnist, writing at various times for the Murdoch and Fairfax presses. A collection of his articles was published under the title *Blainey: Eye on Australia* in 1991. His writing can be seen as significant in shaping the concepts employed in the New Right's battle for moral supremacy. Blainey had a genius for the phrase which captured the essence of detailed argument. Previously exemplified in his academic work, perhaps with best effect in the title of his *The Tyranny of Distance*, in his role as conservative propagandist he invented or did much to popularise the terminology of the 'Surrender Australia Policy', the multicultural 'industry', the 'nation of tribes' and the 'black armband' view of history.

This linking of Morgan and Blainey is not, however, to argue that they were acting in tandem. On some issues there were significant differences of opinion between the two. Morgan rarely spoke on immigration; in 1988 he seemed to support discrimination on the basis of cultural difference, applying a rule of 'marriageability' in selection criteria and illustrating his argument by reference to the plays of Shakespeare, but he advocated unrestricted entry for immigrants from the major English-speaking countries. In 1992 he spoke of 'massive immigration' of about half a million annually. Blainey, unlike Morgan, did not oppose the principle of land rights, nor did he directly disparage Aboriginal culture. Morgan was heavily involved in the organisational side of the New Right; Blainey, although encouraged and patronised by the New Right, was an independent academic of international stature who developed a career late in life as a public controversialist and freelance journalist. In response to questioning in 1986 he stated:

> I would rather remain unlabelled: a lot of my views would be seen as right-wing, but a lot aren't. I support Aboriginal land rights, but moderate land rights—not the Federal Government's version. Aboriginals shouldn't have a veto over mining, but they should be granted royalties.

Despite this disclaimer, he did much to legitimise aspects of the New Right agenda. Although often a moderate voice on public issues, he was capable of taking extreme positions, with apparent disregard for the inflammatory effect of his words. Thus, for example, he could compare policies providing benefits to minorities with the policies of Nazi Germany: 'Hitler was a master of affirmative action. So was South Africa in the heyday of apartheid. Affirmative action has a sad history as well as a constructive history'.

How are the roles of Morgan and Blainey to be understood? Not as the creators without whom racial issues would have been absent from the mainstream of Australian politics. The development of racial politics was common to a number of western democracies and this feature of late twentieth-century politics was not likely to bypass Australia. Morgan and Blainey were, however, of major importance. In my view, they led the way by breaking mainstream taboos and did much to give form to Australian debates on immigration and other issues. In this task they were assisted by a number of conservative figures, not least by Member of the House of Representatives Graeme Campbell and Senator John Stone; Peter Coleman, editor of *Quadrant* and prominent Liberal Party politician; public controversialists, including Bruce Ruxton, president of the Victorian Returned Servicemen's League; influential conservative commentators in the print media, notably Padraic McGuinness, Frank Devine and Michael Barnard; and talk-back radio hosts among whom Alan Jones, Ron Casey and Stan Zemanek were prominent.

Although Blainey and Morgan continued to develop their ideas after 1984, their initial speeches and writings largely prefigured the structure and emphases of the critique of policies which originated in the Whitlam years. This critique comprised three core elements: criticism of supposed policies of racial discrimination, identification and criticism of interest groups and exposure of the techniques by which they sought to gain their ends and warnings of the consequences for the nation if sectional interests were allowed to prevail.

The first element concerned the definition of legitimate and illegitimate policies, proceeding on the taken-for-granted assumption that good governments treated all citizens 'equally'. Such governments supposedly maintained a balance which served the interests of the bulk of the population. Illegitimate policies were ones which catered to minorities, to extremists. Prime examples of such policies were land rights for Aboriginal people (or, in the view of some, more correctly described as land rights for some individuals who claimed to be Aboriginal), immigration policies favouring Asian immigrants, multiculturalism and affirmative action.

The second element was based on identification of opposed interest groups. On the one side were the Australians, a people with an honourable history, who through hard work had established for themselves a high standard of living in a hostile physical environment. Australians were a people rightly respected for their traditions of a 'fair go', whose open society provided boundless opportunities for those wanting to enter their world, be they Aboriginal or immigrant. According to Morgan, again quoting Biblical authority:

> Australians are heirs to a culture, a technology, and a language which enables them 'to replenish the earth and subdue it: and to have dominion over the fish of the sea, and over the fowl of the air, and over every living thing that moveth upon the earth'.

Given the record of hard work and achievement, there was no reason for Australians to feel guilt. In Morgan's view 'the guilt which provides political capital for the guilt industry is not guilt for actions for which we ought to feel guilty. We are dealing with a neurotic condition in which people feel guilty for crimes they did not commit'. Blainey also celebrated great economic successes and the country's proud democratic traditions.

In contrast, the sectional interests which sought to overthrow the 'Australian way of life' were motivated by their own narrow interests, perhaps loyalty to foreign masters or even a death wish induced by self-hatred. In Blainey's view there were people to be found among members of parliament, the staff of leading newspapers, employees of the ABC and in the secondary and tertiary education system 'who rarely celebrate Australia's past'. In September 1984 he referred to a divisive and parochial 'multicultural industry'. Such groups together comprised less than 10 per cent of the adult population, according to Blainey, but 'they have stormed the moral heights, even maybe the spiritual heights and captured them'. The great majority of Australians were being 'bluffed into doubting their own legitimacy and even their own rights'.

Was there some sort of conspiracy to destroy the country? Morgan identified a long-term strategy to divide and denigrate, but steered clear of the language of conspiracy, employing the categories of class and interest group. Thus he wrote in 1988 of:

A campaign conducted by the guilt industry; a campaign which has been designed above all to delegitimize the settlement of this country. The rhetoric of guilt . . . is coming from church leaders, academics, journalists, and Government ministers.

Blainey was similarly minded in most of his writings, although in his 1984 book *All for Australia* he employed terminology dear to the minds of conspiracy theorists, arguing that there existed in Canberra, 'unknown to the public, unknown probably to the parliament', a 'secret room' inside which 'are devised plans that run counter to the immigration principles announced . . .'.

In keeping with the New Right emphasis on the power of ideas, attention was directed to the subversive impact of the rewriting of history. Blainey spoke of those who regarded the history of Australia before 1950 as a 'desert'. They had:

a deep sense of grievance about much of Australia's history . . . They see Australia's history as largely the story of violence, exploitation, repression, racism, sexism, capitalism, colonialism, and a few other isms.

In April 1993 he characterised such views of the past as 'the Black Armband view of history', a description that was to enter the political lexicon.

In a speech delivered on Australia Day 1985 Morgan asserted that in the quest to destabilise the nation an 'Orwellian reconstruction' was underway with the intent, through control of knowledge of the past, to control the present and the future. 'Our national sovereignty, and the legitimacy of the settlement that began formally on 7 February 1788 is under political threat'. His inspiration was the visiting British philosopher Roger Scruton who counselled that 'recuperation of our history has become a most important and significant duty for us'. The task, Morgan wrote, was to 'remember our famous men and women, and to praise their courage, their endurance, their faith', to regard the pioneers with pride and feelings of gratitude. Those who could not 'respect their parents and grandparents, who cannot identify with them in the difficulties and problems they faced, cannot respect themselves'.

The attempt to rehabilitate the forebears led to criticism of the depiction of Aboriginal people and frontier conflict in the new histories. In part this was an attempt to reassert the values which informed traditional understandings; at times it descended into crude attempts to besmirch. It was as if, having assimilated the New Right injunction to learn and apply the techniques of the enemy, its champions now proceeded to repay supposed denigration in kind.

It was taken as proven that ideologically driven historians and anthropologists had presented a false and romanticised view of the culture and history of the Aboriginal people in an attempt to create a feeling of guilt and provide the basis for compensation claims. The reality, asserted by Morgan and others, was that Aboriginal culture was heathenish and barbaric, distinguished by its toleration of infanticide, cannibalism, cruel initiation rites and vengeance killings.

The Asian immigrants who were brought to the country in supposedly excess numbers came from alien cultures, snatched jobs away from the native-born and threatened to change the character of the country. Morgan, while specifically eschewing racial discrimination, counselled against admission into the country of people who 'may not, should not, or cannot, marry with each other'; he found 'difficult to imagine' the integration through marriage of those who could not speak English and had no 'religious ties' and 'cultural affiliation' with the Australian people.

The third element was prophecy, based on an estimation of the likely outcome of government policies. The idea of betrayal (often discussed in the context of threat from an external enemy) leading to national destruction was a theme increasingly emphasised.

The consequence of a policy of affirmative action (depicted as a form of racial discrimination) was the dividing of Australia, with no long-term benefit for the recipients of government aid. Blainey referred to the creation of 'a cluster of competing tribes', a series of ethnic islands. In a 1986 Australia Day address he commented that:

> Our current emphasis on granting special rights to all kinds of minorities, especially ethnic minorities, is threatening to disperse this nation into many tribes ... A nation is ultimately bound together by a sense of shared obligations and duties. Ultimately it can be pulled apart and even shattered by an emphasis on the rights of each minority and on the virtues of divisiveness.

In Morgan's words 'the Grassbian ideal of a polylingual, polycultural, polypolitical social porridge', presumably a reference to multiculturalism, could never produce a community capable of defending itself. In the view of some, if ideologically motivated minorities continued to press their agenda Australian tolerance would be pushed beyond the breaking point, with the prospect of an outbreak of vengeance motivated violence.

MABO

The major racial controversy before 1996 was sparked by the High Court's Mabo decision, delivered in June 1992. Analysis of the arguments employed shows the extent to which a racialised form of reasoning had become established in Australian public life.

For almost a full year after the decision reaction was muted, despite the efforts of Morgan and others to bestir public protest and government action. In October 1992, in what was described as the 'first ... considered response from industry', Morgan asserted that the High Court had 'put at risk ... the whole legal framework of property rights throughout the whole community'. He called for repeal of the *Racial Discrimination Act* to allow the states to legislate and to restore security of property title. The Mabo decision, he claimed, 'effectively creates recognition of Aboriginal law, as if it were the law of a foreign country'; there was now the prospect of a separate Aboriginal taxation system, passports and diplomatic representation.

Late in January 1993, in the run-up to the March federal election, Morgan criticised the Opposition's acceptance of a bipartisan approach to Aboriginal issues which supposedly stifled debate. In April, in a speech to the centenary conference of the Australian Institute of Mining and Metallurgy, he accused Prime Minister Keating of jeopardising the nation's future by promoting policies motivated by guilt. Until the late 1960s, he asserted, well founded policies had sought through 'patient assimilation' to bring Aboriginal people into the mainstream of Australian life: now policies promoted separatism which could only lead to greater incidence of poverty and alienation. The way forward required that Aborigines 'give up much of what contemporary official rhetoric describes as their unique culture'. In response to criticism by Robert Tickner, Minister of Aboriginal Affairs and Minister Assisting the Prime Minister on Aboriginal Reconciliation, he wrote that 'the drift of contemporary policy in Aboriginal affairs, in general, and the consequences of the Mabo decision, in particular, have the capacity (once these things are widely understood) to divide and embitter this nation to a degree we have not previously experienced'.

Bipartisanship in politics was insulating politicians from the realities of public opinion; sooner or later, he predicted, 'the force of opinion will constrain governments'. In May Geoffrey Blainey, speaking in Perth at the Chamber of Mines' Mineral Outlook '93 seminar, commented that the Mabo issue was '20 times' more significant for Australia's sovereignty than the republican debate and should be the catalyst for a major shift in government policy.

At that time such comments failed to spark public reaction. While noting the criticism of Morgan and Dr Colin Howard, former professor of law at Melbourne University, the *Sydney Morning Herald* observed in an editorial that 'the High Court judges dumped the doctrine of terra nullius because it was a product of an age of extreme racial discrimination and totally out of step with current international law'. It would cause difficulties for the determination of future land claims but there should be no fear of 'legal anarchy, a loss of investor confidence, or the creation of an Australian variant of apartheid'. Canada's experience, for example, provided a positive lesson: 'The Canadian Government has negotiated land claim settlements with indigenous communities across the country' which served to 'integrate those communities into the national life without unduly burdening the rest of the population'. Such negotiated settlements had provided indigenous people with a self-sustaining economic base. This was the path that beckoned, 'if only we are prepared to choose it'. Prime Minister Keating similarly argued that Mabo offered Australia the prospect of becoming a country 'which is in its soul at peace with itself ... an opportunity to deal very late in the piece, but better late than never, with the injustice of Aboriginal dispossession'.

A calm, measured response was not, however, acceptable to the critics. At the beginning of June 1993 a vehement outcry arose across the nation, sparked by the federal government's principles to guide native title legislation. Indicative of the extent of public debate, in the three months June–August 1993 Aboriginal issues appeared on the front page of the *Sydney Morning Herald* on twenty-nine occasions, for five weeks in this period on at least every second day. Leading the attack were conservative politicians (including state premiers and National and Liberal members of parliament), leaders from the mining industry, financiers, media columnists and radio talk-back hosts. Their arguments contained four main elements.

The first element concerned the illegitimacy of the ideas which underlay the High Court's concept of native title. A number of commentators rehearsed the argument that the normal and appropriate course for governments was to maintain the equal treatment of all citizens, the 'level playing field' and not tolerate the regression from this ideal represented by 'native title'. Western Australian Liberal State President, Bill Hassell, described native title as based on 'racial discrimination. You have to be an Aboriginal person or a Torres Strait Islander person to be qualified to get native title'. In the words of Morgan, Mabo 'brings in a separate law for one group of Australians. It encourages aboriginal Australians to think of themselves as separate and distinct from their fellow citizens'.

Second, the critique was directed at those who supported 'native title'. The once respected judges of the High Court had become transformed, in the words of John Stone, into 'Aboriginal industry spokesmen'. A criticism was mounted that the judges, on a number of counts, had betrayed the demands of their high office. The critics professed a view of the law as non-problematical: the legal 'facts' were there for all to see, parallel with the 'facts' of history. The role of the judge, as of the historian when chronicling the story of Australia, was presented as one of neutrality, one of simply establishing the correct reading of the law or ordering of facts, not of embarking on a highly complex interpretative exercise, involving the evaluation of contradictory principles and evidence.

The Mabo decision was, in the words of Western Australian premier Richard Court, 'fatally flawed'. The decision gave insufficient weight to the body of legal precedent which should have guided the judges' deliberations and they had allowed themselves to usurp the role of legislators and embarked on a legal revolution. Barrister and Liberal Party frontbencher Peter Costello argued: 'Once upon a time, Parliament made the law and the courts interpreted it. But all that has changed . . . You've got unelected, and maybe unrepresentative, people making the rules that we all have to live under. And if you don't like what they're doing, you can't vote them out'.

Blainey encapsulated the argument of the critics in one sentence: 'in effect, the High Court has become a parliament, an unelected parliament'. Heightening his criticism late in the year, he declared that the High Court had 'not done its work properly'; its judgment seemed to rest on 'hearsay, prejudice and misguided research'; some of the judges were 'noteworthy in their ignorance'. The climax of this assault came with the proposition that unless the judges could indicate where they found the evidence for the 'strong historical statements' then the Chief Justice 'should seriously consider making way for a chief justice who is willing to carry out all the duties'.

Third, there was the critique of the beneficiaries of 'native title'. In part a reaction to the assertion of Justice Brennan who argued that the law should not be allowed to remain 'frozen in an age of racial discrimination' and that a failure to adapt to changing social values would be 'unacceptable' to the Australian people, the critics thundered: 'what age of racial discrimination?', 'what was unacceptable to the Australian people?'. This was 'guilt industry' talk. How, they asked, had the learned judges come to these views?

Apparently unable to contain their fury, in the third week of the public disputation the critics moved beyond arguments focused on legal principle to attacks on Aboriginal culture, at times to overt dismissal of the rights of Aboriginal people on the basis of race.

Tim Fischer, National Party leader, assumed the mantle of archaeologist to reveal that 'at no stage did Aboriginal civilisation develop substantial buildings, roadways or even a wheeled cart as part of their different priorities and approach. ... Rightly or wrongly dispossession of Aboriginal civilisation was always going to happen. White settlement of the Australian land mass was inevitable'.

Morgan, in his element, won front page coverage on 1 July where during previous months he had struggled for attention. The

Sydney Morning Herald headed its lead article 'Mining Chief Lashes Mabo', the *Australian Financial Review* ran with 'Morgan Splits Miners After Mabo Outburst'. Ever active in the search for established truths in the writings of the great thinkers of the west, he now put forth an argument based in the world view of a seventeenth-century British political philosopher. Thomas Hobbes in his *Leviathan* had described the life of primitive and uncivilised European man as 'solitary, poore, nasty, brutish and short'. 'These words', Morgan counselled, 'provide a description of life which is very close to all contemporary accounts of eighteenth- and nineteenth-century Aboriginal life ... they lived in continual fear of violent death, particularly the women'. Reviving the nineteenth-century justification of colonialism, Morgan pointed to the fact that Aboriginal society had no written language, had not invented the wheel, and had no political institutions. Such a culture could have no future:

> Guilt industry people have great difficulty in accepting, or recognising, that aboriginal culture was so much less powerful than the culture of the Europeans, that there was never any possibility of its survival ... Because the Europeans had the ships, the navigation skills, the weapons, the technology, the wealth, the people, the ambition; the future of Australia was going to be either a French or an English future, not an aboriginal one ... The English got here before the French, and the rest is history.

Others focused on contemporary Aboriginal society, introducing arguments overtly based on race to justify their positions. Northern Territory Chief Minister Perron observed, in the context of a comment on Aboriginal health standards, that 'part of the problem is they really are centuries behind us in their cultural attitudes and their aspirations in many respects'. Former prime minister John Gorton commented that he could not see the point of throwing the country into turmoil for the sake of 1 per cent of the population who were, in any case, 'not as good as the white people'.

The attack on the worth of Aboriginal people was perhaps taken furthest in the comments of Henry Bosch, former chairman of the National Companies and Securities Commission. Bosch observed that the Aborigines were 'a Stone Age people' who were 'the most backward one per cent of the population'. He clarified his position in a subsequent newspaper interview. Aborigines were:

> the most backward by any objective set of achievements by which I can think. I realise that this is not a politically correct thing to say. I have the utmost contempt for political correctness, the white-washing of Aboriginal people who are a Stone Age people ... [The High Court decision recognising native title was] regrettable, entirely regrettable. I think we should forget completely about any concept of Aboriginal land rights and if that requires legislation, then let's do it ... I don't want reconciliation, I don't believe it's necessary, nothing should be done, let's get on with something serious. Aboriginal reconciliation is a complete waste of time and a diversion from important things.

Others counselled Aboriginal people against living in the past; in the past everybody had been dispossessed, for example the Anglo-Saxons had to contend with the Norman conquest. Aborigines should concern themselves with the present. They should congratulate themselves that it was the British who got here first; they had been treated no differently to other indigenous populations, indeed much better than most.

Last, the country's future, were the policy of advantaging Aboriginal interests not overturned, was presented in the most threatening light. In the view of the critics, the legacy of the Mabo decision presented a crisis of the gravest proportions. Thus Ian

McLachlan, Liberal member of the federal parliament and Opposition spokesperson on national development, observed that Mabo 'risks the stability and future development of the nation'. In Morgan's words, the decision carried 'the seeds of territorial dismemberment of the Australian continent and the end of the Australian nation as we have known it'. In an address to the annual conference of the Victorian Returned Servicemen's League, where he was accorded a standing ovation, he declared that there was a prospect of 'very rapid economic decline and . . . a partitioning of the continent'. In his newspaper column Blainey, although not opposed to the principle of land rights, wrote eloquently that:

> we could well end up with two permanent systems of land tenures and the genesis of two systems of government . . . Aboriginal lands form almost a continuous corridor from the Arafura Sea to the Southern Ocean, with only tiny breaks in the continuity . . . One large Aboriginal area has the rainfall and general capacity to support a nation of many millions at East Asian standards . . . To extend land rights is also to weaken . . . the real sovereignty and unity of the Australian people.

ONE NATION

In the first chapters of this book a mode of thought common to a number of western countries was discussed. Its features included glorification of the nation, pride in its history and culture, a demand for unity, negative designation of 'minorities', calls for 'balanced' policies and equal treatment for all. This chapter has illustrated the growth of this way of ascribing meaning to contemporary events in Australia.

I have argued that Hugh Morgan and Geoffrey Blainey played a major role in breaking mainstream taboos and did much to give form to Australian debates. In this they were assisted by a number of conservative critics and it is clear that, by the time of the 1993 disputation over native title, while they remained important spokesmen, they no longer enjoyed the prominence they commanded in 1984 but were now two voices among many.

The ways of talking about racial issues were discussed in Chapter 1. Elements of an overtly racialist approach could still find their way into mainstream discussion in 1993. Aboriginal people were depicted as a 'backward', 'Stone Age people'; in appraising their rights in the contemporary world some protagonists in the disputation considered it relevant to note that they had not invented the wheel—presumably if they had done so then land rights would have been conceded. But the language of racial difference was not the major feature of public discussion, nor did culturalist modes of speaking about the unbridgeable gulf between peoples feature prominently.

In Australia variants of the 'equal rights' argument were to the forefront, enabling arguments to be based on principles of supposed universal validity. As discussed in the Introduction to this book, the critics of Mabo sought to enlist 'common sense' and logic for their cause, while ignoring the possibility that Aboriginal people were not claiming special rights but rights similar to any other litigant pursuing their interest in property as recognisable in common law.

The logic of Australian constructions of meaning based on 'equal rights' led increasingly to emphasis on national unity, the idealisation of the 'one nation', to the denial of pluralism and the legitimacy of multiple identities.

In the early period of his public intervention Blainey had invoked the image of the nation divided. In his 1985 description, the 'great majority of Australian-born citizens believe we should be one nation, not a nation of many nations'. Leader of the Opposition John Howard announced his vision of 'One Australia' in 1988. By the early 1990s the juxtaposition of one nation/many nations/divided nation had become a central feature of political consciousness. Responding to this reality, in 1992 even Labor under the prime ministership of Paul Keating titled its four-year plan for economic growth 'One Nation'. Keating argued that:

> the most successful societies are notable for their unity, for the co-operative quality of all their relationships, from the workplace up. This is the kind of Australia we seek, and which I firmly believe we can have. An Australia which is more truly one nation.

In the context of Mabo Morgan warned that if the crisis sparked by the High Court's decision was not resolved 'Australia will soon become a divided nation, no longer in undisputed possession of this island continent, and unable to face with any confidence the external dangers which history teaches us will, inevitably, one day threaten us'. He called on his audience 'to stand up for the ideals of federation—one nation—one continent; one law, one people, one destiny'.

4

John Howard, Leader of the Opposition, Prime Minister

*B*y the time he was elected prime minister John Howard had served for 22 years as a member of parliament. First elected to the House of Representatives in 1974 he was a minister within two years, treasurer from 1977–83 and twice leader of the Opposition. While Morgan and Blainey first broke with accepted norms in mainstream public discussion, it was Howard who was to bring racial issues to the forefront of federal politics, first in 1988. In contrast with the other Liberal Party leaders during the party's thirteen years in opposition—Peacock, Hewson and Downer—Howard was willing to campaign on issues of race and break the bipartisanship which had characterised the Whitlam–Fraser years. Once in government he continued to entrench policy differences and lent an air of legitimacy to the phenomenon of Hansonism in its crucial formative period. As his former leader John Hewson observed in June 1998, 'the Liberal Party actually tried to get on the back of [Hanson's maiden speech], . . . to ride it to their electoral advantage. And they are still trying to do it'.

Labelled by Prime Minister Keating as the most conservative of coalition leaders, Howard described himself as radical in economics and conservative in social and cultural matters:

I think of the Menzies period as a golden age in terms of people. Australia had a sense of family, social stability and optimism during that period ... I believe in the traditional values of Australia: egalitarianism, strong families, entrepreneurial opportunity, hard work, Protestant work ethic. I believe economically that the government should leave it to the markets. If you have a choice between government enterprise and private enterprise you should give it to private enterprise.

Thus the Liberal leader who presided over radical budget change and privatisation was also responsible for the socially conservative 'Future Directions' document in 1988 whose cover depicted, in the words of David Barnett, Howard's biographer, 'a happy family, a nice-looking couple with two nice-looking children, standing before their nice home with its white picket fence, with a nice family car in the driveway'.

Of the succession of Liberal leaders after the defeat of the Fraser government in 1983, it was Howard who most clearly drew on the cultural values propounded by the New Right, stressing the need to fight the ideological battle to ensure long-term economic restructuring of society. He presented a simplistic, bipolar defence of Australian history and culture, rejecting the 'guilt industry' and drawing sharp lines of division between unambiguous truth and unacceptable interpretation. He sought to position the Liberals as the party of Australian nationalism, the upholders of 'mainstream' values and of freedom of speech—in opposition to the divisive Labor Party, beholden to sectional groups, acting against the national interest. While making pragmatic retreats and learning to temporise, particularly during the 1996 election campaign, Howard maintained what he described as 'a broad consistency of belief and sense of direction', 'crucial to political credibility'. His response to Hansonism, which surprised some, was fully in keeping with the policy direction he had set in the eight years preceding his election to office.

BACKGROUND

John Howard came from a relatively humble background for a leader of the conservative forces in Australia. He was certainly not born into the establishment and one of his early employers, who thought that Howard 'would have made a wonderful Labor leader of the Ben Chifley type', recalls his surprise when he discovered that Howard was an active member of the Liberal Party.

His father, a mechanic and returned serviceman from World War I, lost his job in the Depression, but managed to purchase a small garage in the Sydney suburb of Dulwich Hill. The youngest of four children, Howard was born in 1939 and was only sixteen when his father died after a period of serious illness. His biographer writes that the family was 'honest, unpretentious and upright, and strongly imbued with the Protestant work ethic . . . Small business, free enterprise and Liberal'. Paul Kelly argued in his *The End of Certainty* (1992) that Howard was the embodiment of Robert Menzies' 'forgotten people', typifying the middle-class values of hard work, decency and thrift, with a respect for profit, property and authority. Unlike his Labor predecessors, Hawke and Keating, Howard was to prove largely immune to the attractions of the high life, presenting himself as an unpretentious family man, at home in humble surroundings, the exemplar of the values he sought to perpetuate; even after his election to the prime minis-tership he maintained his (much publicised) annual holiday pilgrimage to the coastal town of Hawk's Nest where his family stayed in modest hotel accommodation and Howard rejoiced in his freedom to mix freely with his fellow Australians.

Howard was educated in the state system and at Sydney University where he studied law. He excelled 'neither in the classroom nor on the playing field', but was a highly skilled debater. After travel overseas he obtained employment in a small suburban law firm and worked within the New South Wales Liberal Party which he had joined at the age of eighteen, just after leaving school.

Rising in the party ranks he stood unsuccessfully for Drummoyne in the 1968 state election before winning preselection and a seat in the House of Representatives in 1974. Although recognised as a highly skilled political operator, he had repeatedly to struggle against his image as a 'little man', a good minister and deputy but without the capacity to inspire and lead.

LEADER OF THE OPPOSITION, 1985–89

Howard first stood for the position of Liberal leader in 1983; defeated by Andrew Peacock, he won the office two years later. Although not one of the party's first 'dries' or economic rationalists he was a convert by the mid-1980s and making a mark with his speeches on a broad range of topics, including foreign policy, immigration and the failures of left-wing orthodoxy. According to the journalist Anthony McAdam, much of the credit was attributable to the influence of Gerard Henderson, Howard's adviser until late 1986, who did much to broaden Howard's intellectual concerns.

The task of shaping a new direction for the Liberal Party was to prove difficult. Howard's first period of leadership was marked by internal party division, conflict over policy, and his own indecisiveness and inability to project himself as a viable national leader. He lost the 1987 election and in the following months faced destabilisation within Liberal ranks.

Having fought unsuccessfully on the issue of taxation reform Howard was determined in future to campaign broadly on a range of social and economic issues. Paul Kelly wrote that Howard was the first of his contemporaries to realise that 'free market economics required a moral dimension' to achieve electoral success. He set about winning the support of 'the growing reservoir of people who were worried, fearful and suspicious about the changes in economic power and social values occurring in Australia', by offering social policies geared to 'traditional family values' and 'chauvinistic nationalism'.

Howard first resorted to the politics of race in 1988, embarking on a concerted campaign to shatter the bipartisan position on Aboriginal affairs, immigration and multiculturalism. The aim was to accentuate and utilise racial issues to give the party an identity sharply differentiated from Labor. Consistent with the Blainey–Morgan line, on a number of occasions he argued that Labor policies were contrary to the long-term national interest. He promoted a vision of 'One Australia', of 'one nation and one future', based on rejection of a treaty with Aboriginal people, a halt to Aboriginal land claims, and a commitment to skill-based immigration.

In May 1988, at the first meeting in the new parliament house, Howard refused to endorse a resolution which stated that Aboriginal people had been dispossessed of their land. He refused to accept the view that there was any aspect of past policy for which he bore responsibility:

> I do not accept the doctrine of hereditary guilt. I acknowledge that, in the past, wrongs were done to Aboriginals, but they weren't done by me. They weren't done by my parents. They weren't done by my generation . . . I am all in favour of giving [Aboriginals] special help. They need it. But I am strongly against dividing the country between black and white. I think that is a recipe for disaster.

The Aboriginal Affairs Policy, released in October 1988, stated as its first basic principle that:

> The Coalition rejects the notion that this generation of mainly European Australians should feel a sense of guilt concerning actions of previous generations against the Aboriginal people. Guilt is not hereditary.

Assistance would be provided not by way of affirmative action programs for specific groups, but 'on the basis of need, irrespective of cultural background'. Labor policy, instead of promoting self-sufficiency, had increased dependence. While endorsing the ideal of reconciliation, there would be no treaty between 'Aboriginal and other Australians' as a treaty could only serve to divide the Australian people, creating hostility and doing nothing to overcome disadvantage. Should Labor enter a treaty the coalition pledged to renounce it. The coalition trumpeted that 'we are one nation and one people sharing one land with a common future'. In September 1988 Howard stated that while an advocate of 'equality of opportunity . . . I abhor the notion of an Aboriginal treaty because it is repugnant to the ideals of One Australia'.

Multiculturalism was denounced as a symptom of loss of national direction: 'to me multiculturalism suggests that we can't make up our minds who we are or what we believe in'. In January 1989 he stated:

> The objection I have to multiculturalism is that multiculturalism is in effect saying that it is impossible to have an Australian ethos, that it is impossible to have a common Australian culture. So we have to pretend that we are a federation of cultures and that we've got a bit from every part of the world. I think that is hopeless.

It was his stance on immigration, however, which was to prove the most controversial. In the course of the first half of 1988, armed with Liberal Party research and a carefully thought out strategy, Howard moved from calling for an immigration program 'which preserves and promotes unity and cohesion of Australian society', to talking of imbalance in immigration policy, to openly referring to a need to slow the pace of Asian immigration.

The coalition immigration and ethnic affairs policy, released on 22 August 1988, began with the assertion that the coalition stood for 'One Australia and welcome[d] all those who share our vision and are ready to contribute to it'. Echoing the Blaney critique, the policy document asserted that 'community acceptance of Australia's immigration policies has been seriously undermined' and that 'a major factor in immigration policy' needed to be 'the capacity of the Australian people to accept and absorb change … The size and composition of our immigration policy should not jeopardise social cohesiveness and harmony within the Australian community'.

By implication alleging undue influence by the ethnic lobby, it was stated that in future it would be a 'fundamental principle' of immigration policy that only 'the democratically elected government has the right to determine both the overall and the specific composition of our migrant intake'. The immigration intake would be increased, but priority would be given to 'migrants who are younger and who are skilled, knowledgeable, educated and employable'.

While affirming that 'in selecting between one individual and another, immigration policy will not discriminate against applicants on the basis of their race, colour, nationality, descent, national or ethnic origin, gender or religion', there could be adjustments 'to the size and composition of the immigration program in response to changing requirements, be they social, economic, political or humanitarian'.

On 1 August, explaining the approach on radio while the policy was still in draft form, Howard made clear that in future there could be fewer immigrants from specific regions, certainly in absolute terms and possibly as a proportion of the total. In response to questioning as to whether his policy would lead to a reduction from Asia, he stated: 'It could. Because if you have less family reunion, you may have less coming from Asia. It wouldn't be an aim … but that could happen'. Later the same day he was more direct. Asked whether the rate of Asian immigration was too fast, he stated:

> I think there are some people who believe it is. I wouldn't like to see it greater, I am not in favour of going back to a

White Australia policy. I do believe that if it is in the eyes of some in the community, it's too great, it would be in our immediate term interest and supportive of social cohesion if it were slowed down a little, so that the capacity of the community to absorb was greater.

This perspective was endorsed by the leader of the National Party, Ian Sinclair, who stated that: 'What we are saying is that if there is any risk of an undue build-up of Asians as against others in the community, then you need to control it ... I certainly believe, that at the moment we need ... to reduce the number of Asians ... We don't want the divisions of South Africa, we don't want the divisions of London. We really don't want the colour divisions of the United States'. National Party front bench member Senator John Stone joined the fray with an unambiguous assertion that 'Asian immigration has to be slowed. It's no use dancing around the bushes. Nobody is talking about stopping immigration, just a sensible adjustment in the composition of the program. That's what we're going to have and don't you make any mistake about it'.

This foray into racial politics was hardly an accident, the result of a mistaken word by a harried politician. It was reported in the national press that at the next election Howard planned to campaign strongly on the immigration issue. Laurie Oakes, writing in the *Bulletin*, reported that Howard had 'thought long and hard about the immigration issue before taking the plunge' and that the terminology of 'One Australia' had been his own work, not that of an advertising agency. He commented: 'The Opposition leader has taken a calculated risk and it may pay off'.

On this occasion, however, there were to be no prizes. A number of prominent Liberals opposed aspects of the policy in the party room; when Prime Minister Hawke moved a motion affirming that no Australian government would use race or ethnicity as a criterion for selecting immigrants Howard moved an amendment which restated the Liberal Party's new immigration policy, including emphasis on 'the capacity of the Australian people to accept and absorb change' as a factor in immigration policy. Three Liberal members of the House of Representatives voted with Labor and two abstained. They included two former Liberal ministers for immigration, Ian McPhee and Michael MacKellar, and future immigration spokesperson and minister Philip Ruddock. Some weeks later, when Stone reaffirmed his earlier comments and declined to endorse the generally worded coalition policy he was removed from the Opposition front bench.

The foray into immigration policy had divided the coalition and was seen by political commentators as a major contributor to the destabilisation of the Howard leadership, leading to his replacement by Andrew Peacock in May 1989. The episode was to leave a bitter legacy. In the ensuing years Howard sought to explain away his support for a racially discriminatory policy while nurturing a deep animosity for the lobby groups and sections of the press which had embarked on, what he regarded as unreasonable, criticism of his immigration views.

YEARS IN THE WILDERNESS

From May 1989 to January 1995 Howard served as Shadow Minister for Industrial Relations under three Opposition leaders, Andrew Peacock, John Hewson and Alexander Downer. Although formally limited in his role, he acted beyond the bounds of his portfolio, providing personal explanations for his actions in 1988 and seeking to establish a broad philosophical direction for the Liberal Party.

Distancing himself from his 1988 comments, Howard stated in an address to the Press Club in the following year that he regretted saying that immigration from Asia might fall at a faster rate than immigration from other parts of the world; his remarks had been taken as anti-Asian because of his own loose language and because of zealous misrepresentation by others: 'I regret the anti-Asian slant. I don't have a prejudiced bone in my body, and that did cause me a degree of personal unhappiness'.

He was to return to this issue on a number of occasions. He explained in 1995:

> I did not set out, in 1988, to say something which was racially based or discriminatory, but that impression lingered and in politics perceptions are important. I therefore felt that in order to remove the taint of suggested racism, I had to say something about it . . . I don't want there to be anything around to suggest that I am anything other than totally welcoming in our relations with people from that [Asia-Pacific] region.

Howard was still willing, however, until 1995, to enter into controversy in the immigration field. In 1992 his former adviser Gerard Henderson, then a leading syndicated columnist, questioned: 'why does he do it? Normally the most considered and best informed of the Coalition front bench, he seems to go into emotional overdrive whenever he hears the word immigration'. Amongst economists the short-term impact of immigration on unemployment had been a contentious issue for decades, with some of the view that because of its stimulus to domestic demand it had a small positive effect on employment, while others stressed that because of the increased numbers entering the labour market it had a marginal negative effect. With unemployment exceeding 10 per cent the government signalled a cut in immigration. Not content with this assurance in January 1992 Howard, together with his leader John Hewson, made an unproblematic link between the level of immigration and high unemployment and advocated that the program be 'cut to the bone'.

> Right now, high immigration is aggravating Australia's unemployment problem. Changes to the migration program should

have been made several years ago. Only the Government's fear of certain lobby groups prevented this happening. Continuing high immigration when the labour market is so weak is unfair to new arrivals, as it is to Australians both young and old competing with them for available places in the workforce.

In a bitter exchange Keating accused him of again resorting to race politics; Howard retorted that Keating was using a 'McCarthyist smear' to silence opposition, a theme that was to become a central element in his positioning of the Liberal Party.

In keeping with the New Right agenda, in these years Howard urged the necessity to fight the cultural war, to strive for moral ascendancy in political debate: 'Liberals must not underestimate the significance of Australian nationalism as a potent political issue'. In 1994 he bewailed that:

> There are still far too few Liberals who fully comprehend just how committed Paul Keating and many in the Labor Party are to the quite ruthless use of history—or more particularly their version of it—as a political weapon. Not only do they wish to reinterpret Australian history to promote their contemporary political objectives, but they also wish to do so to marginalise the contribution of the liberal-conservative side of Australian politics and entrench the Labor Party as the only true product of Australia's political soil.

The assault on the Keating vision—depicted as divisive, tainted with the negativism of the 'guilt industry' and intolerant of contrary viewpoints—was to require of Howard that he become the defender of 'traditional' Australian values, embodied in national history and literature. In this task he readily seized on the concept of the 'guilt industry', commenting that 'some of those who want a republic are heavily into the guilt industry. They exult in debunking Australia's past ... A special level of denigration is reserved for those institutions and practices which we have inherited from the British'. In January 1993, looking forward to the centenary of Federation in 2001, Howard presented a view of Australian history along lines established by Geoffrey Blainey:

> The broader debate about Australian society involves a clash between what can only be called the optimists and the apologists. The optimists essentially take the view that Australian nationhood has been a success, and that despite many flaws and imperfections, there have emerged distinctive Australian characteristics of humanity, fairness, egalitarianism and individual risk taking. By contrast, the apologists take a basically negative view of Australian history, and light upon every great national occasion not to celebrate Australian achievements, but to attempt the coercion of all of us into a collective act of contrition for the past. The apologists should not be allowed to capture our centenary celebration.

In developing the contrast between rival visions Howard was quick to adopt the 'Black Armband' concept. He stated in mid-1993:

> Paul Keating's convoluted and usually erroneous excursions into Australia's past exhibit many of the features of what Geoffrey Blainey has so aptly called 'the black armband' view of Australian history. Many republicans seek a rewriting of Australian history which demonises the British connection and marginalises the liberal/conservative contribution to our institutions and political thought.

Central to Howard's position was defence of the monarchy. Under the monarchy Australia had developed a stable, orderly system of government. Why seek to alter that which was working well? For Howard at least part of the explanation was that the monarchy was a central ingredient of the country's history and as such came under attack in the rush to denigrate its British legacy. A 'special level of denigration' was reserved for 'institutions and practices ... inherited from the British'. Keating's republicanism was 'divisive and spiteful'. He was a leader who 'sought to build support for his case, not through inspiration about the future, but through mocking our past. He has been a wounder and wrecker, not a healer and a builder. Not for him the language of national unity and evolutionary change'.

LEADER OF THE OPPOSITION, 1995–96

When re-elected to leadership in 1995 after a series of blunders by Alexander Downer, Howard surprised some of his supporters by taking a soft approach, especially on Aboriginal affairs, immigration and the republic. There would be no attack on the orthodoxies of racial policy in the Liberal Party's 1996 election campaign. Thus the coalition pledged that it 'is committed to maintaining and further enhancing Australia's unique and enriching cultural diversity'. Immigration would remain at least at its current levels and there would be increased funding of adult English teaching and community organisations, as well as a new anti-racism education program. Barnett writes that Howard had concluded that immigration 'was not worth fighting, that the political cost involved in wearing new allegations of racism and prejudice were too high'. The conservative Melbourne newspaper columnist Michael Barnard, apparently unaware of the campaign strategy, deplored Howard's

> skirting around issues on which he previously offered clearly articulated convictions ..., [his] apparent conversion from a sometimes spirited defender of uncomfortable principles, to today's soothing Valium Man ... He has blurred his conservative contours, at a time when conservatism can be described as the true progressive force in politics.

In the lead-up to the election Howard's approach was marked by 'a new sense of caution', a 'risk-averse strategy'.

Howard had learned to bide his time as a result of his personal mauling in 1988 and the party's 1993 defeat when Keating was able to use detailed policy proposals contained in John Hewson's *Fightback* to frighten the electorate and score an improbable victory. It was decided in 1995 that the way to win the election was to minimise the scope for controversy, to deprive Keating of a target. A former senior Liberal Party staffer commented that:

> the Coalition's electoral experience in 1993, together with party research, cautioned against radical policy commitments . . . Armed with private research indicating a popular cynicism about grand political promises and weariness with ideological differences, the Coalition parties chose to modify some policies and to stress only those that could be achieved by measured or incremental change, except in those key areas that were regarded as the core of their mandate for government.

The coalition would make Labor—in particular Keating—an 'obsession of the public' while confining itself to 'directions' and a 'general view' rather than specific policies. This was a strategy with some risks and for a period late in 1995 Labor was able to make inroads into the Liberal lead in opinion polls with charges that under Howard the party was 'a policy free zone'.

Until the launch of the campaign Howard devoted his attention to a series of 'headland' speeches, the first delivered in June 1995. In these he continued to work on the theme of Liberal inclusiveness and regard for the national good, in contrast with the prime minister's tactic to divide and rule. On 13 December he outlined his view of 'our national identity and the shared values and history that have shaped it, . . . [of the] lively traditions and values which bind us together as a people'. This vision of inclusiveness and harmony was to provide the basis for the policies of his government.

Crucial to this vision was its unwillingness to accept that there could be legitimate contrary viewpoints: this was the national, non-partisan perspective. In Howard's unproblematical view the 'truths' of history were evident for all willing to approach the past with an open mind. 'We learn from our history and we build on it. But we should not deny it or misrepresent it. . . . National identity is, and must remain, in a realm above the partisan fray.' Problems of interpretation arose only for 'people with axes to grind who aren't all that interested in the truth'.

> Our national character reflects the generosity of people used to living in a lucky country where there has been an unusually broad distribution of wealth. The only elite to which we have conceded much deference has been that based on ability and achievement—sporting, intellectual or artistic. We are still surprisingly free of class divisions, snobbery and envy, and remain so in spite of the gulf in recent years between the rich and the poor. Increased equality of opportunity has been by consensus a national policy priority for many generations.

National character sprang 'not from particular ideologies but from mainstream, egalitarian values', with which the Liberal Party was equated. The coalition claimed to stand for the Australian people, a positioning evident in the party's 1996 election slogan, 'For All of Us'. It was 'more in touch with the electorate' than Labor, it was the successor to Menzies whose 'political genius lay in that basic affinity with the aspirations of the Australian people'.

In contrast with the Menzies tradition Labor catered for noisy minority groups:

> There is a frustrated mainstream in Australia today which sees government decisions increasingly driven by the noisy, self-interested clamour of powerful vested interests with scant regard for the national interest. The power of one mainstream

has been diminished by this Government's reactions to the force of a few interest groups. Many Australians in the mainstream feel utterly powerless to compete with such groups, who seem to have the ear completely of the government on major issues. This bureaucracy of the new class is a world apart from the myriad of spontaneous, community-based organisations which have been part and parcel of the Australian mainstream for decades . . .

For the past twelve years Labor has governed essentially by proxy through interest groups. Identification with a powerful interest group has been seen as the vehicle through which government largesse is delivered. Increasingly Australians have been exhorted to think of themselves as members of sub-groups. The focus so often has been on where we are different—not on what we have in common. In the process our sense of community has been severely damaged. Our goal will be to reverse this trend. Mainstream government means making decisions in the interests of the whole community, decisions which have the effect of uniting, not dividing the nation, drawing upon the numerous community-based organisations which are the natural expression of the sense of neighbourhood which so many Australians have.

The critique of the 'Keating orthodoxy' was increasingly presented by Howard in terms of 'political correctness', in succession to Cold War rhetoric of the 1950s—'McCarthyism'—which was jettisoned in the context of the community's historical illiteracy.

Political correctness was a symbolic term of opprobrium, a rallying-cry for the opposition, taken from America where, to judge by a content analysis of the *Washington Post*, its usage peaked in 1993. Analysis of three Australian newspapers indicates increasing usage of the terminology from 1993 onwards, with a peak during the 1996 election campaign and its aftermath (see Table 4.1).

In positioning the Liberal Party Howard did not specifically

Table 4.1   Content analysis of the use of the phrase 'political correctness' in major daily newspapers[a]

Year	Washington Post (articles)	Sydney Morning Herald	Age	Australian Financial Review
1990	11			
1991	122			
1992	99	30 (0)		7 (0)
1993	151	84 (2)	85 (0)	28 (2)
1994	129	122 (10)	145 (8)	36 (1)
1995	115	174 (12)	162 (11)	38 (4)
1996	87	205 (74)	220 (65)	64 (29)
1997	90	126 (40)	152 (39)	48 (17)
1998	77	125 (50)	143 (34)	37 (16)
1999	78	78 (25)	118 (24)	

[a] Association with the name John Howard indicated in parentheses
Source: Washington Post online archives; CD-ROM versions of Australian newspapers

target programs which would be cut. Rather, he talked of the inclusiveness which would characterise his government, which would work 'for all of us', for the 'national good'. His government would adopt the standards of the Menzies era. But there was also a sub-text: some would gain, others would lose. 'Many Australians in the mainstream' had been left to 'feel utterly powerless'. Animosity was directed at the illegitimate interest groups which had been the recipients of 'government largesse', increasingly identified as the politically correct. Their fate remained to be spelled out.

PRIME MINISTER

After electoral victory restraint was cast aside. In the first year of office, despite the party's election pledges, immigration programs were cut and the Office of Multicultural Affairs and the Bureau of Immigration, Multicultural and Population Research were both disbanded. Some $400 million dollars was slashed from the Aboriginal budget and the fate of native title was left in the balance.

During the first months Howard rejoiced that the election of the coalition had lifted a 'pall' of 'social censorship' and had 'emboldened people to talk ... moderately and decently, but openly about all sorts of subjects in the Australian community'. He argued that 'a very unhealthy mood' had developed in Australia under Labor and asserted that 'certain subjects were absolutely off limits and ... you couldn't hope to talk about them in a rational, open fashion without being branded as some kind of bigot'. A journalist observed:

> 'political correctness'—the air is thick with the term. The impression we are given is that the freethinkers are emerging at last, in their exultant hordes, from the constraining net of political correctness.

In June 1996 Gerard Henderson noted that the prime minister had denounced political correctness 'at press conferences, during interviews, addressing the Coalition faithful, even at business functions'. He consistently argued that under Labor 'it was not possible ... to talk even about certain subjects without being branded with all sorts of reprehensible labels and descriptions'.

Howard declared that since the defeat of Keating 'a lot of people have said to me they just feel that they can, sort of, breathe again on certain subjects and talk about them, and not in a prejudicial fashion'. One of the 'second or third order reasons' for the defeat of Labor was 'the growing feeling of frustration amongst a lot of people that we had become too politically correct. There was too much social censorship'.

This post-election orientation was of central importance in explaining Howard's response to Pauline Hanson's inflammatory maiden speech (discussed in Chapter 6). Hanson called for the abolition of targeted benefits for Aboriginal people, the abolition of multiculturalism, and the reintroduction of a racially discriminatory immigration policy to save Australia from being 'swamped by Asians'. While her speech was greeted with widespread media criticism and public dismay—Henderson described it as the 'most intolerant outpouring by an Australian politician ... [in] three decades'—the prime minister could only rejoice that some of the issues to which he wished to direct attention had been aired and that political correctness had been dealt another blow. In the key period of Hanson's emergence into the public spotlight and the establishment of her political party Howard did much to lend her movement an air of respectability.

Seven days after Hanson's maiden speech the prime minister undertook his first overseas trip. Addressing a banquet hosted by President Suharto he stated, in opposition to Keating government policy and in tandem with the Hanson rhetoric, that he did not see Australia as a bridge between Asia and the west. It was necessary to realise that there were fundamental cultural differences between Australia and Asia. Australia would 'yield to nobody' in asserting the 'great qualities and enduring values' of its distinctive culture and traditions. 'We do not claim to be Asian'.

On his return he gave what came to be regarded as his landmark 'freedom of speech' address to the Queensland Liberal Party State Council. While warning against 'needlessly insensitive and intolerant language', the prime minister rejoiced that:

> One of the great changes that have come over Australia in the last six months is that people do feel free to speak a little more freely and a little more openly about what they feel. In a sense the pall of censorship on certain issues has been lifted ... I think that is a great thing for a healthy democracy ... I welcome the fact that people can now talk about certain things without living in fear of being branded as a bigot or as a racist or any of the other expressions that

have been too carelessly flung around in this country whenever somebody has disagreed with what somebody has said.

Robert Manne commented that 'when Hanson spoke of Australia
being swamped by Asians or of Aborigines being Australia's new
privileged class, Howard's response was not to deplore the arrival
of a new politics of race but to applaud the arrival of a new era
of free speech'.

As the political storm provoked by Hanson continued unabated,
Howard seemed incapable of distinguishing between freedom of
speech and abuse of that freedom. Interviewed by Alan Jones on
Radio 2UE on 30 September 1996, he was asked if he agreed with
anything in Hanson's maiden speech. He replied: 'I certainly
believe in her right to say what she said. I thought some of the
things she said were an accurate reflection of what people feel'.

He could see no pressing need in 1996 to take a leading role
in combating the public outpouring of bigotry; he was, it seems,
unwilling at this time to look beyond the discomfiture of his
detractors from years past. Michelle Grattan has written that while
Howard 'chose to be contrite for political reasons' over his
performance in 1988, he had 'never really learned from that
experience'. His memory was 'not that he had made mistakes, but
that he had been set upon by sections of his party' and 'the
"elites", including the media'. In the House of Representatives on
8 October 1996 he gave the clearest evidence of the scarring left
by earlier episodes, including Keating's taunts in 1992:

MR BEAZLEY: Will the Prime Minister now agree that it is
time for him to exercise leadership on this issue and state
clearly and unequivocally that the member for Oxley's
[Pauline Hanson] views on racial issues are hurtful to a great
many Australians, are damaging to our interests in the region
and do not reflect the kind of society that Australia is or
wants to be?

MR HOWARD: It is a serious question from the Leader of the Opposition, and I hope the House will enable me to give it a serious response . . . Have I generally followed the debate? Yes. Do I have a few things to say about it? Yes . . .

In my view there should be robust debate in this country about the size of our immigration policy. People are entitled to attack the present immigration levels without being branded as bigots or racists . . . If someone disagrees with the prevailing orthodoxy of the day, that person should not be denigrated as a narrow-minded bigot. That is basically what has been happening in this country over a very long period of time. It has been happening—

MR [DUNCAN] KERR: What about Hanson?

MR HOWARD: The Honourable Member for Denison interjects. When you had people who dared to disagree with your version of how to handle Aboriginal affairs, when you had those people being branded as racists and bigots, then you have a perfect demonstration of the sort of McCarthyism that was creeping into Australian politics under the leadership of the former Prime Minister. McCarthyism was creeping into Australian politics.

I can remember early in 1992 when unemployment went to a very high level and the . . . former opposition leader, John Hewson, and I both called for a reduction in the overall level of immigration because of its link with the level of unemployment. For our pains, we were bucketed by the former Prime Minister as racist. He actually used that expression. That is the kind of behaviour that I regard as absolutely unacceptable . . .

I will always denounce racial intolerance. I will always defend the non-discriminatory character of Australia's immigration policy. I believe that the contribution that Australians of Asian descent have made to this country has been immense . . .

THE HOWARD AGENDA

The attack on political correctness had served the prime minister well, as the rallying cry for his ideological attack on the value system that he sought to jettison. When Howard talked about censorship of views he uncritically conflated a number of meanings. Censorship literally refers to the act of preventing a person from communicating through the spoken or written word. A censor 'examines books, plays, news reports, films, radio programs, etc., for the purpose of suppressing parts deemed objectionable on moral, political, military, or other grounds'. In this sense there was no suppression of political ideas in the 1980s and 1990s. The prime minister and others who attacked 'censorship' by the 'politically correct' sought to shift the opprobrium attached to the practice of censorship to acts of a very different nature: the lack of respect accorded to certain ideas, an unwillingness to listen to and enter into dialogue, a dismissiveness, what may ultimately be termed the disempowerment of ideas and value systems. The proponents of the ideas which the prime minister claimed were suppressed had ample access to the media; they spoke and were reported. What they lacked was a congenial reception.

What was under attack in the battle against political correctness, cloaked by the generality of the championing of freedom of speech, was a value system that had been accepted by the major Australian political parties over the last quarter of a century, albeit increasingly grudgingly by conservatives. Howard openly admitted that the aim was to change the political culture along lines fashioned by Australian conservative thinkers led since the mid-1980s by Hugh Morgan and Geoffrey Blainey. In the context of mooted discussion of cuts to the Aboriginal affairs budget, he announced in April that 'we are not going to be scared off doing things that are necessary in the interests of Australian taxpayers by some kind of politically correct quarantining of certain activities from any kind of scrutiny'. The government was entitled to ask whether the money was helping the people it should 'without being accused of prejudice or bigotry, without being knocked off course by ... phoney charges of racism'. In August he stated that 'you do require a cultural change after thirteen years. It's half a generation'. The 'more difficult challenges we face', he claimed, included 'turning around the cultural attitudes in some areas'.

Some political commentators saw Howard's reaction to Hanson as a massive miscalculation. Closer to reality, as I see it, is the view that he welcomed her first forays into racial politics, her championing of values which they both accepted as those of the majority, her attack on political elites and their values and her championing of 'equal rights' as consistent with his brand of conservatism and as working to clear a path for his own agenda. The extreme statements of Hanson—and her popularity—served to maximise damage to their common opponents, without the need for the prime minister himself to adopt an overtly extremist stance. It seemed to be with the greatest reluctance that Howard agreed, over two years after Hanson's entry into national politics and following her party's spectacular success in the Queensland state election, that One Nation should be placed below Labor in allocation of preferences.

Like Hanson, Howard presented a vision of 'one nation' and 'one truth', albeit with less jarring notes. While attacking the intolerance of Keating, he introduced a new intolerance of his own. There was now freedom of speech and expression, but no legitimacy was accorded to advocacy of Aboriginal rights and 'divisive' multiculturalism, nor to views of history and national character fundamentally different from the values of the 'mainstream', as defined by the prime minister. This involved a move away from pluralism towards the reassertion of a unitary value system. The pendulum had been reset, balance had been re-established. This process was presented as 'natural', the product of 'common sense', 'non-ideological', with a total unwillingness to recognise the partisanship involved in the definition of 'centre' and 'balance'.

Howard and Hanson were courting the same constituency.

Thus, to take but one example, the prime minister appeared on the Stan Zemanek radio show—broadcast on 35 stations in the eastern states and renowned for its pro-Hanson stance—three nights before the 1998 Queensland state election to appeal to One Nation supporters to give their second preferences to the coalition. His purpose was to convince the voters that his was a government that they could trust. He was determined to fix the 'Native Title mess'; he would not accept that there should be one law for Aboriginal people and another law for farmers and miners. He had reduced immigration to 'pretty modest levels'. The family reunion program had been 'out of control' in the past but now it had been 'very very significantly limited'. Without referring specifically to immigration from Asia, he stated: 'we have reduced the emphasis on family reunion and we are now bringing in far more people from different parts of the world who have skills and who can make a contribution'. A two-year waiting period had been introduced to limit immigrant access to welfare benefits. Lastly, the government had changed the approach to international treaties which limited national sovereignty; he was 'angry' about the treaties that governments had entered into in the past.

Howard was clear that his government would respect the prejudices and sensitivities in the community. As he explained on another occasion, a leader on some issues had 'to get out in front and defy people to run him over. On other issues he's got to stay back and listen'. In areas of racial policy he would follow. He stated, echoing Blainey, that 'immigration is always something that needs to be handled carefully ... you have to always take a community along with you in these things'.

The embracing of these perspectives involved a wilful blindness to other truths: a blindness to the plight of refugees who sought shelter in Australia; to families denied the opportunity for reunion; to the risk to democracy posed by the willingness to allocate preferences and consider alliances with extremist forces (as discussed in later chapters); and to the tragedies which marked the lives of Aboriginal people of past and present generations. In the first four years of his prime ministership Howard remained consistent in his refusal to offer an apology to Aboriginal people on behalf of the Australian government. Jackie Huggins, a noted indigenous author and member of the Reconciliation Council recalls a meeting with the prime minister:

> Three of our people from the stolen generation spoke to him, told him their stories. And one of them said, 'Well sir, after hearing all our stories, we would hope that you would reconsider the apology'. He was sitting from me to you away, and I tried to get a sense of his body language. And, you know, there was nothing. He was stiff. He was numb. There was nothing.

In the first four years of his prime ministership Howard had visited just one Aboriginal community. It was not for the prime minister to learn from first hand experience; rather, he would set the standards, Aboriginal people would be the ones to make accommodations, to learn and accept, as had been the practice of past generations.

The gulf that now marked the position occupied by the prime minister and sections of the population which rejected his 'one truth' was perhaps no more clearly demonstrated than in his opening address to the Reconciliation Convention in May 1997, the thirtieth anniversary of the 1967 referendum and an occasion designated as of special significance on the path to national reconciliation between Aboriginal people and white Australians. Insensitive to the demands of the occasion and the hopes of the audience before him, Howard brought the uncompromising message of an approach in keeping with the policies of Sir Robert Menzies in the post-war decades.

RECONCILIATION

Addressing a gathering of 1000 delegates from all parts of the country, many representing the most disadvantaged section of the Australian population, Howard stated that this was an 'occasion for frank speaking'. He explained that he was an optimist about the process of reconciliation because of his faith in the 'decency, tolerance, generosity and common sense of the Australian people', who 'respect the right to a "fair go" for all irrespective of colour, background or belief'. Australia was today 'one of the fairest, most egalitarian and tolerant societies in the world'.

In the face of hostile response from his audience, some of whom booed and taunted and many of whom rose while he was speaking and turned their backs to him, the prime minister became increasingly vehement. Speaking in a 'booming' voice he hectored the audience, stating that reconciliation would not work 'if it puts a higher value on symbolic gestures and overblown promises rather than the practical needs of Aboriginal and Torres Strait Islander people in areas like health, housing, education and employment'. Reconciliation would not work if the views of extremists prevailed: the disadvantages and past injustices had to be acknowledged, but reconciliation could not be based on a sense of guilt and shame, on calls for different laws for different racial groups, on disruption of national events and levelling of charges of racism against those who did not agree with particular points of view. It was necessary to reject 'extremist views on all sides'.

Not even acknowledging the critique of the welfarism lobby—the view that more and better targeted welfare had been tried and found wanting over several decades, that sense of ownership and community was the first step in the long road to change—he affirmed that his government would adopt the 'practical, on-the-ground approach' and target the 'true causes' of indigenous disadvantage through programs in health, housing, education and employment.

He expressed his personal 'deep sorrow for those . . . who suffered injustices under the practices of past generations', but in facing 'the realities of the past' it was necessary to reject the view that 'Australia's history [is] . . . little more than a disgraceful record of imperialism, exploitation and racism. Such a portrayal is a gross distortion and deliberately neglects the overall story of great Australian achievement' and will be 'repudiated by the overwhelming majority of Australians who are proud of what this country has achieved', while acknowledging 'the blemishes in its past history'.

To cries of 'shame' he became increasingly angry, thumping the lectern and pointing at Aboriginal leaders in the audience, declaring that he had spent a 'great deal of time in trying to find a just, fair and workable outcome' following the High Court's Wik ruling. His ten-point plan provided an 'equitable balance' between the respect for the principles of native title and the interest of pastoralists and others 'in securing certainty'. In 'the name of truth' he repudiated the claim that the ten-point plan took away the rights of indigenous people. His plan was 'fair and equitable' and 'the only basis of a proper approach'.

Almost twelve months after the Reconciliation Convention Howard's 'fair and equitable' solution was passed into law by the Senate on the third attempt, accepted by the senator holding the balance of power as the lesser of two evils, the greater being the prospect that the prime minister would make good his promise to fight a double-dissolution election on the issue of native title. In the months leading to the breaking of the legislative impasse Aboriginal leaders spoke of a prime minister without empathy or sympathy. Charles Perkins was of the view that 'we've slipped back, at least ten years, in terms of race relations'; Michael Mansell that 'there's hardly any sign of respect for Aboriginal people'; Professor Marcia Langton observed that 'these blokes are reinventing the nineteenth century'.

'IN POLITICS PERCEPTIONS ARE IMPORTANT'

The racial policies of the Howard government drew the attention of United Nations agencies. There was criticism in 1997, 1998 and 1999. In March 2000 Australian government representatives appeared before the Committee on the Elimination of Racial Discrimination, at the request of the committee. The delegation was headed by Philip Ruddock, Minister for Immigration and Multicultural Affairs and Minister Assisting the Prime Minister for Reconciliation. Ruddock was given a difficult time. Why, asked a committee member, does the Australian government quote figures on annual spending on Aboriginal people, without reference to the amount spent on other Australians? Why does the Australian government refer to the amount of land held by Aboriginal people without reference to the quality of the land? Why did Australia rename the International Day against Racial Discrimination, celebrated worldwide, as Harmony Day. It was drawn to minister Ruddock's attention that the United Nations was seeking the elimination of racial discrimination, not harmony.

In its concluding observations the committee expressed concern at several aspects of Australia's record: they included the *Native Title Act*, as amended in 1998, the inadequate participation of indigenous people in decisions affecting their land rights, the apparent loss of confidence of indigenous people in the process of reconciliation, the disproportionately high rates of imprisonment of indigenous people, and mandatory sentencing laws in Western Australia and the Northern Territory which 'appeared to target offences that were committed disproportionately by indigenous Australians'. The committee 'seriously questioned' the compatibility of such legislation with Australia's obligations under the Convention to Eliminate Racial Discrimination and other international treaties. A second United Nations agency drew attention to violation of the right to a fair trial by an independent and impartial court; contravention of the independence of judges; and breach of the Convention on the Rights of the Child.

These reports, alongside a spate of other criticisms, presented the government with a minor crisis during March and April 2000. This was the time when the remaining refugees from Kosovo, granted temporary entry, were pressured to return to their homeland. Adverse publicity followed the revelation that the government had failed to ensure that food and housing was provided while the refugees sought to re-establish themselves. When questioned by a Melbourne radio reporter minister Ruddock responded that it was not right to look at such matters from a 'Eurocentric' view. Some listeners who rang the radio station were unable to contain their tears. Was it an Australian government that had treated refugees in this manner, asked callers who identified themselves as lifelong supporters of the Liberal Party?

Senator Herron, Minister for Aboriginal Affairs, created a furore with a submission to a senate committee which argued that there had been no 'stolen generation' because the 'proportion of separated Aboriginal children was no more than 10 per cent'. The submission was based on the argument that 'it is an inflated estimate which has led to the assumption of vast numbers having been affected and whole generations of trauma across the entire indigenous community'. Critics immediately pointed out that trauma inflicted was not to be measured solely by the number of children removed, but also by the impact on those left behind. Such was the public outcry that both Senator Herron and the prime minister felt it necessary to apologise in parliament—not, however, in acknowledgment that the submission was misconceived, but for the distress caused to Aboriginal people.

The major issue in terms of its political ramifications was, however, mandatory sentencing, which came to public attention following the suicide on 9 February of a 15-year-old orphaned Aboriginal boy, taken 800 kilometres from his home on Groote Eylandt for stealing property worth less than $90. Subsequent reports disclosed the disproportionate rates of imprisonment of Aboriginal people under mandatory sentencing laws, often for very minor offences.

Following revelations of adverse United Nations findings on mandatory sentencing, and of the attempts by Australian diplomatic representatives to limit criticism before the findings were made public, the government attacked the integrity of the UN. Attorney-General Daryl Williams stated that the report of its agency was an 'unbalanced and wide-ranging attack that intrudes unreasonably into Australia's domestic affairs'. Minister of Foreign Affairs Alexander Downer announced a review of Australia's obligations to send reports on the honouring of its treaties.

Such moves did not, however, still domestic criticism. The climax came when more than ten Liberal members of the federal parliament criticised mandatory sentencing and three declared their intention to support an independent member's Bill to override Northern Territory laws. Prime Minister Howard's reaction was to muster all the pressure at his disposal to prevent them voting against the government, telling a party room meeting that they were going to stay there until the issue was sorted out. Subsequently he undertook to meet with the chief minister of the Northern Territory to request modification of the laws.

The events of March and April had exposed contradictions at the heart of the Howard prime ministership. Here was the leader who had promised a 'common sense', 'non-ideological' approach and the flourishing of freedom of speech. Why then, critics asked, had he allowed a free vote to override the Northern Territory's euthanasia laws during 1996 and 1997 but so strongly supported state rights in the matter of mandatory sentencing? Why did this critic of political correctness not allow his backbenchers to vote according to their consciences, especially given the traditions of his own party? Why had he used the authority of the United Nations to oppose safe heroin injecting rooms proposed by two state governments and then apparently rejected out of hand the findings of two United Nations committees on matters affecting Aboriginal people?

During Corroboree 2000, the climax of the ten-year process of reconciliation held over the weekend of 27–28 May 2000, the actions of the prime minister cast a pall over the proceedings. There could be no national acceptance of the Reconciliation

Council's 'Declaration Towards Reconciliation' because the prime minister refused to endorse some of its key elements. There could be no national apology at the major public ceremony, held at the Opera House and televised nationally, because the prime minister maintained his refusal to tender one. Nor could the People's Walk for Reconciliation across the Sydney Harbour Bridge, in which an estimated 150 000 to 250 000 participated, fulfil its potential for national healing in the absence of the country's leader and key ministers. Laurie Oakes described Howard as 'a roadblock to progress'. Paul Kelly commented that 'it should never have happened . . . The nation, after a 10-year reconciliation process, is split. There is no closure . . . Australia was uplifted yet diminished'. After the record of the past four years there seemed little point in working for change under the Howard government; rather, attention was directed to the future. Sir Gustav Nossal, the Deputy Chair of the Reconciliation Council, who took the major media role on behalf of the Council in the weeks leading to Corroboree 2000, predicted that 'if an apology is not made by this Prime Minister, it most certainly will by the next'.

5

The politics of paranoia

*I*t has been the argument of this book that to understand the
re-emergence of racial issues as a central concern of Australian
politics it is necessary to consider a complex conjunction of factors.
Three of these have been examined in the previous chapters: the
New Right mobilisation; the construction of meanings based on
the ideal of 'one nation' in the mainstream of Australian politics;
and the role of John Howard in the electoral positioning of the
Liberal Party. It remains to consider the values, policies and influence of the far right in Australia, the traditions of populist politics,
particularly in Queensland, and the birth of Pauline Hanson's One
Nation.

The far right, the concern of this chapter, is considered to enable
understanding of modes of thought and world views on the fringe
of Australian politics—and of the nature and place of racial
ideas within such thought. Consideration of the far right is also
necessary to locate One Nation in its full context: to enable
identification of the elements of the far right value system which
One Nation adopted and introduced into the mainstream and of
key individuals who sought to promote their ends through its
organisation.

THE POLITICS OF PARANOIA

Over the last half-century, while neo-Nazi groups have been established in Australian cities, they have had little impact beyond their own narrow circles; such groups have attracted few followers and their open racism and violent actions have denied them an opportunity, with rare exceptions, to present their ideas in the mass circulation press and electronic media. There is, however, a semi-respectable face of the extreme right which has succeeded in spreading its message, particularly in rural areas and often through front organisations. These organisations are distinguished by the practice of the politics of paranoia.

How does it come about, its adherents ask, that certain groups have wealth beyond the average person's imagination, although they do little or no real work, while we seem forever to lose out, to be denied the good things in life and our children are left facing a bleak future? How is it that the country seems to be going from bad to worse, that we witness daily the destruction of our culture and traditions and nothing is done by politicians to halt the process?

One form of explanation, attractive to some, is in terms of conspiracies. Three basic propositions underlie this way of understanding the world: first, it is argued that throughout history there has been a constant struggle between the forces of absolute good and absolute evil, between light and darkness, between God and the devil; second, the reality of this struggle is hidden, known only to a few—the forces of darkness are able to cloak their activities because they control national leaders and the media; and third, the struggle has now reached a climactic stage and catastrophe beckons, to be avoided only if 'the people' can be aroused to fight for their freedom.

This belief system was perceptively analysed by Richard Hofstadter in his book *The Paranoid Style in American Politics*, first published in 1965. Hofstadter noted that the idea of a conspiracy—whether by Jesuits, Freemasons, international capitalists,

Jews, or communists, or some combination of all five—was a recurrent theme in the modern history of many countries. The impact of conspiracy theories was a fluctuating rather than constant feature of national histories, at its strongest in times of acute conflict between rival value systems, leaving sections of the population to feel that their country and way of life was being taken from them; government, the law, even the church had fallen under the control of the enemy, leaving 'the people' powerless, denied even the opportunity to be heard. Hofstadter argued that:

> the paranoid disposition is mobilised into action chiefly by social conflicts that involve ultimate schemes of values and that bring fundamental fears and hatreds . . . into political action . . . The paranoid tendency is aroused by a confrontation of opposed interests which are (or are felt to be) totally irreconcilable, and thus by nature not susceptible to the normal political processes of bargain and compromise. The situation becomes worse when the representatives of a particular political interest . . . cannot make themselves felt in the political process. Feeling that they have no access to political bargaining . . . they find their original conception of the world of power as omnipotent, sinister, and malicious fully confirmed.

In recent years the pace of social change and its adverse impact on sections of the population and regions has fostered the growth of politics of the paranoid style. Paradoxically, one of the contributors to the pace of change, the revolution in communication, has facilitated the spread of far right ideas and the self-confidence and sense of mission of its adherents. It is far easier today for members of extremist societies, comprising a minuscule section of the communities in which they live, to establish 'virtual communities', to maintain daily contact with those who share their views, to exchange ideas and provide mutual support. McKenzie Wark, a leading Australian commentator on the electronic age, has written that 'it's not just that there's the Internet. There's cheap offset printing. There's the mail-out list managed on a home computer. There are videos sold through gun shops. And in the US, there's short-wave radio'.

THE LEAGUE OF RIGHTS, GRAEME CAMPBELL AND AUSTRALIANS AGAINST FURTHER IMMIGRATION

This section examines the oldest and most influential of the far right organisations promoting racism and bigotry, the Victorian based League of Rights, and its links with member of the House of Representatives Graeme Campell and the anti-immigration party Australians Against Further Immigration. It considers the league's message and the means by which it has been promoted, including its efforts to draw into its orbit potential sympathisers from other organisations and to use them in the attempt to spread its influence.

Since its formation in 1946 racist and anti-semitic policies have been central to the league's agenda. The extreme nature of its views, however, are kept from view in its propaganda directed at the general community, in which it presents itself as the defender of traditional social values of 'God, Queen and Country'—state rights, free enterprise, the family farm and small business. The league advocates the Social Credit philosophy of C.H. Douglas, which in its later form presents economic and political ideas which focus on sinister forces manipulating the distribution of credit in the economy (the 'money masters') to enrich a small elite; economic salvation is promised through equitable distribution of the profits of industry and of credit (created by governments printing money) to the citizens of the country.

At times the league has succeeded in attracting mainstream federal politicians to its meetings, not least a future leader of the Liberal Party, Alexander Downer. It has, however, been more successful in winning active or tacit endorsement of some local government councillors and independent members of parliament, notably Graeme Campbell, Labor (subsequently independent) member of the House of Representatives, who became a prominent participant at a number of league gatherings.

The key figure throughout the league's history has been Eric Butler, who has been obsessed for over half a century with his vision of a Jewish conspiracy to control the world. His writings include *The International Jew*, first published in 1946, which promoted the notorious anti-semitic forgery *The Protocols of the Elders of Zion* and argued that Hitler was a tool of Jewish interests and implemented 'a Jewish policy' in furtherance of the aim of Jewish world domination. In the 1990s league publications were still promoting *The Protocols*, describing the Holocaust as a 'hoax', the invention of Zionist propagandists, identifying prominent Jewish individuals in public life and declaring that modern Christianity was 'little more than a form of Liberal Judaism'. The Jewish plot was also described using various code words, notably the 'one world conspiracy' hatched by 'international elites', international bureaucracies, international bankers, members of the Fabian society, or the United Nations. The journalist Tim Duncan wrote in 1984 that the league saw itself:

> engaged on a historic mission to save western civilisation— and, within that, British civilisation—from the forces of darkness and evil. It feeds on conspiracy and the menace of apocalypse. Where the league had found those who would take over the world in international Jewry, international socialism and international capitalism, now its journals talk mostly of international bureaucracies . . . When Butler looks at the world, he sees the Anti-Christ.

League propaganda in the 1980s sought to depict the entry of Indo-Chinese refugees as 'a Peking Communist plan for the invasion of Australia. The first steps are for agents posing as students, migrants or refugees to gain entry into Australia surreptitiously to prepare the ground for a larger invasion force'. In 1988 its publications warned of a 'programme to destroy traditional Australia'; to betray Australia's sovereignty and fragment the country. An 'Asian invasion' was underway, a 'multicultural madness' that could only end in race riots. Australia was being 'torn from its roots' with the aim of 'killing the Australian soul'.

In 1984 the league won prominence in rural Victoria in the context of proposed legislation on land rights. Under the guise of the 'Save Victoria Committee', the league spread the message that landowners were at risk from future Aboriginal claims. In this task the league promoted a book by Geoff McDonald, entitled *Red Over Black*, which argued that the land rights movement was supported by communist countries with the objective of United Nations intervention in Australia. After months of campaigning its target was broadened to encompass proposed federal legislation, with 'Save Victoria' renamed 'Save Australia 1984'.

During 1987–88 there were claims of league activity in rural communities influenced by the teachings of fundamentalist Christian churches. At this time one of its major initiatives was promotion of the 'Swiss principle' of 'Initiative, Referendum and Recall', to be introduced following a referendum to enable Australians to determine 'their own future'. In this advocacy of participatory democracy the league acted alongside the fundamentalist Logos Foundation, which supported a national 'Voter's Veto—Australians Speaking Up' campaign as the antidote to the One World Government Conspiracy. One of the key Logos speakers was Jeremy Lee, for many years a prominent league activist. In 1989 Logos claimed to have a direct mailing list of more than 30 000 from various Christian churches and to have distributed more than a million pamphlets and other publications bearing its message.

In 1988 the league believed that the hour of deliverance was at hand, thanks to the publicity gained by 'courageous' nationalists in the mainstream media. In January 1988 Butler rejoiced at the positive response to his message:

> For many years the League was like a voice in the wilderness attempting to warn Australians of the far reaching implications of the New International Economic Order ... of the revolutionary forces attempting to divide the nation through a land claims movement ... [of the threat] to destroy completely the family farm, small businesses and Municipal Government, of the destabilisation of a basically homogeneous nation through a policy of multi-racialism and multi-culturalism. But the unfolding of events has, in recent years, resulted in an upsurge of interest and concern which has manifested itself in the emergence of a number of grass-roots movements which had in various ways alerted and encouraged Australians to resist.

In May it was reported that 'the literature is pouring out, League audio and video tapes are being heard and seen by thousands, and League speakers sweep across the nation'.

In leaner times the league has sought to overcome the aversion that its name evokes by infiltrating organisations and adopting ever changing guises to conceal its extremism behind popular causes. Senator Boswell, National Party senator since 1983 and an implacable foe of the league, stated in an April 1988 speech that the aim of the league was not to 'attract members per se', but to get groups and individuals 'to use league thinking, arguments and literature'. The league has been particularly active in rural areas and on a number of occasions has been accused of attempting to infiltrate branches of the National Party. In Boswell's summation:

> The league thrives wherever there is discord, dissension, frustration, fear, resentment and financial hardship. It flourishes in times of drought, low commodity prices, high foreign debt, and high interest rates, and recent events have led to

an unprecedented expansion of its powers, influence and number of supporters . . . [It] preys on people's fears, exploiting and manipulating target groups as tools to promote the League's policies.

Although it is difficult to establish clear links, organisations which have been named as under league control include the Christian Institute for Individual Freedom, Institute for Economic Democracy, Australian Heritage Society, Ladies in Line Against Communism (Lilac League), Conservative Speakers Clubs, Council for a Free Australia and the One Australia Movement. In the early 1990s it issued four periodicals, *On Target*, *The New Times*, *Intelligence Survey* and *Heritage*, and had two publishing outlets, Heritage and Veritas Publications.

The league's involvement with Graeme Campbell, his Australia First Party, and the Australians Against Further Immigration, provides an example of its technique of encouraging like-minded individuals and behind the scenes manipulation—a mirroring of the supposed conspiratorial methods of its foes. Campbell was first invited to attend league functions, to speak to league audiences, then promoted as the national leader to unify organisations of the right. In this way the league attempted to maximise support for its broad agenda, while keeping key elements such as its uncompromising racism from public view.

Since 1992 Campbell had occasionally addressed league meetings. In May 1995 he spoke at the league's annual Queensland state seminar in Toowoomba on 'Policies for a Better Government', condemning multiculturalism, high immigration and the Asianisation of Australia. Interviewed on radio, Campbell defended the league as an organisation that was simply 'expressing ideas that you will find expressed right across rural Australia'. In apparent ignorance of league policy of the past fifteen years, he declared that 'they've actually copied my ideas on immigration . . . they've just endorsed the position I've been pioneering'. In the same year he co-authored a book entitled *Australia Betrayed* which featured on its cover a bloodstained knife plunged through the heart of Australia. The book argued that Australians 'would be shocked to discover that their country is effectively being taken from them' by traitors of the 'new cosmopolitan Ascendancy'—including members of the elite in politics, the bureaucracy, academia, big business and the media. Such statements, and his abusive condemnation of Prime Minister Keating, his party leader, contributed to the decision by the federal ALP national executive to disendorse Campbell in December 1995.

Campbell also involved himself with Australians Against Further Immigration (AAFI), endorsing its candidates in March 1994 by-elections. The league was happy to encourage this link given its interest in the group, promoting, for example, a Campbell rally organised by AAFI at the Heidelberg Town Hall on Australia Day 1996.

AAFI, a single issue party, had run candidates for parliamentary office since 1990, performing poorly at general elections but winning sufficient votes in several by-election contests to gain media interest. Like Campbell, AAFI leaders were cultivated by the league with considerable success. Robyn Spencer addressed the league's Gippsland regional dinner where she criticised the media's negative coverage of the league. In turn the league praised Spencer's comments on immigration, multiculturalism and 'destruction of all things Australian'; she had spoken with 'great authority and presence' and a tape-recording of her talk was sold through the league's bookshop. Another of AAFI's leaders, Denis McCormack, addressed a number of far right meetings throughout the country, such as the Inverell Forum, an annual gathering in which league activists were prominent, and the Melbourne Conservative Speakers' Club. In May 1995 McCormack shared the platform with Graeme Campbell at the league's Toowoomba conference.

Leading members of AAFI argued that speaking to members of a group such as the league did not entail endorsing its principles, that they were willing to speak 'to anyone or any organisation that wishes to hear our views'. They failed, however, to address the question of whether some organisations, as a consequence of their racist beliefs and authoritarian structure, placed themselves outside the realm of democratic politics. Further, the freedom of speech defence lost cogency in the context of growing links between McCormack and the league.

Increasingly AAFI shifted its attention from general immigration issues to the 'Asianisation' of Australia. At the time of its establishment AAFI stressed that 'we are a non-racist group and the racial background of immigrants is immaterial to our cause'. By 1994, while claiming that it was 'not anti-immigrant', it argued that:

> By abolishing tax payer funded multiculturalism our proud and unique Australian culture can once again prosper without the threat of being swamped in a sea of opposing cultures. The violence, gang warfare and minority politics we see in a Los Angeles must not be allowed to develop in Australia. The major political parties are promoting the policy of Asianisation for Australia. Our traditions, way of life and ability to control immigration are threatened now as never before.

At a 1995 league gathering, also attended by Campbell, McCormack brandished an empty machine gun magazine and implied there would be violence if immigration was not controlled. He claimed that Australia's population would be 25 per cent Asian by the year 2020: 'they're changing the genetic make-up of our people ... that's why we've got to get our hands on the levers of power to change these policies'. AAFI's January 1996 newsletter carried an editorial entitled 'Asianisation' which linked this process with the destruction 'before our eyes' of Australia's 'egalitarian society' and the decline in the standard of living.

McCormack increasingly embraced a conspiratorial view in his explanation of contemporary politics. In July 1996 he presented a paper, under police protection, to an academic conference hosted by the Asian Studies Association of Australia. The paper was entitled 'The grand plan—Asianisation of Australia' and argued that through an act of treason Australian elites embarked upon:

> the grand plan for the long-term Asianisation of Australia . . . A path towards radical change . . . was trod by many elites who considered themselves and their world view 'progressive'. They entered into long-term cooperative networking and planning on a whole constellation of internationalist economic and social issues which they hoped would bring about the radical changes they desired. They accurately identified the destruction of Australia's traditional immigration restriction policy as their top . . . priority.

In the abstract of his paper, McCormack put forward the view that:

> The diggers, the founders of the Labor Movement, the Fathers of Federation, Furphy, Lawson and Paterson, along with countless other true-blue Australians, from their day to ours, warned about the future swamping, dispossession and eventual disappearance of all things traditionally Australian should mass Asian immigration ever be sanctioned. Those warnings of yesteryear are today not only officially ignored and suppressed, but are being systematically erased from our common national memory through manipulation of Immigration Policy, Multicultural Policy, Education, Trade, Foreign Affairs, Defence, and Industrial Relations as well as Finance and Economic Management Policy in relation to globalisation, privatisation, deregulation, foreign ownership and foreign investment. Australia is being demographically and economically recolonised through gradualist bipartisanship against often demonstrated public opinion . . . The Australian public is largely uninformed about the scale of the scam or depth of

deception, . . . let alone the irreversible long term ramifications implied . . . for their collective future . . .

Graeme Campbell was sufficiently impressed with McCormack to table his 'Grand Plan' in the House of Representatives, 'in the national interest'. He declared that 'Australia needs Denis McCormack in federal parliament'.

In June 1996 Campbell launched his Australia First Party in which McCormack would become a senior officeholder. It would be the means to enable 'the Australian people to take back control of our country, to institute sane and productive policies of national reconstruction and consign the old political parties to history'. The new party's core policies included support for the manufacturing industry, control of foreign ownership, lower immigration, an end to the policy of Aboriginal reconciliation, introduction of the citizens initiated referendum, reduction of the gap between city and country and easing of gun controls. In June 1996 a merger was announced between Australia First and the Australian Reform Party, founded by Ted Drane, a major player in the gun lobby. It was to last but seven days, highlighting the inability of peripheral right groups to coalesce, in part because of political differences but also because of the jostling for position by prospective leaders.

According to newspaper reports, in the following month a secret meeting was convened at a Christian bush retreat near Lithgow, New South Wales, to discuss Australia First strategy, perhaps to further attempt the amalgamation of the major far right groups. Two of the most prominent invitees, Ted Drane and Pauline Hanson, declined to attend. Campbell was left in the company of some twenty stalwarts including Denis McCormack and a number of senior league members including Eric Butler. Drane publicly expressed concern at Campbell's links with the league and with AAFI, complaining that he had checked on people who were to be involved in a forthcoming meeting and found two prominent league activists. Drane subsequently provided journalists with details of his dealings with

Australia First and claimed that 'I kept being invited to meet Butler and I kept saying no'. McCormack responded that neither he nor Campbell were puppets of the league: 'If we were there, so what—we're moulding the league, the league is following us'. Campbell commented that 'I know some people in the League of Rights and I know some people in the Catholic Church. So what?' In Senator Boswell's assessment, Campbell 'has been fawned upon by the Eric Butlers and Denis McCormacks of this world until he believes what they tell him—that he can found a successful new political party in Australia'.

The league had also sought to promote Pauline Hanson, distributing thousands of copies of her maiden speech and writing of her that she had given 'renewed hope to ordinary Australians'; she 'acted as a catalyst in politics to the benefit of traditional Australia'. But full endorsement was reserved for Campbell; he was 'an outstanding leader', 'head and shoulders above all other Federal members', a man around whom 'an effective nationalist movement could emerge to counter the treachery of the internationalists'. Eric Butler applauded the launch of Australia First in 1996 and described Campbell as the 'great white hope of Australian nationalism'. The 17 January 1997 issue of the league's *On Target* declared of Campbell: 'we can see no other national figure of sufficient stature to act as the catalyst for the emergence of a new type of political movement which can divert Australia off the present disaster course'. League members or former members filled key positions in four Australia First state branches but the league had badly miscalculated: Campbell lacked the personality to interest the media, he was not in the race to match the Hanson charisma.

CITIZENS ELECTORAL COUNCILS

It seems that Citizens Electoral Councils (CECs) were first established by League of Rights activists with support from kindred organisations, although it is not possible to be certain. The councils sought to harness the popularity of the Voter's Veto campaign and by 1988 it was claimed that there were branches in 55 electorates. The citizens' initiative movement drew its support from disillusionment with the political system; it seemed to promise a way to recapture control of the political process from politicians working to further the interests of the 'new class' and the 'one world government'. A journalist reported in 1991 that 'the concept of CIRs [citizens' initiated referendum] has a receptive audience in rural areas where people feel remote from the political process and are fearful of the future'.

The Citizens Electoral Councils achieved a major success in 1988 with the victory of their candidate, Trevor Perrett, in the by-election for the Queensland state seat of Barambah vacated by the former Queensland premier, Sir Joh Bjelke-Petersen. In the words of the key CEC activist John Koehler, a Queensland farmer, support was based on:

> the realisation that all the political parties slavishly served the international, New World Order Masters and not us—the people of Australia . . . The One World Government Agenda of the Fabians, Rhodes Scholars and others has never been put to the people . . .

In his maiden speech Perrett outlined the principles of the citizens' initiated referendum:

> We are supposed to be a constitutional parliamentary democracy where the people rule, yet no machinery or means exist whereby the people in any district or electorate can communicate their majority views to their elected member in Parliament . . . The real solution is relatively simple, and so beneficial to all—a solution which would bring greatness to this State and to this nation. We have to adopt the principle of direct legislation—citizen-initiated referendum . . . If we

are to lay claim at all to being a genuine parliamentary democracy and a properly constitutional one, we can scarcely deny this right of the people to decide policy ... When the Government has not perceived the true mood of the people, and when the Parliament has acted or is failing to act on important matters in the way that the people particularly want ... the people will be stirred to make use of this direct legislative process. Surely in the interests of harmony, true consensus and common sense, we would all welcome that ... The Government must give the people what they want.

The following year a second candidate, Dennis Stevenson, was elected to the Australian Capital Territory Legislative Assembly on a 'Voters' Veto' platform and was to play a significant, if erratic role, in fringe politics, chairing, for example, the CECs' national conference in Bendigo in 1990.

Why extremist organisations should promote democratisation of politics through the referendum is at first sight puzzling. Part of the answer is its efficacy as a propaganda weapon; what better way to mobilise discontented grass roots support than to show up the corruption of politicians and of the political system by demanding this most democratic of reforms, the path to 'harmony, true consensus and common sense'; and what better way to side-step the complexities of decision making and carry the message that there was a quick-fix, simple solution to the problems facing rural communities. A second component of the answer is the self-identification of leaders such as Eric Butler with the community, the belief that mass support would be forthcoming once the blinkers were removed and truth allowed to prevail. With such an outlook there were no dangers in the extension of democracy. Indeed, the League of Rights denounced party politics and put its trust in the mobilisation of mass support which would produce a people's revolution, a moment of cataclysmic change which would advance humanity to a higher stage.

In the interim, hopefully no one would closely examine the organisations supporting the citizen's referendum. The League of Rights, for example, placed supreme power in the hands of its leader, held no elections, did not publicly circulate a balance sheet of income and expenditure, and included no self-criticism or conflict of views in its publications. After his election Perrett soon found that the CEC Party organisation began ordering him to report almost daily and he was bombarded with right-wing propaganda; he was also told to assist in raising financial contributions in his electorate. 'I became a puppet on a string. They proclaimed to represent the will of the people but the will of the people was only okay provided that they agreed with it. They were trying to use me to push their own agenda—an extremely right-wing agenda'. His response was to defect to the National Party before completion of his first term. He retained the seat as an endorsed National candidate at the next election and subsequently became a minister in the Borbidge government.

In 1988 the CECs sponsored a highly successful speaking tour through parts of New South Wales and Queensland by a former social security department clerk, Peter Sawyer. His speech in a Brisbane suburb packed a high school auditorium with an audience of more than 800. People entering the hall passed tables set with League of Rights publications and were handed copies of the quarterly newspaper, *Wake Up Australia*, published for the Brisbane-based Council for a Free Australia. This organisation, under the national chairmanship of Jackie Butler, proclaimed itself to be Pro-Christian, Pro-Family, Pro-Free Enterprise, Pro-Freedom, Pro-Life, Pro-Common Law and campaigned on moral issues, opposing legalisation of abortion, homosexuality, marijuana and pornography.

Sawyer was described by Laurie Oakes as 'the nation's champion conspiracy theorist'. His message, in Oakes' summary, was that:

> Australia is sliding into a planned totalitarian state; that it is all part of a conspiracy to bring about a world government; that Australia's billion dollar Parliament House is to be the

new world government headquarters; and that the hub of the conspiracy is Canberra's Deakin Centre where, he says, the government has already secretly interlinked departmental computers in a gigantic Big Brother national surveillance.

In January 1988 Sawyer prophesised that Aborigines, who had supposedly smuggled thousands of AK 47 Russian assault rifles into the country, would launch an armed uprising on Australia Day and warned his supporters to stay indoors. In 1991 he was urging people to prepare for 'imminent' invasion from Indonesia in consequence of Australia's disarmament and advocated that his listeners purchase and hide firearms. Indicating the extent of support for far right conspiratorial ideas in Queensland, Sawyer stood as an advocate of citizens' initiated referenda in a July 1990 by-election on the Sunshine Coast and secured 16 per cent of the vote.

To the chagrin of the league, control of the CEC movement was captured by followers of the American Lyndon LaRouche and the movement's national headquarters was moved to Melbourne. The LaRouche organisation was distinguished by its professionalism in research, publication and fundraising. According to one 1992 source it raised close to $20 000 per week, published *The New Citizen*, a newspaper with a distribution of 50 000 copies, and ran a training program for activists.

The LaRouche movement has been likened to a cult, providing its followers with a strange mix of conspiratorial theories, complicated economic analysis and populist policies geared to appeal to farmers, pastoralists and blue collar workers. It views its leader as a major historical figure, a 'statesman' and the 'world's greatest living economist'. According to one of the leading Australian authorities, David Grearson, the movement:

takes the conventional conspiracy theories much favoured by the far-right and goes ten steps further. . . . [They] claim, for example, that the Queen heads an international drug-trafficking ring, that Dr Henry Kissinger is a KGB agent, and that AIDS is a Soviet plot . . .

In the early 1990s the LaRouche publication 'Sovereign Australia: an Economic Program to Save Our Nation', based on material prepared in the United States, presented the view that the 'twin tyrannies of communism and the International Monetary Fund' had brought Australia to the brink of ruin. It urged admission only of English speaking migrants, the rebuilding of the nation's military capacity, the setting up of a citizens' militia and an end to the 'totalitarian practice' of gun control. The 'average Aussie' was urged to take up the battle for citizens' referenda, otherwise 'the Australia our forefathers left us will soon be finished'.

In the late 1990s the LaRouche policy provided for abolition of land rights, the ending of free trade and economic rationalism, the reintroduction of tariff protection, exchange and currency controls, promotion of large scale infrastructure development projects and implementation of an immediate moratorium on debt for family farms.

CONFEDERATE ACTION PARTY

The Confederate Action Party (CAP) was established in Queensland in July 1990, possibly to provide a rival to the LaRouche-influenced Citizens Electoral Councils and a substitute for the Logos Foundation, expected to decline following revelations of the mis-conduct of its director. The Confederate Action Party's name recalled the revolt of the Confederate states in defence of their way of life and of slavery in the period of the American Civil War; it was also a call for a 'Confederation of organisations and citizens who value liberty, the flag and our constitution' and for 'positive ACTION'. Its slogan was 'ONE FLAG ONE NATION'.

While it was short lived, the CAP revealed the potential of far right politics in Queensland. In 1992 it ran twelve candidates at the state election and won strong support, an average vote of 9.6 per cent, with over 15 per cent in five seats, compared with the average for the Liberal Party in the same seats of 8 per cent. Several prominent supporters of Pauline Hanson, including Tony Pitt and Bruce Whiteside, had been Confederate Action candidates. At the March 1993 federal election its Queensland Senate team received 39 000 votes, about 2 per cent of the total. By the second half of 1993 it was reduced to a group publicly squabbling over control of the organisation and charging each other with financial irregularity; a handful of branches were established in other states, one in rural Western Australia winning national headlines in January 1995 when its most active member was murdered.

The party's policies provide further evidence of the issues engaging far right politicians in Queensland. Its 'main aim' was to 'introduce "Citizens Initiated Referendum" into Australian politics'. This reform would ensure 'that the people of Australia can say no to laws that the majority do not want'. A CAP pamphlet argued that:

C.I.R. gives back to the people the real power to determine the laws under which they are governed.

C.I.R. requires our elected representatives to take notice of the will of the people.

C.I.R. stops intimidation by extremist groups and also stops decisions being made by political parties and pressure groups.

C.I.R. gives immunity from politicians' attempts to dictate against the wishes of the Australian people.

C.I.R. is a proven, successful system being used in many countries whereby voters have a direct say in determining their own laws by which they are governed.

AUSTRALIA NEEDS CONSENSUS DEMOCRACY!

Its electoral appeal called for Queenslanders to 'Stand up for Australia—One Flag—One Nation'. If elected to office the party undertook to hold a vote on the introduction of the citizen initiated referendum, reintroduce the death penalty, provide people with the right to defend themselves with firearms, introduce national service, create a strong military, abolish the family law act, limit provision of unemployment benefits to six months in each year, reform the taxation system, work towards the introduction of a flat tax and cancel foreign aid until the national debt was eliminated. Policies bearing on racial issues, sovereignty and national identity promised to:

- Cancel the refugee programme, and in future draw immigrants from traditional and Christian countries; overall immigration to be reduced at present and to be in accord with national sensitivities and requirements.
- Abolish the Aboriginal Affairs Department. WE ARE ONE AUSTRALIA—ONE NATION.
- Remove social engineering and political ideologies from government education. Make mandatory the study of the Australian Constitution and Common Law in High Schools. Rebuild pride in our Nation and respect for The Flag.
- Rescind any legislation which removes total Australian Sovereignty over the Nation's land and resources—including World Heritage areas.
- Review, towards recision, all foreign originated Conventions whose adoption overrules the Australian Constitution. Support the Constitution by denying 'interpretation' of External Affairs clauses so as to usurp State Rights.
- Eliminate government benefits from non Australians other than long term 'tax contributing' permanent residents and introduce a five year wait for citizenship.

One of the key figures in the party was Tony Pitt, a resident of Maryborough. A candidate at the 1992 election for the seat of Maryborough, where he received 16 per cent of the vote, in 1993 he was second on the senate ticket, the party's press secretary and emerged as leader of one of the factions struggling for control of the party. After the CAP disintegrated Pitt formed 'The Australians' and continued his activity as a publicist for right-wing causes through his own publications. He was editor and owner of *Fight*, which had presented itself as the vehicle of the CAP; he also took over *Wake Up Australia*, published the *National Interest* and maintained an Internet site. In 1992 he was the press secretary of the Firearm Owners Association. Following the emergence of One Nation he became president of its Hervey Bay branch.

In expressing his views Pitt felt no need for subtlety. In the second issue of *Fight* he urged his readers to view a videotaped exposé of the New World Order produced by former League of Rights deputy director Jeremy Lee. In later issues Pitt observed that 'these scheming, thieving cretins have a neat plan to clean out our bank accounts, take our minerals, eliminate our industries and turn our farmers into slave labour on New World Order Bank owned farms'; there were 'forces at work in Australia to clean us out and make us slaves to foreign financiers'. And who was behind the New World Order? A cartoon accompanying Pitt's article presented a Trojan horse being wheeled into the national parliament, with a shield on its side emblazoned with the Star of David.

Pitt explained that the major political parties were working in tandem to further the ends of the conspiracy and their own financial interests. The nation's leaders had their noses 'deep in the trough and simply change places to ensure that they get their share of the bribery'. If an honest party appeared 'the financiers sool their media dogs onto that party in a mad feeding frenzy, until the honest group is defunct, then it is back to the trough for pollies, media barons and financiers'.

Such was the hold of the conspirators that their agents removed books from public libraries 'so you cannot find out what they are up to'. They worked to deprive citizens of their guns so they would be unable to defend themselves when the day comes to establish a soviet-style republic. The socialists were planning 'to totally disarm us, number us, catalogue us, control us and shoot us'.

Pitt equated socialism with Hitler's Nazi regime; for example, a photograph of a woman being shot by a German soldier was accompanied by the caption 'This is socialism'. He produced a poster in which Hitler raised his arm in salute to indicate support for gun control. The caption read: 'Six million Jews can't be wrong. Don't find out the hard way. The Australian socialists mean business'.

The threat came not only from the conspirators within but also from neighbouring countries. The 'civilised world' ended at Australia's shoreline; 'on the other side of that water there are about 140 nations. Over one hundred of those nations are at the same stage of social and cultural evolution as the Japanese were in the thirties'. In several issues he reproduced a horrendous photograph of a dead girl, hanging from a rope, in full profile, her clothes tattered shreds after she had been 'raped, tortured, mutilated, murdered'. Pitt's caption was: 'she typifies the treatment that is inevitable when a nation is overrun by Asian invaders or even European invaders . . . This could be your wife or your daughter, and it will be, if you allow the ALP, the Liberals, the Nationals and the Democrats to disarm us'. Other wartime photographs of civilians being murdered by Japanese and German soldiers were used to demonstrate the fate of the unarmed.

Amongst a series of disastrous policies, defence was possibly the worst. Malaysians threatened to invade Australian by boat people, Indonesia by direct attack. The 'ALP/DEM/LIB/NAT/GREEN' party worked 'actively and knowingly to destroy our defence capability'. War was inevitable:

War . . . is nature's way of stopping the planet overpopulating to extinction. The tough, ruthless, smart and innovative survive. Idiots join the dinosaurs. Australians face extinction because our politicians are idiots. They disarm us as World

War III blossoms into reality . . . The only language aggressive Asians understand is naked force and a willingness to play as hard as they play and just a bit harder. Faced with the choice of anthrax or the atom bomb our neighbours are smiling, friendly and peaceful but, as the song goes, 'Never smile at a crocodile. Don't be taken in by his welcome grin'.

Immigration policy was a disaster, bringing in people who 'have no trade, can't or won't speak English, won't intermarry, wouldn't defend their own country and won't defend ours'. Pitt published material prepared by the Queensland Immigration Control Association showing the Asian dominance of the immigration intake and printed a racist doggerel depicting immigrants prospering on welfare fraud, lowering Australian standards and destroying white neighbourhoods. He warned that mixing people of different backgrounds was a recipe for disaster: 'the ethnic influx did not create racial harmony and prosperity in England and it won't here either. Politicians should stop playing God and stop monkeying with racial mixtures'.

The idea of 'land rights' had been devised by international socialists in 1959 'for the establishment of an Aboriginal republic under Communist control', as revealed by Geoff McDonald in his book *Red Over Black*. The plan was to create an independent black nation in Australia which would invite Marxist troops to safeguard its borders; once strong enough the troops would wage war on the Australian nation on the pretext of returning the land to its rightful owners.

Later Pitt presented a different scenario. Militant Aborigines were 'backed, armed, trained and funded by the Black Muslims, Gadaffi, Indonesia and others who covet our mineral, oil, land and fishing'. Once they gained ownership of land 'the mixed breed white, yellow and brown trouble makers' who posed as Aborigines would sell the land for a pittance to their masters. Land rights was about '*big money*' and the High Court judges had been specifically chosen to implement an agenda—to begin the process of piece by piece dispossession of white Australians.

As for the demand by Aborigines for an apology for past treatment, there was nothing to apologise for. In their traditional society Aborigines were savages who practised cannibalism, eating their children:

> The 'stolen' children were taken because they were in moral, physical and mental danger, from parents who were primitives. In the eyes of the whites, they were saving the children to give them some chance of becoming human beings with a future. There is no shame in that ... We saved the Aborigines from themselves. Anything done by whites against blacks in Australia pales into insignificance when compared with their treatment of others in their own tribe and anyone else who was unfortunate enough to fall into their hands ...

THE GUN LOBBY

Gun lobbyist groups have been active in Australian politics since the enactment of gun control laws in 1988, organising to oppose government moves to restrict further the right to own firearms. The major gun rights group in the early 1990s was the Sporting Shooters Association of Australia, with over 45 000 members in 1996. Its subsidiary organisation was the Institute of Legislative Action, established in 1993 on the model of and with the assistance of the American National Rifle Association's lobbying arm. The Shooters Association portrayed itself as comprising law-abiding citizens who wanted guns for sporting pursuits or self-protection. Its president and chief executive of the Institute of Legislative Action, Ted Drane, sought to distance his association from the fringe groups, seen in his refusal to join Graeme Campbell while he maintained his association with the League of Rights. An Australian Shooters' Party was formed in 1992. Its leader, John Tingle, a radio personality and relative moderate, won a seat in the New South Wales Legislative Council in 1995.

Other groups included the Australian Right to Bear Arms, run by Bob Doring, and the Firearm Owners Association of Australia, headed by Rod Owen and Ian McNiven. The Firearm Owners Association, with a membership of 3400, claimed to speak on behalf of half a million unlicensed shooters. It advocated minimal restriction on gun ownership and regarded as totalitarian any attempt at government control. Legislation to ban ownership of automatic and semi-automatic guns by the states and the commonwealth following a massacre of tourists in Port Arthur, Tasmania, was met with outraged opposition by the shooters associations. At a rally in Gympie on 15 May 1996 McNiven won national media attention with his threat of civil war:

> Little Jackboot [the prime minister] is launching a brutal totalitarian attack on our fundamental freedoms. It's not about this bullshit that it's only semiautomatics that's going to go. It's everything. Make no mistake. Once it's given up, it must be bought back and you can only buy it back with the most expensive currency in the world. The only currency you can buy your freedom back with is blood.

Various rallies to protest legislation were organised by shooters, the largest in Melbourne on 1 June 1996 when an estimated 70 000 marched.

Those on the right of the shooters associations argued, with varying degrees of vehemence, that ownership of guns was essential to a people's freedom; it was essential to protect the home against criminals, to protect the individual against authoritarian government and to protect the nation against external aggression.

Shooters groups were particularly active following the federal government's 1996 banning of semi-automatic weapons. Extremists argued that the Port Arthur massacre in that year had been staged by government agents to provide an excuse to disarm the Australian people. It was a 'psyop', an operation designed to psychologically manipulate public opinion. In a manner analogous to the conspiracies used to explain the assassination of President Kennedy, it was argued that the killings could not have been the work of one man, certainly not of the man charged, Martin Bryant. The idea was developed in a series of articles in the extremist magazine *The Strategy*, beginning in May 1997, with subsequent articles published in *Exposure* and other far right publications.

Bob Doring queried whether the Port Arthur killer 'was . . . programmed to commit the killings and did he act alone . . . ?' There was indication of 'a definite conspiracy and cover-up'. Jeff Knuth, One Nation member of the Queensland parliament, argued in his maiden speech that Port Arthur was 'only the excuse to slap Australians with extremist laws long hidden away in the dark boltholes of Canberra waiting the day they could scare Australian lawmakers into passing laws hatched in a faraway foreign capital . . . We now know Port Arthur had nothing to do with it'.

The extremist elements among the shooters found voice in the periodical *Lock, Stock and Barrel*, published in Gympie, Queensland, by Ron Owen of the Firearm Owners Association. While Owen dismissed the argument that it was physically impossible for Bryant to have been responsible for the killings, he had no doubt of the existence of a conspiracy to impose rule by the One World Government. In typical style, he began an interview with a far right Queensland politician by asking: 'When were you first aware of a One World Government movement?'.

Owen undertook twelve months of research into the history of the One World Order, the fruits published in serial form in his magazine. He discovered that the New World Order, the cancer of nations, had been active since 1 May 1776, which explains why May Day was celebrated by Communists, Socialists, Zionists and Illuminists. The New World Order originated with 'the Order of the Illuminati', founded by Adam Weishaupt, and was based on a brotherhood between socialists and monopolists. Its organisation had 'different legs or tentacles to the main body. Some authorities call them circles which are a part of other circles ... It is more accurate to think of it like a vine or a creeper which expands in every direction ... Once it covers a beautiful tree, the tree withers and dies'.

At the extreme end of the spectrum, the gun lobbyists were linked to paramilitary groups who threatened to resist violently any attempt to disarm them. The best known of the paramilitary groups was the Cobar (New South Wales) based AUSI (Australians United for Survival and Individual) Freedom Scouts, led by Ian Murphy, who claimed that the group's monthly newsletter was mailed to 3000 supporters. Murphy admitted that he had visited right-wing groups in the United States to 'try to forge a farmers' alliance against crippling World Bank interest rates'. The Freedom Scouts pledged 'Honour to God—Loyalty to Australia—Preservation of families—Total opposition to Fabian/Marxist Socialism'. They asserted that the country's lack of defence preparedness had reached 'emergency status'. Less than 3000 combat troops were available to defend the Australian land mass; the one hope was to organise and train armed citizens. In 1993 the call was issued for the formation of small units of five to fifteen men able to wage guerrilla warfare against an invader of Australia. Two years later AUSI Freedom Scouts supporter Ross Provis was reported as saying that AUSI Freedom Scouts had 'heavy and light machine guns, mortars and artillery pieces', and arms caches scattered throughout New South Wales.

Ian McNiven, Vice-President of the Firearm Owners Association, publicly expressed support for the ideology of Freedom Scouts and warned that the country's armed forces were in a 'parlous state'; 'if Indonesia invaded us tomorrow they would be raping women in Melbourne within a month'. An appeal for members, made incoherent in parts by its stream of consciousness vehemence, was published in the April–May 1993 edition of *Lock, Stock and Barrel*:

JOIN THE A.U.S.I. FREEDOM SCOUTS
LET NO QUARTER BE GIVEN

Do not kid yourselves about what is at stake. Your career, your property, your material wealth, your status among family and friends, your freedom from incarceration and even your life are at risk . . .
Keep in mind those principles [that] created this great Nation. We owe no apology for that success. If you speak of rights, of the legitimacy of national and cultural continuity and dominance, you like me, will be labelled a fanatic, a racist, an extremist, a radical and even a terrorist . . .

The socialist vomit being fed to our children in the public schools, corrupt politicians, abusive police and government officials, distorted media reporting the rape of our land, the poisoning of our water and air, the strangulation of free enterprise by megabusiness, the insanity of affirmative action and the arrest and prosecution of citizens for self defence are the same rabble who will take your rights, confiscate your weapons and castrate your spirit. [sic]

TAKE OUR WEAPONS AND WE WILL TAKE YOUR LIFE
TAKE WARNING, the line has been drawn. If blood is to be shed, let it begin here. Should the flames and violence consume us, history will mark for future generations the courage and passing of free men. If the Almighty grants an undeserving people mercy once again before the light flickers into darkness, free men and women will take their weapons in hand, place the point of the sword against the throat of the enemy and no quarter shall be given.

THE COMMON STRAND

There are a number of groups on the far right, each with some element of distinctiveness in their policies and the militancy of their demands. There is, however, a common strand: the central place accorded to conspiracies and plots to destroy the Australian people.

Race figures at two levels in this world view: first, as the motive force for the conspiracy and second, as a key element in the means adopted to achieve the ends of the conspiracy. The plotters are most frequently referred to in general terms, commonly depicted as the agents of the One World Government. When the veil is lifted the conspirators are often revealed to be Jewish financiers. Indeed, the One World conceptualisation is little different from the anti-semitic propaganda of the Nazi period with its message of secret cabals working to enslave humanity through destruction of the nation-state and subversion of a people's national identity—their sense of unique culture and heritage—and the imposition of a universal value system. The means adopted have included 'flooding' of the country with immigrants who can never 'assimilate' to the Australian way—people who in time of threat will work to undermine unity; the promotion of divisive 'multiculturalism' in opposition to 'Australian' values; and the ceding of huge areas of land to Aboriginal people, to a small, disloyal minority which may one day compromise Australia's territorial integrity.

There is much additional evidence of the progress of the conspiracy. The education system is no longer teaching national history and patriotic values. The economy is being run down and industries moved overseas, resulting in high rates of unemployment. Economic rationalism is destroying the infrastructure necessary to sustain communities. The family farm is being bankrupted through manipulation of international trade and denial of credit on reasonable terms. The national debt is rising to unsustainable levels, handing control of the nation's destiny to overseas financiers.

While this internal destruction is proceeding the country's defence capacity is quietly being eroded. Spending on defence is cut, the size of the military forces and armament production reduced, while a real deterrent to invasion, the stockpiling of nuclear and biological weapons, is rejected by politicians. Meanwhile patriotic Australians are disarmed.

Revelation of this interlocking set of policies is seen to provide unambiguous evidence of a carefully thought out plan to enslave the Australian people. The politicians and bureaucrats who have facilitated this process are traitors to their people, having allowed themselves to be bought-off by huge sums of money. While the present is a time of great danger, it is also a moment of destiny— the climactic period in Australian history. Salvation can be achieved by sweeping away the corrupt system of government and replacing it with direct democracy, the citizens' initiated referendum which will be the means to translate the people's will into national policy.

6

Pauline Hanson's One Nation

POPULISM

Pauline Hanson was the latest Australian practitioner of a style of politics known as populism, distinguished by four surface features. First, populism gives birth to a movement led by a charismatic leader. Second, the leader disdains to operate through the party system, instead establishing direct contact with 'the people', in keeping with populist rhetoric which condemns the corruption and betrayal of existing politics which it promises to replace with true democracy. Third, the policies of the leader are characteristically little more than general ideas, acceptable to the movement's followers as the simple, 'common sense' approach that is needed to solve national problems. No detailed elaboration of policy is placed before the electorate, in keeping with the populist anti-intellectualism and condemnation of university-educated elites and their deception of common people. Fourth, populism promises its followers a speedy return to a prosperous, stable, well-governed society, the supposed 'golden age' of recent memory.

These features define the appearance of populist politics. In reality the leader is involved in covert practices no different from the party political system—including secret deals and contradictions between policies declared and policies pursued. While populist leaders base their appeal on honesty and a direct link with the people, this form of politics is as much about images and illusions as the system of corruption which it denounces and undertakes to replace.

Perhaps the most notable of Australian populist leaders were Jack Lang, Labor premier of New South Wales during the depression of the 1930s, and Sir Johannes Bjelke-Petersen, Country (subsequently National) Party premier of Queensland from 1968 to 1987.

'Joh', as he was popularly known, ruled Queensland almost as an autocrat, little concerned with the traditions of Westminster democracy. In his period of office parliament met infrequently, demands for accountability were disregarded and the Labor Opposition was treated with contempt. His government had little regard for the separation of powers. Bjelke-Petersen brooked no opposition, at times using the police special branch as an arm of the National Party. The extent of corruption revealed by the Fitzgerald Royal Commission following his departure shocked even the National Party faithful and led to a sharp fall in the party's electoral support in 1989.

Part of the appeal of the premier and of his ministers rested on overt bigotry. Thus in 1982 he asserted that Aborigines were 'as wealthy as Arab oil sheiks'; he announced in parliament that the Aboriginal land rights movement was part of a communist plot to create a separate nation within Australia, which could then be 'capable of contracting with overseas nations hostile to Australia in the future'. In the same year his Aboriginal Affairs Minister informed a journalist that Aboriginal people were not ready for freehold land rights because they would not know what it was. Charles Porter, a former minister of Aboriginal Affairs, wrote in 1985 that demands for land rights 'come largely from those with only a vestigial trace of Aborigine blood and who would be unable to identify the ancestral aboriginal woman supplying that blood trace'.

The Aboriginal policies of the Bjelke-Petersen government were distinguished by a refusal to budge from the assimilationist goals of the 1960s and intransigent opposition to policies developed in Canberra. The only acceptable path for Aboriginal people was to discard their culture and become part of the mainstream. The premier viewed the granting of land rights as 'out of the question', portending the establishment of a 'nation within a nation'; his government's aim was to make 'all Queenslanders, at exactly the same level as myself and everyone else'.

Bjelke-Petersen played on the insularity and xenophobia of Queenslanders and the appeal of simple remedies. His form of politics was particularly effective in a state distinguished by low rates of post-secondary education and the largest percentage of its population outside the capital: in 1981 67 per cent of Victoria's population lived in Melbourne, 56 per cent of New South Wales' population in Sydney, but only 41 per cent of Queensland's population resided in Brisbane.

Bjelke-Petersen's language has been described as rambling, anecdotal, vague on detail, often confused and ungrammatical, in sharp contrast with the verbal polish of national leaders. His signature phrase, employed frequently when pressed on matters of detail by journalists, was 'Don't you worry about that . . .', often delivered with a smile and a wave to his constituents watching the television news as their leader fed the 'chooks' from the big cities. Allan Patience has commented that Bjelke-Petersen 'appealed to provincial suspicions of governments, experts and intellectuals, which is tinged with fear and resentment . . . against big cities, big business, all of the complex sophisticated urban symbols'.

Pauline Hanson was very much a Queensland populist in the style of Bjelke-Petersen, a reality lost on the southern public. While there were differences of detail in the policies of Bjelke-Petersen and One Nation, there was a basic unity in orientation and style, one not lost on the former premier who endorsed Hanson: she was 'the only one talking about the issues that concern people'. Queensland historian Henry Reynolds commented that Hanson was 'closer to Bjelke-Petersen in style than the present parliamentary members of the National Party'. Hanson's first campaign manager observed that she was:

> not a feral neo-Nazi extremist, a fellow traveller of the League of Rights. Many of her ideas might be offensive to a lot of Australians, but they come straight from the heart of conservative Queensland politics. Until her opponents realise that, her attraction to voters in regional Australia will never be understood.

The crudities of local politics which passed as normal in Queensland, however, shocked when presented on the national stage, in part accounting for Hanson's novelty value. Southern interest is also explained by the development since the early 1980s of ways of speaking and talking about race which provided a legitimacy for key elements of Hanson's populism, fostering an environment in which there was a willingness to listen and report, a willingness which might not have otherwise existed.

THE GENIE IN THE BOTTLE

With Pauline Hanson's victory in the 1996 federal election race-based, nationalism reclaimed a central place in public life, a position it had not occupied since the political demise of Robert Menzies and Arthur Calwell in the mid-1960s.

Nineteen eighty-four had witnessed the first episode of heated public controversy over immigration policy when the demand for reintroduction of racially discriminatory policy proceeded from advocacy by far right groups on the fringe of the political process to sympathetic consideration by prominent individuals, newspaper columnists and radio hosts. By the time of the second episode in 1988 the reintroduction of racial discrimination was advocated by the leader of the Opposition and other members of the Liberal–

National Party coalition. Ideas which had been seen as bigoted and unacceptable became the subject of veiled and coded reference and then proceeded to open discussion.

With the advent of Hanson episodic debate was transformed into a continuing feature of federal politics. While the newly elected member for Oxley was unable to locate herself in the value system developed since the early 1980s, her political advisers immediately made the connection. In a speech written by John Pasquarelli and delivered to Ted Drane's Australian Reform Party in October 1996, Hanson stated:

> Ladies and gentlemen, I wish to pay tribute to those people who were prepared to take on the priests of political correctness and their political lackeys long before I came on the scene. In 1984 Professor Geoffrey Blainey delivered a speech to a Rotary Club in country Victoria, in which he made a reasoned call for a debate on the levels of Asian immigration . . . Others who manned the barricades on the immigration and multiculturalism issues were Bruce Ruxton, Peter Walsh, John Stone and . . . Graeme Campbell.

But these predecessors had apparently been too mild or ineffective in their approach, for she went on to assert that 'I hope you will not be too offended, if I say that it took a woman to come along and let the genie out of the bottle'.

Such was Hanson's influence that the party which she founded, at the peak of its popularity during the June 1998 Queensland state election, won 22.7 per cent of the vote and eleven of 89 seats, outvoting the previously governing National Party. Indicative of the shock produced by this result, the Queensland Labor Party State Secretary Mike Kaiser asserted that at the next federal election five Queensland coalition seats could fall to One Nation, which stood to win the balance of power in the House of Representatives. An 'electoral analyst' quoted in the *Financial Review* predicted that the coalition could lose '10 or more seats to One Nation'. It was widely accepted that the party was well placed to gain the balance of power in the Senate; in the event of a double-dissolution election, which seemed possible given the impasse over native title legislation, the party stood to win up to ten Senate seats.

OVER THE SHOP COUNTER

Pauline Hanson was born in 1954 in Brisbane, the youngest of four girls in a family of seven children. Her parents ran a large, prosperous café, and she was educated in the state system, leaving at the age of fifteen to take up employment as a clerk. Her teenage years instilled the work ethic. Hanson recalled that her father worked 106 hours per week for 25 years; she started helping in the business at the age of twelve and it was not unusual in her teens for her to work in an office from eight till five, then waitress in her father's café from six to midnight for very little pay: 'it made you respect money. It made you realise that you don't get anything for nothing. And I think that's what's been instilled in all of us'.

She first married at the age of seventeen and had two children by the time she was 21. From the proceeds of part-time jobs while she raised her family—which included two further children from a second marriage—she purchased a seafood business in Ipswich, located 45 kilometres west of Brisbane, in which she worked six days a week, 80 to 90 hours. She claimed the credit for introducing fresh fish to Ipswich, an innovation which required her to make pre-dawn trips to the Brisbane fish market four times weekly.

Of particular significance for her future role was her lack of formal education and ignorance of the world of ideas. At the time that she entered federal politics she had difficulty writing a grammatical sentence, to judge by a letter she wrote to a local newspaper, and had little understanding of the political process. The values of southeast Queensland left their mark not through attendance at political or church meetings but through conversations with customers. When asked how she formed her views on Aboriginal issues Hanson replied that 'over the years, women used to come into the shop and we'd talk about this, the inequalities at the school and problems that were happening around. Because you'd hear of the Aboriginals maybe getting into problems in the streets, or stealing handbags, or disrupting business, or coming in and stealing things. It was just that talk was around over a period of time'.

To some extent her lack of political knowledge and worldly wisdom was an asset, allowing her to assume the mantle of the quintessential anti-politician, but it left a legacy of problems that ultimately seriously, perhaps fatally, weakened her movement. Ignorance left her almost totally dependent on political advisers. Her political adviser during 1996 had no success in encouraging her to read. He would leave her briefing papers and books only to return later to find them untouched; Hanson would complain that she had no ability to understand the issues and to grasp and retain detail. He lamented that she was 'intellectually indolent', 'she would let me down time and time again by not reading the simplest of briefing notes'. One journalist who obtained time for a lengthy interview found that 'on many issues, Hanson, surprisingly, has no view. "I haven't read enough about it", or "I haven't thought about it" are common responses to questions about talking points'. The following year a second journalist travelling with her on an interstate flight was astounded to observe that she lacked sufficient powers of concentration or interest to read a long newspaper article about her own party.

It is wrong, however, to assume that Hanson was merely a creature of her advisers. While they moulded her rhetoric and introduced her to issues to serve their own ends and understandings of effective politics, Hanson was nothing if not strong willed and single minded. As she stated, 'I am my own person . . . and I only do what I really want to do'. She was not one to endorse policies with which she did not agree and it is clear that her stance was constant from the time of her candidature for the seat of Ipswich, although there is scope to argue that she could not keep up with the range of issues adopted by One Nation and by the time of the 1998 federal election campaign was happy to delegate key areas of policy formation to trusted advisers.

While she brought to the national forum the value system typical of far right politics in southeastern Queensland, there were distinctive elements, not least because of her position as a fiercely independent woman. She did not, at first, embrace the apocalyptic, conspiratorial vision of elements on the far right, nor did she campaign on moral issues. Over the previous decade few women had risen to prominence on the far right and those who had, such as Jacqui Butler of Women Who Want to Be Women and Wake Up Australia, focused on morals. Hanson, in contrast, did not speak from a fundamentalist religious background. She described herself as an agnostic in religion and talked on one occasion of what seemed to be a woman's right to abortion ('every woman's right to determine her body, to decide her body'), described two of the happiest times in her life as the dissolution of her two marriages, claimed to have close friends who were homosexuals and stated that 'what they do in their life is their own business'.

INITIAL POLITICAL MOVES

Hanson's political career began in Ipswich, where she served a term of less than one year as member of the local council during 1994–95. After an unsuccessful attempt at re-election she joined the Liberal Party—in her eyes the party sympathetic to small business—and secured endorsement for what was seen as the safe Labor seat of Ipswich. It was her 1996 campaign that first gained her national prominence.

Prior to the announcement of the election date, while campaigning as the endorsed Liberal candidate, Hanson wrote a letter to the editor of the local newspaper, the *Queensland Times*, published on 6 January 1996. The letter, apparently sparked by anger at the actions of Robert Tickner, Minister for Aboriginal Affairs, was concerned exclusively with government policy towards Aborigines. It echoed the values of the Queensland right and encapsulated many of the issues which were to establish her national identity. They related to the demand that all be treated on the basis of equality rather than on racial criteria; the need for Aboriginal people to take responsibility for their own actions and futures; the view that welfare bred dependence and was of no benefit to the recipient; the questioning of the racial status of those claiming to be Aboriginal; the loss of balance in government policy; the assertion that the present generation bore no responsibility for whatever happened in the past; and the claim that racism, far from being endemic in the community, was caused by resentment of government favouritism of Aboriginal people:

Black deaths in custody seem to be Robert Tickner's latest outcry. Pity that as much media coverage or political grandstanding is not shown for white deaths in custody. As for Mr Tickner's statement that Aborigines should not go to jail because apparently it is not working: imagine what type of country this would be to live in if Aborigines didn't go to jail for their crimes. One of these men was serving a 12-year sentence and it wasn't just for a speeding fine. Can you imagine then if we had equality, then we would have no prisoners at all. The indigenous people of this country are as much responsible for their actions as any other colour or race in this country. The problem is that politicians in all their profound wisdom have and are causing a racism problem. I would be the first to admit that, not that many years ago, the Aborigines were treated wrongly but in trying to correct this they have gone too far. I don't feel responsible for the treatment of Aboriginal people in the past because I had no say, but my concern is for now and the future. How can we expect this race to help themselves when governments shower them with money, facilities and opportunities that only these people can obtain no matter how minute the indigenous blood is that flows through their veins, and this is what is causing racism. Until governments wake up to themselves and start looking at equality not colour then we might start to work together as one.

This letter was drawn to the attention of the national media by Hanson's Labor rivals—not the last effort by her political opponents to discredit her which badly misfired. The resulting media outcry gained her continuing publicity during the election campaign and led to her disendorsement as the Liberal candidate. This did not happen, however, until some weeks after the date of the letter's publication, by which time it had become too late to endorse a replacement and to remove her Liberal affiliation from the ballot paper. She was thus left in a position to win both the Liberal and disenchanted blue collar vote against the lacklustre Labor incumbent and unpopular prime minister in a traditional Labor electorate. Hanson secured the biggest anti-Labor swing in the election which, by a quirk of fate, was within 0.2 per cent of the vote (and swing) won by One Nation at the 1998 Queensland election (see Table 6.1).

Immediately after her election Hanson won further notoriety when, during an interview with a journalist from the *Australian*,

Table 6.1   Vote, 1996 federal election—seat of Oxley

Candidate	Party	% Votes	% Swing	After preferences
Scott, Les	ALP	39.36	−15.18	45.34
Hanson, Pauline	LP	48.61	+22.86	54.66
Pullen, David	DEM	6.08	+0.56	
McKeon, John	GRN	2.68	+2.68	

Source: Australian Electoral Commission

she was seen to disown her Aboriginal constituents. In response to the question 'So you're fighting for the white community generally?' she stated:

> Yeah, look, the white community, the immigrants, Italians, Greeks, whoever, it really doesn't matter, you know, anyone apart from Aboriginals and Torres Strait Islanders, you know. I just want everyone to be equal and I think then we could get rid of this umm, I think there's a racial discrimination out in the community and we might start to get on to work together as one.

Hanson was willing to admit that there was a serious problem with Aboriginal health, but 'millions and millions' of dollars had been spent and 'nothing has improved'; people were 'working too hard for their money and pay too much tax for it to be wasted'.

FIRST YEAR IN POLITICS

Hanson's first year in politics was tumultuous. She started as a political innocent, with basic attitudes and orientations but little in the way of specific policies. Further, she had almost no experience in handling the media. She was fortunate to immediately attract the attention of a seasoned political operator, John Pasquarelli, who was recommended to her by Graeme Campbell.

Over the previous ten years Pasquarelli had brief periods of employment with other champions of far right causes, Senator John Stone for nine months from mid-1989 to March 1990 and Graeme Campbell during the 1996 election campaign, as well as various other jobs including employment as a private investigator. Pasquarelli had lived for a number of years in Papua New Guinea, had been elected to its first House of Assembly in 1964 and in 1987 had stood as the unsuccessful Liberal candidate for the House of Representatives Victorian seat of Jagajaga, safely held by the Labor Party.

In the late 1980s Pasquarelli was known for his views critical of government immigration and multicultural policies and his willingness to outrage the complacent. Thus after the 1987 election he attempted to circulate a letter within the Liberal Party asserting that 'one of the hard issues that is going to affect future generations of Australians is the question of coloured immigration'. With such views his securing of employment with Senator Stone and his association with Bruce Ruxton and other identities of the right is hardly a surprise. As he rightly observed, 'politics is an incestuous business'.

Pasquarelli was also renowned for his overbearing and aggressive character. Denis McCormack of Australians Against Further Immigration said of him that 'he has an unfortunate personality that seems to inevitably rub people up the wrong way'. Michelle Campbell, wife of Graeme Campbell, said that 'he was not easy to live with or work with. He was overpowering, but he suddenly found his match with Graeme'. Hanson sacked him after some nine months, explaining to the press that he seemed to have become confused as to who was the employer and who the employee. In her view he sought to control the people around her and keep her in the dark about his contacts and actions on her behalf: 'he would tell me little. I was never informed exactly to whom he was talking'.

Pasquarelli did, however, understand the basis of Hanson's electoral appeal and her strengths and weaknesses, was adept at handling the media and was an excellent speech writer. He maximised Hanson's appeal as anti-politician and was able to broaden the range of her concerns while keeping her firmly within the New Right's form of racial nationalism. Her repertoire was developed to embrace the critique of 'political correctness', immigration policy, the historians who were busily rewriting the country's history, and other policies including national service and defence. It was not difficult with this agenda, as Pasquarelli wrote, to provoke a 'shock wave of media indignation and emotional attacks from the Aboriginal "industry" and its conglomerates' and ensure that Hanson remained in the spotlight.

The broadening of Hanson's agenda ran the risk, in Pasquarelli's eyes, that she would be trapped into a statement that would prove counter-productive. He recalls one potential disaster when Hanson informed a local journalist that in her view 'all Asian immigration should be stopped'. According to Pasquarelli's account, when he later asked what she was trying to achieve she could only smile and giggle.

The major achievement of Hanson's first year in office was her maiden speech, delayed because of a tortuous process of drafting, with a battle over its content between Pasquarelli, Hanson and her secretary, Barbara Hazelton. Hanson later commented that 'I told him the topics that I wanted ... and then he wrote them up for me. But it just wasn't coming from my heart and it was not what I wanted to get across'.

The final result was a political masterpiece, one of the most memorable of parliamentary speeches, its opening words almost immediately elevated to legendary status. This was an event to mark the entry into the halls of the federal parliament of the 'average Australian', the liberation of those previously captive to the cabal of Canberra politicians:

> I come here not as a polished politician but as a woman who has had her fair share of life's knocks. My view on issues is based on commonsense, and my experience as a mother of four children, as a sole parent, and as a business woman running a fish and chip shop. ... I may be only 'a fish and chip shop lady', but some of these economists need to get their heads out of the textbooks and get a job in the real world ... I consider myself just an ordinary Australian who wants to keep this great country strong and independent.

Pasquarelli drew on New Right values to attack 'political correctness' and parasitic taxpayer funded 'industries', as well as older targets, the 'fat cats' and 'do-gooders'. Hanson's maiden speech continued:

We now have a situation where a type of reverse racism is applied to mainstream Australians by those who promote political correctness and those who control the various tax-payer funded 'industries' that flourish in our society servicing Aboriginals, multiculturalists and a host of other minority groups. In response to my call for equality for all Australians, the most noisy criticism came from the fat cats, bureaucrats and the do-gooders. They screamed the loudest because they stand to lose the most—their power, money and position, all funded by ordinary Australian taxpayers.

Always the bottom line was the taxation dollar, the hard-earned cash taken from the 'ordinary Australian taxpayer'. In developing the prognosis of ills and prescription for the future Hanson touched on six major areas.

Primacy was given to the 'equal rights' argument—there should be 'equality' for all Australians, with no special benefits available on racial criteria. In future there should be only one policy, for a united Australia with all treated 'equally', with an evocation of the nationalist rallying call. The Nazi regime had promised to deliver 'Ein Volk, Ein Reich, Ein Fuhrer' ('One People, One Country, One Leader'), National Action in Australia promoted 'One Aim, One Symbol, One Method, One Movement', now Hanson in 1996 offered 'One People, One Nation, One Flag'.

If politicians continue to promote separatism in Australia, they should not continue to hold their seats in this parliament. They are not truly representing all Australians, and I call on the people to throw them out. To survive in peace and harmony, united and strong, we must have one people, one nation, one flag.

Special benefits available only to Aborigines should be abolished; economic policies changed to protect Australian jobs by introduction of tariff barriers to stimulate industry, low interest loans made available to business, and government-run national development schemes; radical change made to the *Family Law Act*; defence capacity increased to protect Australia from the menace of countries with huge populations to the north; foreign aid ended to free money to help Australians; and multiculturalism abolished and immigration law changed.

It seemed that comments on immigration and multiculturalism were deliberately kept vague and contradictory to enable Hanson to rouse indignation while leaving room for different readings and hence the basis for rejection in the mainstream media of claims that the policy was racially based. Immigration, Hanson declared, should be halted while unemployment remained high. When it was resumed, a strong indication was given that Asian immigration would not be permitted. The key justification was in keeping with the rationale of the now historic 'White Australia' policy—that because of innate human characteristics multicultural societies could not work, people from different 'races' could not be blended into a harmonious whole:

> I believe we are in danger of being swamped by Asians . . . They have their own culture and religion, form ghettos and do not assimilate. Of course, I will be called racist but, if I can invite whom I want into my home, then I should have the right to have a say in who comes into my country. A truly multicultural country can never be strong or united. The world is full of failed and tragic examples.

After justifying a racially discriminatory policy on the grounds of general principle, on supposed infallible laws of human nature—'they . . . do not assimilate . . . can never be . . . united'—a contradictory statement was added, affirming the 'first-class' qualities of those already resident:

I must stress ... that I do not consider those people from ethnic backgrounds currently living in Australia anything but first-class citizens, provided of course that they give this country their full, undivided loyalty.

Elements of politics of the paranoid style were present, but under-developed. The United Nations was identified as part of the problem facing the Australian people, as were 'financial markets, international organisations, world bankers, investment companies and big business people'. While the apocalypse was not imminent, it was time for strong words and action: 'I am fed up with being told, "This is our land". Well, where the hell do I go? I was born here, and so were my parents and children'. The politicians who did not serve the people should be thrown out. Time was 'running out. We may only have 10 to 15 years left to turn things around'. Echoing the title of the far right 'Wake up, Australia' campaign of the late 1980s, she urged: 'Wake up, Australia, before it is too late'.

This was a speech for the times, most carefully crafted, designed to provoke, with different messages for different audiences. Its objectives were splendidly achieved.

MEDIA STAR

Following the maiden speech Hanson was immediately embroiled in public controversy, a controversy that was to ebb and flow for over two years. For much of this period there was little that she could do wrong in the eyes of her supporters. To her critics she was the dark face of Australian racism reanimated, the siren song beckoning in Geoffrey Barker's words to 'a mythic past where employment was full behind high-tariff walls, where the bush was prosperous, where Asians were excluded and Aborigines were invis-ible, and where a real man could keep his guns'. Based on its weekly survey, the country's leading media monitoring service, Rehame, reported that Hanson ranked in the top five 'of the most talked about people' over the years 1996–98 (see Tables 6.2 and 6.3).

Contrary to Pasquarelli's fears, it seemed that Hanson could do no wrong. While the media elite thought they could show her up as an ignoramus—an 'Oxleymoron' in the alliteration of the intelligentsia—gaffes and lack of knowledge became positive assets, reinforcing her status as one of the people.

Why was Hanson able to command so much public attention?

Table 6.2 Five most talked about people of 1996—New South Wales

	In the press	On radio and television
1	John Howard, PM	John Howard
2	Bill Clinton, US President	Bob Carr
3	Bob Carr, Premier of NSW	Paul Keating
4	Paul Keating, former PM	Pauline Hanson
5	Pauline Hanson	Andrew Refshauge

Source: Sydney Morning Herald, 20 December 1996

Table 6.3 What made news, 1997–98—radio and television—Australia

	Most talked about people		Year's top stories	
	1997	1998	1997	1998
1	John Howard	John Howard	Native title	Waterfront dispute
2	Pauline Hanson	Kim Beazley	Pauline Hanson	Federal government tax policies
3	Jeff Kennett	Jeff Kennett	Death of Princess Diana	Pauline Hanson and the One Nation Party
4	Bob Carr	Pauline Hanson	Thredbo landslide	Esso Longford Gas Explosion
5	Kim Beazley	Peter Costello	Australian republic	Native title

Source: Rehame, 1998 Annual Review

Why did she succeed, where others before her had failed, to win sufficient votes for election and then to build on her success once in federal parliament? Why was she able to go from strength to strength, while others with policies similar to her own such as Graham Campbell remained in the wilderness? The answer lies in large part in her personal attributes.

Hanson was able to turn lack of polish and education, her ignorance of basic political issues, even her limited vocabulary, to advantage. She exemplified, without the need for artifice, the anti-politician. Unlike more seasoned performers she was able to gain the devotion of a large number of Australians who identified with her, who saw in her a person like themselves confronting the university-educated elites, out of touch with the real world. This was perhaps most clearly indicated when, in response to a television interviewer's question of whether she was xenophobic Hanson responded with 'please explain', a request for definition of a word she had not previously encountered. 'Please explain' soon became a Hanson trademark, a symbol of the gap between the world of the lettered classes and Hanson's constituency.

There were, however, other personal attributes. Hanson had a rare ability to relate to those attracted to her meetings; she thrived on personal adulation, glowed in the company of admirers of whom there was no shortage. It seemed as if whole townships in rural Australia gathered for a handshake or autograph. Her supporters were cheered by her confrontations with journalists. Possessed of fierce temper and iron determination, Hanson would never take a backward step. When challenged she would bristle with indignation. She could never admit that she was wrong. It was not difficult for her media minders to develop the image of the fearless redhead whom no one could cower. She was likened to a modern day 'Joan of Arc' or Australia's Evita Peron and seen by seasoned political observers as a charismatic leader. In some respects she met the classic definition of charismatic leadership, through her personal capacity to inspire devotion, to discard the prepared speech and relate to her listeners on an immediate, personal level.

To the press she was, in the words of the *Sydney Morning Herald*'s Margo Kingston, 'like a shot of oxygen for a jaded media reporting to a jaded public', 'an exotic, a curiosity', not a manufactured product of political minders and spin doctors but a real human being. In the context of the mundane and predictable, it was 'like an alien had entered the citadel'.

While her ability to play the role of the anti-politician served her well in the short and medium terms, it was a role with limited durability. Her lack of political knowledge left her overly dependent on advisers: she could choose between them, but not between their policies. Further, she could not acknowledge her own limitations. In the months following the Queensland election triumph she talked more than once of her sense of being the 'mother of the nation': 'it's like I'm a mother . . . and the Australian people are my children'. This, it seemed, was one delusion too many. The image of national motherhood could be acclaimed by few. The tenuous nature of Hanson's appeal was based on ordinariness, not exceptionality; she was more the voice of resentment and defiance than the visionary leader. Within a narrowly circumscribed role she could inspire, but when she strayed beyond designated bounds support quickly fell away.

As pressure built up following the spectacular Queensland success she found it increasingly difficult to cope with media probing. The shock value of headline-grabbing claims wore off. Once her party yielded to pressure to develop policies she found it almost impossible to explain detail. Ignorance could only take her some of the way to her political ambitions.

ON THE GRAVY TRAIN

At the moment of triumph, the maiden speech, a second egocentric political operative, David Oldfield, made himself known to

Hanson. Like Pasquarelli, Oldfield had been a fringe player in Liberal Party politics for a number of years: a local councillor, he had unsuccessfully stood as an endorsed Liberal candidate for the state seat of Manly. On the night of Hanson's maiden speech he intervened to rescue her from abusive patrons at a Canberra nightclub. A friendship developed and he began to provide secret advice, behind the back of Pasquarelli and his own employer, Liberal member of the federal parliament Tony Abbott.

It seems that in November 1996 Oldfield began moves to establish a new political party headed by Hanson in which he and a close friend, David Ettridge, would play key roles. At a secret meeting the triumvirate drew up a memorandum of understanding, setting out the duties of Hanson as leader, Oldfield as strategist and Ettridge as fundraiser and administrator. Oldfield and Ettridge persuaded Hanson—possibly without full awareness of what she was doing—to limit membership of the party to three, with a majority vote (of two) being necessary for binding decisions. Hanson had delivered control of her movement to two men whose acquaintance she had only recently made.

For some months after the sacking of Pasquarelli, Oldfield and Ettridge stayed hidden from public view, although it seems that by the beginning of February 1997, if not earlier, Ettridge was acting on Hanson's behalf. It was only with the successful launch of One Nation in April 1997 that Ettridge and Oldfield, confident in the prospects of their alliance, quit their employment and assumed new roles at Hanson's side.

Oldfield was to prove himself a highly skilled political operative. Like Pasquarelli he exuded supreme confidence in his own abilities; he was the adviser who could make no mistakes. Those close to Oldfield paint a picture of a man with an unquenchable need for media attention, obsessed with power, driven solely by unswerving pursuit of his goals, possessed of an almost pathological calmness in moments of crisis, not caring for damage that his actions provoked. On one occasion, basking in the media spotlight, he teased the headline writers with the statement that he was attracted to the ideas of national socialism, which he leisurely clarified with the statement that although he was a nationalist and in some respects a socialist he was aware that the term had unfortunate connotations. During the 1998 election campaign he complained to Hanson that 'she'd gone "soft on Abos"'.

In the period of Oldfield's dominance Hanson's message was narrowly focused, made more abrasive, and openly embraced the politics of paranoia. It was as if Oldfield had schooled himself in the lessons of the master propagandists of the twentieth century, who taught that for propaganda to be effective, it had to be simplified, one-sided, limited to a few points and repetitions. It had to identify malevolent forces and present criticism of established elites. Lastly, it had to present a vision of national salvation and utopia. Perhaps the most successful practitioner of the art of propaganda, Joseph Goebbels, explained the requirements for success:

> the rank and file are usually much more primitive than we imagine. Propaganda must therefore always be essentially simple and repetitive. In the long run basic results in influencing public opinion will be achieved only by the man who is able to reduce problems to the simplest terms and who has the courage to keep forever repeating them in this simplified form, despite the objections of intellectuals.
>
> Nobody can say your propaganda is too crude, too low, too brutal, or is not sufficiently decent, for all these attributes are not characteristic of its specific nature. By no means should propaganda be decent or mild or soft or humble, it should lead to success . . . Anything is permissible which is successful.

Oldfield and Ettridge openly espoused the view that any tactic that served the party's ends was acceptable. In the words of Ettridge, one thing 'overrides every other consideration, that's the need to succeed'.

THE LAUNCH OF ONE NATION

In April 1997 Hanson launched her own political party. By this time, under Oldfield's influence, there seemed to be little concern about the extremism of statements. Shortly before the launch, while Oldfield was still an employee of a Liberal parliamentarian but heavily involved in charting Hanson's political career, Hanson asked her then adviser David Thomas to look at the draft of her speech. According to the journalist Marian Wilkinson, Hanson 'was a bit uneasy about it. Thomas read it and freaked. It was, he recalled, "really racist, Nazi Party stuff, anti-Aborigine and anti-Asian. I was shocked."'. It is unclear who wrote the draft but Oldfield was given responsibility for the final version, which remained the most extreme speech delivered by Hanson to that date. As delivered, it was notable for its emphasis on the 'one truth', for its identification of malevolent forces working to destroy Australia, for its sense of impending crisis and vision of national salvation.

Truth in the context of the Queensland far right meant belief in a sacrosanct vision; it meant dedication to nothing short of total victory and refusal to compromise. Hanson proclaimed that 'I am about the truth. I am about us being Australians. I am about us being one people'. The Australian people now faced a plot by their 'enemies' to take 'our country ... from within'; there was a 'betrayal', a 'conspiracy of divisiveness ... encouraged by our governments'. In this time of national crisis people were called upon to:

> stand against those who have betrayed our country, and would destroy our identity by forcing upon us the cultures of others ... If we fail, all our fears will be realised, and we will lose our country forever, and be strangers in our own land ... They think Australians will just lay down and see their country disappear before their eyes ... Are they right? We've come too

far to be stopped, and we won't be stopped. We will reclaim our country, and the future of our children. We have been pushed far enough.

In contrast with 'what we all know to be the truth' were the government policies destroying Australia: the removal of tariff barriers which led to manufacturing jobs going to 'countries like Indonesia' and the consequent increase in unemployment; the decline of rural Australia while money was wasted on ATSIC; and immigration policies which 'fill our country with people who have given us nothing in return'. There was an immediate need to end funding of the 'industries' dividing the people and to implement policies in the national interest. A continuation of present policies could lead to civil war.

To maintain media attention, and also as a money-making venture, a book of some 242 pages, *The Truth*, was published to coincide with the party's launch. The book was issued in Hanson's name and she was designated the copyright holder. The first part contained the full text of a number of Hanson speeches, the second was a compilation by Hanson's South Australian supporters, with Denis McCormack acknowledging that he provided editorial assistance. Hanson and her advisers seemed little concerned about the controversial nature of its content. One of the then inner sanctum subsequently revealed that 'it was just looked at from a total business point of view, saying "right, if we could sell 100 000 books at $10 per book, then we're going to make a lot of money"'. The book was as much Hanson's as her speeches and when asked if she stood by the publication Hanson was unambiguous: 'I put my name to the book and I support my book'. When confronted with criticism of its contents she responded: 'it's all documented evidence and it's true fact'.

The book's statement of purpose, printed on its back cover, indicates clearly that the Hanson movement was now clearly in the embrace of the paranoid right. Australia, readers were told, was in peril of enslavement by the One World Government, acting through the United Nations:

> For too long the devotees of the United Nations' agenda have held court, claiming the intellectual capacity and internationalist birthright to do so. This blind following has led a once proud and wealthy country down the road to despair. Why? The answer is simple: we have allowed our own indifference, apathy and fear to prevent us from challenging the status quo. The phenomenon that is Pauline Hanson is simply the capacity and courage of a politician of the people to express the uncluttered, unsophisticated and simple commonsense philosophy of the Australian people. The manifestation of the race debate has been the end product of the social experiment of putting the people of the world into a common melting pot. It is not the Australian people who are racist, for they are merely the pawns in the ideological and pathological agenda of globalised money politics.

The four chapters prepared by 'members of the Pauline Hanson Support Movement' were entitled: 'In Defence of Pauline Hanson: New Class Elites and the Betrayal of Australia'; 'Surrendering Australia: Mabo, Wik and Native Title'; 'The Gun Control Debate: Political Correctness and the Assault on Traditional Australia'; and 'Pauline Hanson—Giving Government Back to the People'.

Employing the apocalyptic imagery of the Nazi era, the book presented the argument that 'a class of raceless, placeless cosmopolitan elites' were exercising 'almost absolute power over us':

> Fragmentation, produced by new class policies such as immigrationism, multiculturalism, Asianisation and Aboriginalism (romantic primitivism) ultimately divide us ... Ordinary Australians do have a common enemy, but it is not

Aborigines, Asians or people of any particular colour, race or creed. Our common oppressors are a class of raceless, placeless cosmopolitan elites who are exercising almost absolute power over us; like black spiders above the wheels of industry, they are spinning the webs of our destiny. We can only escape these webs by organised action.

The chapter on the gun control debate put forward the argument that 'behind the gun controllers is the black claw of the internationalist elite of "The New World Order" . . . The groundwork for a global gulag, a cosmopolitan police state has been already put into place . . . We are entering an era where our fundamental freedoms will come increasingly under attack. We must organise now to meet this threat, head-on'.

The new class elites have deliberately earmarked Anglo-Saxon Australia for destruction. By successive waves of migration the ethnic composition of the population has changed. Assimilation has been rejected; multiculturalism advocated. Step by step social cohesion has broken down. To the side of this development has been the undermining of Australia's industrial and manufacturing base by the economically genocidal policies of economic rationalism, free trade and the level playing field.

And what would the future hold if the 'New World Order' succeeded in implementing its agenda? A scenario of Australia in the year 2050 was presented. By this time the Republic of Australasia had become part of the United States of Asia, established by an official World Government proclamation. Its constitution had been altered by the World Government Security Council to allow free entry and citizenship to any refugee or displaced person. Its population had grown to 1.8 billion and 'its ethnic composition . . . changed to a Chinese and Indian mix'. The country's president was Poona Li Hung, 'a lesbian . . . of multiracial descent'. She was also part machine, the world's first cyborg president.

The book won immediate notoriety, with media attention focused on the Aboriginal chapter which sought to de-legitimise contemporary Aboriginal demands by denigration of traditional Aboriginal society—through a dredging up of spurious historical evidence of Aboriginal cannibalism. Without any consideration of the reliability of sources it presented claims that 'some Aboriginal tribes killed mixed-race babies by placing them on ants' nests', that 'baby cannibalism was rife among the central-western peoples' and when women ate their new-born babies they shared the flesh with other women in their group, that women who were unfaithful were 'killed and eaten', and that 'older women were often killed for eating purposes like livestock'. Such 'evidence' was designed to 'refute the romantic view of the Aborigines held by the new class'. David Ettridge commented that 'the suggestion that we should be feeling some concern for modern-day Aborigines for suffering in the past is balanced a little bit by the alternative view of whether you can feel sympathy for people who eat their babies'.

One critic observed that such claims usually accompanied attempts to justify the denial of normally accepted human standards to those accused of cannibalism; another that 'images of baby killing' was a standard element of European anti-semitism. Gerard Henderson depicted the book as 'packaged paranoia from cover to cover', distinguished by its 'racial insularity', and urged conservatives to make a stand against its claims. The conservative intellectual Robert Manne urged leaders of the Liberal and National parties to read the book, to understand the nature of Hanson's political movement and to distance themselves decisively. Such advice was ignored at that time. Prime Minister Howard continued to see no problem in exchanging preferences with One Nation and in late June 1998, according to Paul Kelly, remained unconcerned at the prospect of working with One Nation senators.

Shortly after the launch of One Nation the party placed a half-page advertisement calling for support in perhaps the most rabidly racist publication in the country, the Bendigo based *Strategy*. Indicative of the nature of this publication, one of its contributors argued that 'We, the white race, are enveloped in a vicious deadly race war. This involves maniacal minds conceiving the destruction of our gene pools and seed stocks of our white creative race'.

Had Oldfield and Ettridge hijacked the people's movement, distorting Hanson's 'home-truths' and 'commonsense'? When asked directly by a journalist in September 1997 about her views on the 'New World Order conspiracy theory', Hanson replied:

> I wouldn't dismiss it as rubbish. There's too many people out there who are concerned about it. We've signed over 2,000 treaties with the United Nations and I don't know that the Australian people know what we've signed away.

THE QUEENSLAND ELECTION

The Queensland election of June 1998 was the first test of One Nation's electoral appeal. In the twelve months after the launch of the party support had ebbed, if opinion polls are to be believed. Late in 1997 Oldfield resorted to a media stunt in an attempt to reverse the trend. At his instigation Hanson recorded a message from the grave, to be released to 'her people' should she fall victim to assassination. Within days excerpts were broadcast, leading to endless parody and condemnation. In the view of some analysts One Nation had no future.

Hanson had little new to say, but was able to remain in the media spotlight by holding public meetings, an invitation to mass protests in major centres of population. Those who came to hear her message were subjected to abuse, in some cases violence, by anti-Hanson demonstrators. The front pages of newspapers were dominated by images of mayhem outside meetings as police fought to maintain order. These meetings served not only to create a media forum for Hanson but also diverted attention from her policies to civil liberties issues concerning the freedom of speech and the right of people to hear what she had to say. While it is next to impossible to evaluate the impact of demonstrations, it is possible that on balance they damaged One Nation's cause; that despite the publicity they gained Hanson they succeeded in the long term in undermining support beyond her core constituency. She faced the problem that the agenda, to an important extent, was set by demonstrators and she was required constantly to respond to charges of racism.

Still under Oldfield's guidance, Hanson delivered her most extreme speech two weeks before the Queensland election of June 1998. Speaking in the House of Representatives, she drew on the motif of the 'guilt industry', its genealogy traced through Prime Minister Howard to Morgan, to allege that there was 'a carefully coordinated assault on the conscience of . . . Australians for the express purpose of producing guilt so as to extract monetary compensation'. In mocking terms—developing elements of the prime minister's position—she dismissed the 'so-called stolen generations, sorry days, sorry books', seemingly endless demands produced by the detractors of the Australian people, 'the ongoing PR campaign aimed not at reconciliation but at remuneration'. The result of this campaign was that 'up to 79 per cent of Australia is under the threat of native title by less than two per cent of the population'.

There was a grave problem facing the country, she alleged, orchestrated by outside interests, embodied in the MAI (Multilateral Agreement on Investment) and the United Nations Draft Declaration on the Rights of Indigenous Peoples. These treaties would 'take power and choice from the majority of our own people and place that power and freedom of choice firmly in the hands of foreigners and self-seeking minorities'.

Hanson asserted that the draft declaration, which she termed 'a treaty', represented 'a treacherous sell-out of the Australian people . . . It will tear the heart out of our country and deliver that heart to one of our very smallest minority groups'. This was the responsibility of 'internationalists with no loyal commitment to our country or the future of our people', 'Aboriginal separatists, the United Nations and the disloyal and self-seeking globalists in our own midst'. Hanson had identified the One World plot for the benefit of the Queensland electorate. Although even John Howard was moved to denounce the speech as 'deranged', it played well in Queensland to judge by the election result.

In the weeks leading to the election One Nation released a range of policy documents focused on 'equal rights', the need to make politicians responsible to the electorate and to free the nation, rural Australia and the family home from external influence.

Under a One Nation government assistance to Aborigines and Torres Strait Islanders would be slashed, as would multicultural programs. The Anti-Discrimination Board would be closed down. Politicians would be made to listen to the people through introduction of the citizens initiated referendum. The 'obscene' superannuation benefits enjoyed by politicians would be terminated and their expense accounts opened for public scrutiny. A people's bank would be established to provide the farming and small business community with 2 per cent fixed interest loans. There would be government funding for industrial development and heavily subsidised wages to encourage employers to take on apprentices. Schools would re-emphasise basic literacy and numeracy and teach responsibility and respect. Tertiary education would receive less government support and financing of arts programs would be terminated. The authority of the family would be reinforced by allowing parents to 'administer just and fair domestic discipline within their homes', without outside interference. Police would be empowered to detain children under the age of sixteen found in public places and return them to their homes. Citizens would be allowed firearms to protect themselves and their homes. Farmers would have the right to purchase self-loading and slide or pump-action shotguns. Those trespassing on private property would forfeit any claims for compensation for injuries suffered. Legislation would ensure appropriate prison terms for criminal acts and mandatory sentences would be imposed for serious crimes. A body of twelve 'Ordinary Citizens' would be elected to oversee the performance of judges and recommend dismissal where undue leniency was exercised towards criminals. A maximum security prison with 'extra security walls' and electrified fences would be built in a remote part of the state, at least 1000 kilometres from Brisbane. A referendum would be held on the reintroduction of capital punishment.

Hanson campaigned well at a time of mounting support, capitalising on disillusionment with politicians, particularly with the performance of the governing coalition parties. Instead of allowing herself to become embroiled in details of policy, she lent a willing ear to the disaffected. Margo Kingston noted that on the road she 'let people come to her. She'd wander along and they'd approach her, whereupon she'd bend her head, cross her hands and listen. Hanson excelled as a channel for grievances'.

Crucial to the party's electoral success was the decision of the National and Liberal parties, with the exception of one seat, to allocate preferences to One Nation ahead of Labor, a decision which provoked condemnation and was seen by commentators as explaining the significant decline in the Liberal vote in Brisbane. One Nation won a spectacular 22.7 per cent of the primary vote, exceeding almost all expectations, winning eleven seats in the one-house Queensland parliament.

The Queensland election marked the peak of the party's success. It was expected that at the pending federal election One Nation would take a large part of the National Party vote and gain increased representation in the House of Representatives and the balance of power in the Senate. Indicative of the post-Queensland election political climate one of the country's senior political commentators, the measured Paul Kelly of the *Australian*, wrote that Hanson had a chance to 'convert her movement into a parliamentary party with potentially great influence at the federal level'.

Such predictions, however, raised the pressure on the coalition parties, which became sufficiently concerned to decide, after considerable internal party debate and talk of defections, to place One Nation last in the allocation of preferences for the forthcoming federal election. This was a decision reached with considerable misgivings and was, for a time, apparently opposed by Prime Minister Howard. The precise reasons leading to the decision have yet to be revealed, but for a period of weeks there was mounting pressure from Liberal Party backers and declarations of opposition to a preference deal from senior party members, including deputy leader Peter Costello, before the prime minister resolved to act. Four National Party candidates in Queensland, however, refused to accept direction and allocated preferences to One Nation ahead of Labor. There were apparently attempts to broker deals with the National Party to preference Pauline Hanson in the seat of Blair but they came to naught.

THE UNRAVELLING

The support for One Nation was to prove extremely volatile, with a fall in its vote of almost 50 per cent within three months. It seems that this loss of support is largely explained by a series of blunders committed by Hanson and her advisers in a context of mounting difficulties following the demonstration of the party's electoral potential.

Part of the blame rested with the two Davids. In the aftermath of electoral triumph Ettridge thought he could adopt a public role. Seemingly parroting the Social Credit ideas of the League of Rights, he suggested that One Nation could fund its proposed people's bank by printing the required money: 'the Government doesn't have to go overseas to borrow money. They can print their own money as they did during the wartime, I believe'. This was ammunition for the party's political opponents, who sought to capitalise on his gaffe by alarming one of the party's core support bases, the retirees whose savings could be imperilled by the inflationary pressures released by government policy of printing money. Hanson hurriedly announced that Ettridge did not mean what he said and that he would have no public role in the forthcoming federal election campaign.

Oldfield's ambitions left a more permanent legacy. Following the Queensland success he increasingly adopted a public role. Late in June he appeared alongside Hanson in a televised 'Meet the Press' program and dominated the discussion. Subsequently he made solo appearances on Nine's 'Sunday' and on the ABC's 'Lateline'. Michelle Grattan observed in June 1998 that Oldfield 'now pops up as One Nation's talking head more often than Hanson herself'. In the Canberra press corps he was referred to as 'the proxy for Oxley'. The situation was mocked by Labor leader Kim Beazley, who described One Nation as 'not so much a party but a franchise, with a puppet [Hanson] . . . the puppeteer being David Oldfield'.

It seemed as if Oldfield had convinced himself that he could better serve the interests of the party by increasingly taking a public role. On one occasion previous to the Queensland election TV cameras had filmed him sitting at the feet of Pauline Hanson during radio talk-back shows, handing her hastily-written slips of paper. Kingston reports that by the time of the federal election Oldfield 'was overtly contemptuous of his leader to journalists', describing her as 'the product'.

Oldfield created enemies within One Nation, leading to rejection of his advice on several occasions. In July 1998 he revealed that his views on the allocation of preferences had not been followed in the Queensland election. Wishing to retain a semblance of neutrality, One Nation did not accept his recommendation that preferences be directed against the Labor Party in all marginal seats and issued split 'how to vote' cards in all but fifteen seats, leaving it to electors to decide their preference allocation. Oldfield believed that had his advice been followed One Nation would have won the balance of power in the Queensland parliament. As it was, One Nation preferences elected Labor candidates in a number of seats, giving Labor a slender working majority with the support of an independent. Another major decision in the early stages of the federal election campaign, to embrace a radical taxation policy, was again taken against the advice of Oldfield. He, unlike others around Hanson, understood that there was no need to provide the media with ammunition, that the party's electoral appeal was dependent not on policy detail but on rhetoric and the leader's mass following.

Whatever the precise reason, after July 1998 Oldfield appeared less prominently in the media. Then in late August, in pursuit of his own political ambitions, he gained selection as One Nation's lead Senate candidate in New South Wales and decided that he would stand down from his role as Hanson's political adviser.

For the first time Hanson was left without streetwise political guidance. In Oldfield's absence One Nation's campaign became a shambles. In the view of Kingston, who daily accompanied Hanson in this period, the party 'never knew what it was doing . . . Hansonites were a bunch of hare-brained amateurs without cash, talent or experience'. Hanson's handling of the media was grossly mismanaged; schedules were not followed and friction between Hanson and journalists steadily escalated.

NATIONAL POLICIES

More serious than the handling of the media was the decision to announce a series of detailed policies, mirroring the major parties and contrary to the successful Queensland election strategy which was to keep policies largely at the level of principle and talk loudly of conspiracies and of the betrayal by politicians. One Nation lacked the capacity to develop detailed policies of its own so in key areas it accepted policies offered by special interest groups, such as the anti-immigration and divorced men's lobbies.

There was much evidence of infiltration from the far right. Thus in December 1996 sacked Hanson staffer Jeff Babb commented that Hanson's close supporters 'have let in extreme LaRouchite and League of Rights-style conspiracy theorists, who have established footholds in her support organisation'. In January 1998 it was reported that the Mackay branch of One Nation was disbanded following the joining of a number of AUSI Freedom Scout members. Rod Owen of *Lock, Stock and Barrel* fame observed in August 1997 that 'near enough every one of our members' had joined One Nation. In August 1998 Ted Briggs, One Nation's Queensland treasurer, resigned after discovering that fellow state executive members had been leaders of the Confederate Action Party. Brendan Bogle, president of the Petrie branch, made a similar charge of infiltration. Several endorsed One Nation candidates were forced to resign following the revelation of extremist links.

Those familiar with fringe politics immediately recognised the origin of One Nation's policies. Extremists in Queensland had long advocated taxation reform along the lines of the policy adopted. Elements of the financial policies were similar to those of the League of Rights and Eric Butler conceded that 'they have borrowed . . . on our ideas'. The totality of policies differed little from the Confederate Action Party platform, itself influenced by a range of Queensland fringe groups (see Appendix 2). Once such policies were released and subject to scrutiny doubt over the party's competency and the extent of extremist influence heightened.

This, however, was only the beginning of the party's problems. Hanson's own inadequacies were highlighted when she attempted to explain policies. She proved herself unable to deal with detail and could not overcome a basic ignorance of the political system, nor could she deflect questioning and send the media on their way with pleasantries in the style of Joh Bjelke-Petersen. The release of policy was disastrous for another reason. Vagueness and strong rhetoric enabled the party to maximise its appeal; specific policies, whatever their content, alienated some section of the support base—for example, taxation policy imperilled the support of retirees, hard-headed farmers and the small business community.

On 1 July One Nation released an immigration policy similar to the policies of Australians Against Further Immigration (AAFI). Indeed, One Nation absorbed AAFI and appointed AAFI's Robyn Spencer as its immigration spokesperson. Under the policy, explained to a hostile media conference by Spencer, the party would aim for population stability through zero net immigration, refugees would only gain temporary entry and be expected to return to their country of citizenship as soon as circumstances allowed, and the family reunion program would be restricted and only available to those with basic English competency (with the exception of 'young children').

In a classic contradictory statement, it was proposed that the immigration intake would be non-discriminatory, but only to the extent that 'the numbers do not significantly alter the ethnic and cultural make up of the country', on the pattern of racially discriminatory American immigration quotas enacted in the early 1920s. A One Nation government would abolish multiculturalism and encourage 'widespread use of English within all communities and institutions of the land'. Granting of citizenship would be dependent on ability to 'pass a spoken and written English test' and 'basic understanding of Australian institutions, history and environment'. While campaigning against limitation of freedom of speech which had supposedly characterised the era of 'political correctness', One Nation undertook that 'organisations or individuals who deflect loyalty from Australia should be sidelined in debates on national issues'. Further, all citizens would be 'expected to have an overriding commitment to Australia and to accept the basic structures and principles of Australia'. It was not explained how these forms of thought control imposed by the champions of freedom of speech would be implemented.

The immigration policy was consistent with the pronouncements which had been crucial in establishing Hanson's public identity. Not content, however, to campaign on the basis of past statements and this elaboration, policies were released in the areas of small business, taxation, primary industry, family law and child support, health, veterans' affairs, industrial relations, aged care and disability, manufacturing and rural and regional employment.

Largely, it seems, on the decision of Hanson herself, One Nation adopted Easytax, a radical taxation policy developed by two Queenslanders. Under this policy, existing means of raising revenue—personal income tax, company tax, withholding tax, superannuation tax, fringe benefits tax, payroll tax and sales tax—were to be abolished and replaced by a 2 per cent tax on the sale price at each change of ownership of property, goods and services. To the embarrassment of the party, the policy was soon shown to favour large 'vertically-integrated' companies with control over all stages of production at the expense of small producers.

Other policies included the reintroduction of protective tariffs to favour primary producers and manufacturers; the abolition of the existing family law system and the setting up of people's tribunals to adjudicate matrimonial disputes; limitation of the right to sole supporting parent's benefits; abolition of the universal health care system through exemption from the Medicare levy of taxpayers with private health cover; and the establishment of rural health departments of existing medical and health schools in regional universities.

Three weeks from the date of the election Hanson's campaign was in tatters. Detailed policies drew critical media scrutiny and probing questions with which Hanson could not cope. Small numbers attended meetings and Hanson's attempts to meet electors face-to-face produced embarrassment before the cameras of the national press.

In an attempt to turn the party's fortunes it was decided to recall Oldfield and play the 'race card'. The media was informed that the party's controversial Aboriginal policy would be announced in the town of Longreach on 11 September, 1170 kilometres by road northwest of Brisbane. This was the location of Prime Minister Howard's 1997 meeting at which he had promised a hostile gathering of pastoralists that he would not compromise on legislation limiting Aboriginal native title rights. Oldfield told Margo Kingston that 'you've got something to look forward to . . . You're going to stand on your head and spew green vomit when you hear her speech on Friday'.

Karl Marx, in one of his more famous aphorisms, stated that when history repeats itself it is as farce the second time around. Where Howard had spoken to an audience of 2000 Hanson spoke to 30. Where earlier in her career Hanson had spoken to 'her people', observed by television cameras, now she addressed television cameras and turned her back on the small number who came to listen. Where before she had shocked by her pronouncements on Aboriginal issues now she had nothing new to say, merely rehearsing lines spoken many times before.

The text, drafted by Hanson herself and given final shape by Oldfield two nights before it was delivered, included the now familiar demands for abolition of ATSIC, repeal of the *Native Title Act*, and the ending of special benefits issued on the basis of Aboriginality, with specific reference to the Indigenous Land Corporation, housing loans and access to educational allowances including ABSTUDY. Howard was accused of selling out 'Pastoralists, Miners and non-Aboriginal Australians' through his 'weak 10 Point Plan'. The 'shameless grab for land' was 'not about reconciliation, but . . . an exercise in remuneration'.

Although the speech itself was mild by Hanson's standards it failed to send the media scurrying to their mobile phones. Failing to get the desired reaction Hanson attacked journalists. One asked if the speech was an excuse to kick Aborigines in order to revive her campaign; others asked her to respond to the charge that 'your message is actually racist'. Hanson at first ignored the questions, then screamed at journalists that the *Native Title Act* was a deception and they should do their duty and inform the Australian public forthwith:

> the people have been deceived over it ... go and tell the people of Australia the truth ... Howard ... lied to the Australian people. Go and print the facts and go and tell the Australian people the truth, and let them make up their minds ... Get this clear—we are Australians, and it makes no difference whether you are from Aboriginality, or whether you were born here or whether you were a migrant. We are all Australians together. And don't try and divide this nation.

The last period of campaigning, involving visits by Hanson to Western Australia, Tasmania, Victoria, South Australia, and New South Wales, then return to Queensland, failed to produce a significant improvement in Hanson's performance and tensions between Hanson and Oldfield were readily evident. At a meeting in Perth Oldfield referred to his leader as 'just a little redhead from Ipswich'. Afterwards Hanson drove off with her police escort without waiting for her adviser. At another Western Australian meeting when Hanson started to discuss Easytax Oldfield, sitting beside journalists, 'groaned audibly, put his head in his hands and said loudly, "Oh God, I've got to go home"'. In Tasmania during a press conference he publicly humiliated his leader by standing in front of her to prevent completion of an answer.

In the last days of the campaign Oldfield adopted the tactic of trying to create sympathy by blaming Hanson's difficulties on the media. At meetings, before carefully selected audiences comprising One Nation supporters, he tried to limit which journalists could ask questions and when he did not get his way incited the audience against the 'Sydney' and 'Canberra' media, placing journalists in fear of physical violence. While publicly announcing that because of its distorted coverage the media would no longer be invited to all functions, behind the scenes he maintained contact with journalists and made sure they were fully informed of Hanson's itinerary. Kingston commented:

> It seemed clear to me that Oldfield, having nothing else left in his armoury, was now intent on playing the anti-media card. How else could one explain him inviting the media to a press conference then goading his supporters into howling us down?

Hanson, on the other hand, took the matter further, deciding to have nothing more to do with journalists in the last week of the campaign. One Nation had sought to use the media as the main publicity arm of the party. It was expected that journalists would write what the party wanted, which in the leadership's eyes amounted to 'the truth'. There was a refusal to accept the right of journalists to scrutinise the party's policies. Hanson had a long and successful record of boycotting sections of the media and specific journalists. Under Pasquarelli the ABC was excluded; following the Queensland election Hanson's armed Australian Protective Service guard obeyed an order to escort a *Queensland Times* journalist from a press conference while other journalists sat quietly and did nothing. Others to be banned included one of the country's most respected media commentators, Laurie Oakes, and the *Toowoomba Chronicle*.

The last major controversy of One Nation's campaign arose over policy costing. There had been an undertaking to provide the costing at Hanson's campaign launch, held only one week before the election. On the appointed day, however, the document was not produced at the expected time. In response to media questioning Oldfield ordered journalists to leave, only to be met with resistance from a minority who demanded that he live up to his undertaking. His response to the party faithful was recorded:

You can see quite clearly the way the media treats the people of Australia. You can see that they have absolutely no truth whatsoever. The media are basically anarchists . . . looking for problems . . . This is another example of the Sydney media leading an assault on democracy.

Late in the day a document was released, revealing the total inability of the party's leadership to live up to the levels of accountability reasonably expected. The costing for the full range of policies was provided on one page (see Table 6.4). It was as if, at the last moment, some low-ranking official, without capacity to understand budget requirements, was given the task of compiling a list, any list, which would enable the pretence to be maintained that costings had been provided and which would appeal to the party's core constituency. There was no reference to the impact of the 2 per cent Easytax or the cost of the people's bank which would provide low interest loans to farmers. Figures were seemingly plucked from the air and placed in random order. Expenditure items of '1 million (approx)' and '$ unknown' were placed beside round figures of the magnitude of $1.5 billion. Savings of $5.549 billion dollars were to be made, paving the way for $5.117 billion to be spent on new initiatives. Cost cutting measures included reduction in politicians' superannuation ('unknown'), slashing foreign economic aid ($1.8 billion), abolishing multicultural funding ($1.5 billion), International Monetary Fund ($630 million), Aboriginal and Torres Strait Islander programs ($180 million, 'approx.') and ex-prime ministers' allowances ($1 million, 'approx.'). There was no substantiation offered for these figures. New expenditure items included $1.5 billion for aged care, $855 million for veterans' affairs, $500 million for a national development trust, $160 million for apprenticeships, $42.5 million for rural and regional initiatives and $20 million for rural and regional tourism.

Table 6.4   One Nation budget statement

Savings through existing budget reallocations (funding to be at last year's figures)

Foreign Economic aid	$1.8 billion
Parliament	$6 million
Communications and the Arts	$36 million
Prime Minister and Cabinet	$168 million
Immigration and Multicultural Affairs	$31 million
Cut off ex prime ministers' allowances	$1 million (approx)
Abolish multicultural funding	$1.5 billion
Reducing identifiable commonwealth expenditure on ATSI affairs across all portfolios with regard to related costs of dual administration	$180 million (approx)
Abolition of national competition policy	$217 million
Reallocate unused portion of Federation Fund	$355 million
Money saved by reducing politicians' super to a level equivalent to public service	$ unknown
Retain costs related to the sale of Telstra	$265 million (approx)
IMF contributions/aid	$630 million
Portion of government surplus	$360 million
TOTAL	**$5.549 billion**

Cost of One Nation's policy initiatives

National Development Trust	$500 million
Apprenticeships	$160 million
Rural and regional tourism promotion	$20 million
Veterans' Affairs	$855 million
Health	$1.8 billion
Commonwealth dental	$100 million
Aged care	$1.5 billion
Family services	$200 million
Rural and regional initiatives	$42.5 million
TOTAL	**$5.177 billion**

Source: One Nation policy release, 29 September 1998

The election result was to prove a great disappointment. Her prognosis having been proved correct prior to the Queensland poll, Hanson predicted on the federal polling day that One Nation would win twelve to fifteen seats in the lower house and six in the Senate. The result was just one Senate seat. Both Hanson and Oldfield were defeated. In the Queensland parliament, as a result of resignations from the party, within six months of the June 1998 state election its representation was cut from eleven to ten, then to five in February 1999 and nil in December.

One Nation's declining electoral appeal in the period June 1998–March 1999 is presented in Table 6.5. In February 2000 the party did not field candidates in the by-elections for two Queensland state seats in which it had polled strongly a little more than eighteen months earlier. The breakaway City–Country

Table 6.5 One Nation vote, June 1998–March 1999

Queensland election (June 1998) (one house parliament)	Queensland federal vote (October 1998)	Queensland federal vote (October 1998)
	House of Representatives	Senate
22.7%	14.35%	14.83 %
Queensland state seat of Mulgrave: state election, June 1998	Queensland state seat of Mulgrave: by-election, December 1998	
31%	15.5%	
New South Wales federal vote October 1998 House of Representatives	New South Wales state vote: March 1999 Legislative Assembly	
8.96%	7.35%	
New South Wales federal vote October 1998 Senate	New South Wales state vote March 1999 Legislative Council	
9.61%	6.34%	

Source: Australian Electoral Commission; Electoral Commission of Queensland; New South Wales State Electoral Office

Alliance, formed by the last five One Nation parliamentarians, scored 13.8 per cent of the vote in Bundamba and 1.9 per cent in Woodridge. One Nation had polled 34.3 per cent and 28.4 per cent respectively in these seats at the state election.

'DEMOCRACY REALLY MEANS MOB RULE'

A fundamental contradiction lay at the heart of Pauline Hanson's One Nation. This was a party that trumpeted its democracy, that promised to return power to the people. Like the League of Rights and the Citizens Electoral Councils, its policies were grounded on the promised involvement of 'the people' in the political process. As part of its policy for the Queensland election One Nation promised the introduction of the citizen initiated referendum; its law and order policy provided for 'community based policing initiatives', a referendum on capital punishment, and the election of twelve 'Ordinary Citizens' to oversee the performance of the judiciary and recommend removal of judges not performing their duties; the family law policy announced for the federal election provided for the abolition of the Family Law Court and its replacement with a family tribunal, comprising 'respected members from the local community'.

Yet, in line with the tradition of fascism, One Nation was based on the 'fuehrer' principle, on the role of the leader with capacity to divine 'the people's' will. Like other leaders who have seen themselves as the embodiment of the national will the 'mother of the nation' could see no difference between her own views and those of her 'children'. In this mode of politics rule by the people equates with rule by the leader. She was 'The Truth'.

Any doubt as to the nature of the party was dispelled by its name, the first political party of significance in Australian history bearing the name of an individual: this was not the party of 'One Nation' but 'Pauline Hanson's One Nation'. Despite its claim to be the voice of the Australian people, the leadership of One Nation put no trust in its members, refusing them a meaningful say in internal governance and policy development.

Hanson was strong minded and incapable of tolerating opposition. By temperament she was an autocrat: she was the one who would make decisions, who would arbitrate people's lives. She could state, for example, in the euphoria of the Queensland victory that 'I'm going to really come down on single women out there who are continually having child after child, sometimes with different fathers, at the taxpayers' expense. I will [only] support and look after the first child'. In a revealing comment, she responded to demands for democratic reform after the party's failure in the federal election with the retort that democracy was no more than mob rule:

> People come up to me all the time and say 'we want democracy'. Democracy really means mob rule. People don't like it at times, and neither do I, but I have to make the final decision . . . There are too many people out there who think they can make the decision, but I tell you they can't.

Her co-directors Oldfield and Ettridge were no more democrats than Hanson. One Nation was organised as a company, One Nation Limited, and a political party, Pauline Hanson's One Nation, with only three members. This ruling body was separated from a third entity, Pauline Hanson's One Nation Members, which included the branches and the rank and file. This structure, designed to keep full control in the hands of the triumvirate (or perhaps, more accurately, two members of the triumvirate) was revealed in all its complexity in 1999 proceedings in the Queensland Supreme Court which determined that One Nation had been fraudulently registered in the state.

The company–party structure bears the stamp of David Ettridge, businessman and professional fundraiser. Its authoritarianism reflected the Marxist–Leninist principles of democratic centralism, increasingly to be found in the corporate world, which had been developed to ensure that party (or company) workers uncritically obeyed instructions from the central governing body and remained isolated from each other. Ettridge explained:

> We don't want branches getting into the data base because it is not important for them to have it. It is quite important that they shouldn't have it. Companies in Australia are full of people at different levels of the organisation who don't understand what goes on in the board room ... It is constructed in this manner to provide protection for the political party and make each module a self-contained entity, which, if attacked by unfriendlies, will not contaminate the other modules ... Every successful business and army has control exercised from the top. Not from the ranks.

These sentiments were endorsed by Hanson, who explained that 'One Nation has been set up to protect it being attacked and broken down. It is a structure that is absolutely bullet-proof and is structured that way to protect all of us'. In such an environment there was minimal input of ideas from the membership and little scope to nurture talent. Not surprisingly, the party had difficulty attracting parliamentary candidates of quality and credibility.

Branch office holders were required to sign a 'pledge of loyalty' and an undated letter of resignation, which was held at the Manly headquarters. Those daring to criticise the leadership or regarded unfavourably for other reasons were expelled and subsequently denounced as traitors. A number in official positions were sacked, many others quit in disgust. The long list includes eleven One Nation members of parliament, Hanson's most trusted Queensland lieutenant (Heather Hill), the foundation vice-president (Paul Trewartha), Hanson's first, second and third political advisers (John Pasquarelli, David Thomas and David Oldfield), Hanson's private secretary (Barbara Hazelton), Hanson's most devoted Ipswich adviser (Peter James), Hanson's official biographer (Helen

Dodd), the founder of the Pauline Hanson Support Group (Bruce Whiteside) and senior state officials and ordinary members.

In its brief history One Nation has established a record which may never be equalled on the score of internal fractiousness and dissent. In part this reflected the nature of the personalities attracted to the party and conflict occasioned by the attempts of organised groups to use One Nation as a vehicle for furthering their own ends. While such individuals would have been a problem for any political party attempting to attract mass following, the fundamental cause of divisiveness was the refusal to allow rank and file membership a say in internal governance and determination of policy.

One of the main crimes for which individuals were excommunicated was the attempt to democratise. One of the early victims was Helen Dodd, Hanson's official biographer. On a tour of the country to promote her book she became the focus for grievances against Ettridge and Oldfield. Having collected a dossier of complaints she met with Hanson, urging the need for One Nation to become a genuine mass party, with some internal democracy. The result was her public expulsion from the Ipswich office.

In the aftermath of the federal election debacle it was reported that reformers were holding meetings nationwide, mostly in regional Queensland and New South Wales. A number of draft constitutions were circulating amongst the membership, all proposing an elected council to run the organisation and removal of the power of summary expulsion of party members. At the November 1998 Queensland conference Hanson's retort was that she would not allow the party to be wrecked by democracy.

In February 1999, prior to the first federal conference, the ten remaining Queensland One Nation members of parliament put themselves at the forefront of the demand for reform. The draft constitution, to be voted on at the conference, entrenched the positions of Hanson as president for four years, Oldfield as national adviser for three and Ettridge as national director for two;

at the expiration of these terms the national director and national adviser were not to be elected but were to be appointed by the national executive; thus reappointment of Ettridge after two years was to be decided by Hanson and Oldfield. There were to be no elected members of the Executive until 2001 and in that year only one was to be elected. A national conference was to be held 'at least every three years'. Such was the depth of opposition that the triumvirate deferred vote on the constitution and provided for the immediate election of two members of the executive, but these concessions were insufficient for five of the Queensland parliamentarians, Shaun Nelson, Dorothy Pratt, Jeff Turner, Jeff Knuth and Dr John Kingston, who resigned from the party to sit as independents. At the annual meeting one delegate, Mr Bevan Collingwood, who stated that he represented the Maryborough (Queensland) branch, told the press that he had recently received a letter suspending his membership because he had distributed a constitution opposing the party's official version.

In December 1999 the remaining five Queensland members of parliament, Bill Feldman, Jack Paff, Peter Prenzler, Harry Black and David Dalgleish, quit, citing problems with the party's Queensland registration and alluding also to problems with internal governance. As part of the same move, Heather Hill, at one time Hanson's closest political confidant, Queensland party leader and one time Senator-elect from Queensland, resigned from the party's executive and was subsequently sacked from her party position. She gave as her grounds for resignation the failure to account for the party funds by the Manly central office, stating that 'nearly $5 million has gone through head office and I don't have the foggiest where it has gone'.

When the first Queensland One Nation members of parliament quit Hanson dismissed them as traitors and 'hangers-on not really there for the right reasons'; the resignations were 'a road bump' in the party's history. When the last five left Ettridge commented that they were 'a lot of very ordinary people we didn't know about and bunged . . . into parliament'. Oldfield denied that the move would damage the party: 'It is a speed bump. A lot of their activities have been more embarrassing than helpful anyway. None of them ever really understood anything about politics'.

In January 2000 Ettridge resigned. Nine months later Oldfield was sacked from the party after publicly feuding with his leader. Hanson explained that 'David Oldfield believes he wishes to run this party. Well I've got news for David Oldfield—he doesn't'. Ettridge commented that Hanson 'has become an absolute dictator', Oldfield that her behaviour was 'silly, emotional, completely irrational'. A journalist observed that there was now 'one left standing for One Nation'.

RACIST?

There was much public discussion over the claim that the Hanson agenda was racist, a charge which she and her official circle vehemently rejected. Those who might be regarded as expert in the detection of racism, members of racist organisations, certainly recognised Hanson as a compatriot. Hanson's advent and triumphs were greeted with accolades in Australia and abroad: from the League of Rights and American and British neo-Nazi groups. Still, such identification by the extreme right is not in itself conclusive.

On one interpretation Hanson's rhetoric provides evidence for the view that her primary concern was to deny cultural autonomy and recognition of pluralism; that hers was a policy of assimilation, not exclusion. It involved the imposition of the will of one people on another, the demand for the return to the certainties of a bipolar value system, the rejection of a society structured along complex lines of difference. In the view of many such a stance is the equivalent of racism, but it is different from calls for segregation and exclusion. In comparison with other organisations of the far right in the western world, Hanson's policy towards immigrants was moderate. She did not call unambiguously for an end to migration from Asia. Further, she did not broach the issue of repatriation of immigrants on racial grounds, a policy advocated by some European organisations, notably the French National Front.

One aspect of the rhetoric of One Nation was not overtly racial. Hanson did, at times, seem to be affirming the principle of racial equality, consistently calling for all Australians to be treated equally, for government assistance to be provided on the basis of need, not of race. 'One Nation' was to be achieved not by purging the Australian population of racially unacceptable elements, although in future the immigration policy called for restriction of entry on the basis of race. John Pasquarelli has related an incident in November 1996 when Hanson amended the draft of a speech to read: 'I wouldn't mind if there were more Asians in Australia than Anglo-European Australians as long as they spoke English'. When in panic he sought to explain the folly of such a statement she could not see the problem with what she had written, 'she didn't seem to comprehend how, in one short sentence, she would have surely destroyed the major thrust of her maiden speech'.

Hanson's inconsistency was in part a reflection of her own confusion and inability to think through the logic of her position, but it was also the deliberate product of speechwriters. Australian commentators, impressed by her statements on racial equality, often failed to note the inconsistencies which allowed her to talk to one constituency while providing the means of defence against charges from others.

There is a record of overtly racist statements, even without reference to works such as Hanson's *The Truth*. On one occasion shortly after her election, freed from her minder, she stated unambiguously that Asian immigration should be stopped and on another spoke of the danger that 'the yellow race will rule the world'. Of greater significance, however, than individual statements are her underlying values and orientation to racial issues. As has been noted, a key element of her maiden speech was the idea that there was some law of human nature that precluded the intermixture of peoples, an idea at the heart of racial thought. Further, it seemed that for Hanson Asian people could almost never appear in a positive light. Thus, for example, when in 1998 a 20-year old of Asian background was made Young Australian of the Year for her work with immigrants and refugees, Hanson responded: 'I think appointing the young Asian lady, the government's been pushing us to become Asianised and I'm totally against becoming Asianised . . . I think it's all very political. I'm not very impressed by it whatsoever. I think the majority of Australians will know what I'm talking about'. Senator Ron Boswell commented in June 1998: 'Ms Hanson has referred to Asians in the context of drug pushers, disease carriers, ghetto formers and job stealers. The remarks about the dangers of being swamped by Asian countries conjures up the old frightening image of the yellow peril'.

Evaluation of the party should not, however, rest exclusively on public statements. Full consideration requires attention not only to what was said, but also the context in which statements were made and the political purpose of statements, in part indicated by their timing.

An essential part of the context of Hanson's idealisation of Australian history is denial of the existence and hence structural impact of racism. Refusal to accept the reality of the historical record led Hanson to present a mythical picture of a past before the advocacy of Aboriginal rights and multiculturalism when Aboriginal people and pastoralists amicably co-existed:

> years gone by when the Aboriginals could and did roam on the lands, and they were pastoralists' lands by all means. And usually they worked in very well with the owner of the lands and they camped on the lands and they went about their own traditional ways and culture and they were very happy together with the pastoralists on the lands, and there wasn't these problems that are here today . . . It was a lot happier time for the Aboriginals and the pastoralists.

In keeping with this view of the past, Hanson maintained that 'there is no racism in Australia' and there were no racists in her party; 'if there was anyone who was racist in One Nation, I'd tell them where to go and I'd get them out, because that's not what I stand for'. Thus, to take some examples, if this line of reasoning is accepted those who worked on the compilation of Pauline Hanson's *The Truth* were not racist, nor were some of the gun lobbyists who infiltrated One Nation, nor was Tony Pitt of *Fight* and Confederate Action Party fame who emerged to head a One Nation branch. This denial of racism serves to legitimate the view that Aboriginal people have no grounds to seek recompense on the basis of past and present wrongs.

Attention to context and purpose also reveals that behind the façade of statements of racial equality and inclusiveness One Nation's policies rest on the age old tactic of scapegoating minorities defined in racial terms. In keeping with the definition of racial politics discussed in this book's Introduction, fundamental problems facing Australian society at a time of major change are explained by reference to the cost of special assistance provided to racial minorities. In the Queensland election campaign, ten of 27 areas targeted for cuts involved programs for Aboriginal and Torres Strait Islanders, multiculturalism and anti-discrimination initiatives:

- Abolish the Office of Indigenous Affairs.
- Abolish the Aboriginal and Torres Strait Islander Affairs and Indigenous Advisory Council.
- Reduce the funding for indigenous youth suicide program.
- Remove the Aboriginal and Torres Strait Islander portion from the Transport Infrastructure Development Scheme.
- Remove funding for the Aboriginal and Torres Strait Islander Infrastructure Program.
- Abolish the Aboriginal and Torres Strait Islander Education sub-program.
- Abolish the Aboriginal and Torres Strait Islander Housing Program.

- Defer the formation of the Native Title Tribunal.
- Abolish the Office of Multicultural and Ethnic Affairs.
- Abolish the Anti-Discrimination Commission.

Scrutiny of the Hanson agenda points to the double standards which underlie its policies. One of the hallmarks of the racial value system is the idea that what is applicable to one group is not applicable to another. Hanson's argument from her first entry into politics was that Aboriginal people should be treated on exactly the same basis as other members of the Australian community. But she also argued that Aboriginal people should not have equal access to the Australian legal system. The High Court had ruled, after the most careful scrutiny, that Aboriginal people had rights to land surviving the assumption of British sovereignty, but for Hanson this was not acceptable. At the first opportunity, she argued, parliament should abolish native title. So the principle of equal rights before the law was to be applied on a discriminatory basis, only when she decided that the outcome was acceptable.

As a group Aboriginal people would be stripped of special assistance, but under One Nation policies special assistance would be provided to other sections of the community. Repeatedly she explained that special assistance was not only unjustified, it was a total waste of money as it served only to create dependency. People needed to take responsibility for their own actions, not to look at the state to help them out of difficulties. She asserted in her maiden speech that 'Aboriginals do not want handouts because they realise that welfare is killing them'. Further, her policy was against discrimination for or against minorities, she was in favour of equal treatment for all Australians'.

And yet special assistance would be provided to those One Nation identified as its core constituency: those in rural areas, the elderly, employees in the manufacturing industry. If one section of the community was to receive 2 per cent bank loans those not receiving this benefit would pay by higher bank charges and government taxes.

Similarly if certain primary producers and manufacturers were to receive the benefit of protective tariffs consumers would incur higher prices for their purchases. The dilemma of double standards was clearly captured in an exchange between a journalist and One Nation's health spokesperson:

> Journalist: 'Is this health policy skewed towards providing greater care for aged people and people in rural areas?'
> One Nation: 'The aged people are suffering and obviously rural people are suffering too.'
> Journalist: 'What about Aborigines—aren't they suffering?'
> One Nation: 'Aborigines are going to be treated on the basis of need.'
> Journalist: 'So they'll be treated equally, but rural people and older people will get treated in a special manner?'
> One Nation: 'Not in a special manner, in a manner that they should be treated and haven't been treated in the past. They have been discriminated against.'

Perhaps the ultimate test of racial politics is the way in which issues are exploited for political purposes. When Hanson's federal election campaign was floundering the calculated decision was taken to revive the party's fortunes by playing the 'race card'. The media event at Longreach was organised. Hanson was so concerned that she would not get enough news coverage, as the date chosen clashed with the opening of the Commonwealth Games, that she considered postponing the event, only to be told that preparations were too far advanced to allow postponement. David Oldfield dreamed that Hanson would be so provocative that journalists would spew green vomit. And One Nation would, it was planned, march on to the next electoral triumph.

PART 3

MEANING

7

Interpretations

As this book has shown, the issue of race assumed a central position in the Australian political agenda in 1996. The coalition victory in March 1996 marked a major turning point, with Prime Minister Howard determined to change key policies of the previous Labor administration. Further, the election saw the victory of two independents—Pauline Hanson and Graeme Campbell—who had campaigned largely on racial issues. Such was the magnitude of change over the following months that statements on race which raised a storm of controversy in January 1996 passed almost without notice two years later. Robert Manne has written that by 1998 the conflict of ideas was at its sharpest since the early Cold War years. Australia had become 'deeply divided, not so much by social class or even between city and bush, as into two nations inhabiting separate moral universes'.

There have been a number of attempts to explain the shift in the political environment, most focusing on Hansonism, some showing awareness that any explanation required consideration of the similarities in the experience of Australia and a number of European countries, including the United Kingdom, France, Austria and Germany.

ACCOUNTING FOR THE POLITICS OF RACE

It is possible to isolate four factors which, individually or in various combinations, have been used to explain the rise of exclusive or chauvinistic forms of nationalism and the politics of race. These concern the failures of the political system, the impact of social and economic change, the ending of the Cold War, and supposed innate human prejudices.

One form of explanation for the emergence of chauvinistic nationalism and racial politics focuses on the workings of the political system: on the roles of political leaders and failure to represent views widely held in the community. It is argued that if political leadership had been more capable the emergence of anti-democratic forces would have been avoided. Conservative critics focus on the failure of Labor leadership; to illustrate one position, the blame rests with Prime Minister Keating's aloofness and arrogance, his failure to ensure that policies were adequately explained and supported, his supposed stifling of contrary viewpoints and unwillingness to allow parliamentary debate. Another variant of the political leadership explanation, presented in this book, focuses on the role of John Howard. It is argued that by positioning his party at the head of the campaign against 'political correctness' Howard did much to de-legitimise the Keating agenda and enable the Liberals to re-shape and capture the political middle ground. It was the re-shaped political landscape that provided scope for chauvinist forms of nationalism to assume a major political role.

Other explanations are concerned with the alienation produced by the apparent failure of the party system to represent the wishes of the electorate. This is a development which Judith Brett has described as 'feelings of abandonment and powerlessness' and Hugh Mackay as 'voters' anger, disenchantment and cynicism'. Mackay writes that:

> There's a widespread perception of prevarication, indecisiveness, secrecy, dishonesty (in everything from travel rorts to

policy intentions), aloofness from the concerns of ordinary people, and an inclination to resort to glossy rhetoric that fools no-one.

Polling points to what Michelle Grattan has described as 'the loosening of voters' identification with their old party loyalties'. A 1991 poll found that 62 per cent of respondents expressed little or no confidence in the political system; in 1998 66 per cent of those polled were dissatisfied.

But is disenchantment with politics an explanation or a symptom? Is the present generation of politicians so much worse than its predecessors? Other explanations point not to the political system but to the magnitude of problems which have made the political system less able to satisfy the electorate.

Perhaps the most frequently used explanation deals with the impact of economic change over the last two decades. The prime cause for what is seen as the politics of despair is the impact of economic change on people's lives, which leaves them searching for solutions in terms of the certainties of a past age when they were free of economic insecurities and felt in control of their lives. It is argued that without the consequences of economic change ideas now embraced would be dismissed without serious consideration.

Such explanations draw particular attention to the impact of structural change on the economy: the loss of jobs consequent on cuts in the public sector and the freer flow of capital, goods and labour; the competition which has been introduced into previously sheltered sections of the workforce; the insecurities of those in employment, particularly in threatened sectors of the economy; and the decline of services consequent on the pursuit of economic efficiencies. These changes have occurred in the midst of unprecedented prosperity enjoyed by those with skills and capital for whom new opportunities have opened.

It is argued that the demand for a return to the certainties of a past age, to an economy based on protected employment, to the intolerance of a narrow value system, is voiced most strongly, and/ or finds its most ready response, among the victims of change. Robert Manne, summarising overseas literature, writes that 'contemporary right-wing populism might be described ... as the mobilisation of those for whom the era of globalisation has offered, thus far, not prosperity or hope but the threat of meaninglessness and social fear'. In Australia's case, it is argued, the failures of economic reform 'imperilled the experiments in ethnic and cultural transformation that began in the 1970s'.

Using a broader explanatory framework without specific reference to class, Hugh Mackay writes of 'a widespread sense of insecurity', the outcome of rapid 'social, cultural, economic and technological' change. Australia is 'in the process of reinventing itself ... Everything from the redefinition of marriage to the problem of unemployment reminds us that most of the reference points we used to rely on for understanding the Australian way of life have been swept away'.

Paul Kelly argues that an 'age of uncertainty' has descended on Australia with the attempted jettisoning of the order established at the time of federation. This has involved the replacement of White Australia with multicultural Australia, subservient Aborigines with respected indigenous Australians with special rights, trade protection with trade liberalisation, traditional alliances with a new orientation to Asia and international organisations, the system of arbitration and conciliation with an emphasis on market driven wage bargaining, and reliance on government with emphasis on individual responsibility and private capital.

A third type of explanation is concerned with the ideological and geopolitical significance of the ending of the Cold War. The collapse of the Soviet Union, it is argued, undermined the authority of the left, signalled the triumph of the capitalist system as the only viable basis for economic and social organisation, and released age old rivalries and animosities within the former Soviet empire, resulting in the re-emergence of aggressive nationalist movements.

Optimistic value systems, such as socialism and liberalism, declined in influence, while conservatism in its various forms and economic liberalism, the values of the unfettered marketplace, gained in strength.

A variant of this perspective is the 'indispensable enemy' argument—that a people's sense of identity is formed and cohesiveness maintained by a sense of threat from a malevolent enemy. In the era of the Cold War, international communism served as the enemy; with the collapse of the USSR, however, the rationale which had served the west for some four decades lost its relevance. Racial concepts provided one basis for new understandings, serving to identify the enemy in the form of those whose interests were served by the breakdown of national boundaries. Through such means extremism made an inroad into the political mainstream.

Lastly, as a sign of despair at the reappearance of national, ethnic, even tribal animosities, some seek explanation in terms of primordialism, a theory that innate human characteristics are the ultimate determinants of behaviour. It is asserted that despite the most profound social transformations over the last 1000 years the main determinants of human character have remained constant. Thus life under a communist system inculcating the ideal of human brotherhood and the unity of the working class across boundaries of ethnicity and race proved powerless to eradicate ethnic antagonism and hatred, which resurfaced within a few years of the removal of authoritarian control, seemingly as strong as they had been at the beginning of the century.

EVALUATION

To identify and describe the features of racial politics is relatively simple, as is the recording and categorising of attitudes. The difficult task is to establish causation, to distinguish cause and effect. Given the complexity of the issues under consideration, it is unlikely that a monocausal or single factor explanation will be adequate. The first step towards explanation is to isolate the precise issue under consideration, to avoid the confusion of thought which results from the conflation of related but analytically distinct questions. The following discussion focuses on seven key questions, to some extent overlapping, which when worked through yield cumulative insights.

Is the development of racial politics cross-national or unique to Australia?

Clearly racial politics is not restricted to Australia but is a global development. Awareness of this cross-national pattern is important, lessening the overriding significance attached to Keating's 'thought police' and the 'enforcement' of 'political correctness', or Howard's positioning of the Liberal Party. Australia was unlikely to escape the impact of developments common to western culture, although the precise form and extent of that impact was to be shaped by circumstances specific to Australia.

Which sections of the population were most attracted to the politics of Hanson?

Hanson did not draw support evenly across the nation. Evidence on this point furnishes important insights into a number of the issues discussed here, not least in its bearing on the primordialist position. Were there a basic instinct propelling humanity towards the politics of exclusivity we would expect to find a more even— and larger degree—of support for One Nation across the regions of Australia and social groups. Yet analysis reveals that Hanson's appeal has been strongest in communities distinguished by a number of common characteristics: relatively small numbers with tertiary qualifications, low median family income, high number of children under the age of five, high unemployment, and residence beyond inner urban areas. A relatively high number of indigenous residents was an important distinguishing characteristic of strong One Nation support in some but not all regions, as was limited contact with immigrants from a non-English speaking background, especially from Asian countries. Hanson was most popular among those aged between 45 and 64 and among men. One Nation scored its lowest vote in the most affluent electorates. One Nation polled strongly in rural, hinterland and some outer urban locations, but not in the inner urban areas.

The difference between the demographics of Victoria (the state with the second lowest level of support) and Queensland is instructive. Queensland has a larger proportion of its population in rural areas and provincial cities, lower levels of educational attainment, higher proportion of its workforce in labouring and trade employment, fewer non-English speaking immigrants and larger numbers of Aboriginal people. In his description of One Nation's heartland Henry Reynolds has written of rural and provincial communities that are demographically little changed from the 1950s, have had little or no experience of European and Asian immigrants, and in which anti-immigrant feeling and hostility to Aboriginal people festers. In part because of its distinctive history, Queensland's political culture differs markedly from that of Victoria, a point further discussed below. Talk of conspiracies, of the malevolent forces of the One World government, or of Canberra and cosmopolitan elites, wins a better hearing in the north. It is worthy of note that Hanson was at the peak of her popularity when, with David Oldfield at her side, she talked in terms of populist simplicities than when attempting to develop detailed policies at the time of the federal election.

To what extent did Hanson create her constituency, to what extent did the formation of the constituency predate her entry into federal politics?

It was frequently claimed that Hanson was a creation of the media. Such statements have been made with little reflection or attempt at substantiation. What, for example, is the relevance of coverage in the broadsheet daily press and the Australian Broadcasting

Commission to One Nation's level of support? In all likelihood the answer is, very little, given the reading and viewing habits of those attracted to the party. Proponents of the media hypothesis should focus on the tabloid and regional press, talk-back radio, and far right publications such as *Wake Up, Australia* and *Strategy*. However, here it is argued that One Nation's influence is not to be explained in terms of short- and medium-term media coverage.

If we move beyond untested assumptions concerning the role of the media and examine polling data, the evidence indicates that the formation of a populist constituency concerned with issues of race and national identity predated Hanson's entry into politics. The constituency's existence was demonstrated at the time of the maiden speech, when voters were first asked if they would support a party led by Hanson (see Table 7.1). Hanson's popularity did not steadily rise from this point but fluctuated; the fluctuation was one of *loss of support and recovery*, not of growth beyond the level attained in September–October 1996.

In the attempt to determine when the constituency took form opinion polls and electoral data will be considered. While they

Table 7.1   Support for Hanson-led party/One Nation—Australia

	October 1996 (%)	April–June 1997 (%)	July–September 1997 (%)	January–March 1998 (%)	June 1998 (%)	3 October 1996 election result (%)
Support for Hanson-led party in the Senate	18				13.5	8.4
Support for One Nation		11	8	5		

Sources: Morgan poll, 23–24 October 1996, in *Bulletin*, 5 November 1996; Morgan poll, 17–18 June 1996, in *Bulletin*; Goot, 'Hanson's heartland'. It is estimated that telephone interviewing undervalues support for One Nation by 2 per cent.

do not provide definitive answers, opinion polls throw into question interpretations which focus on the significance of recent disenchantment with the political system and the impact of economic restructuring. The proviso needs to be made, however, that direct comparability over time is difficult as the questions asked and the context of polls is rarely constant, and major differences can result from minor changes in wording and context. The findings of polls need to be read carefully, for diametrically opposite interpretations can be made using the same data; to take one example, under the heading 'Mabo Fails to Find Favour', *Time Australia* published findings which showed that 45 per cent of respondents 'approved of the Mabo case decision', 38 per cent disapproved and 17 per cent 'cannot say'. The following discussion will be directed initially to two issues: attitudes to immigration policy and government assistance to Aboriginal people.

Immigration

The broad pattern of findings does not support the case for a recent shift in public opinion. Opposition to the total immigration intake has for most years since 1984 been in the range 60–70 per cent and was almost at the same level in April 1997 as it had been in June 1984. Katherine Betts, a long-term critic of Australian immigration policies, cites four 'comparable opinion polls' for 1988, 1990, 1991, 1996—in these years the numbers of the view that 'too many' immigrants were entering were 68 per cent, 65 per cent, 73 per cent and 65 per cent respectively. Other polls yield findings in the same range, as indicated by Table 7.2.

Attitudes to the number of Asian immigrants also seem to be relatively stable (see Table 7.3), with some indication of a lessening of numbers concerned with current levels. Of five polls in the period 1982–89, those expressing dissatisfaction were in the range 57–62 per cent, with one finding at a significantly higher level; this is in contrast with two poll findings of around 50 per cent in 1996.

Evidence of polling in a region of recent migrant settlement in

Table 7.2 Attitude to annual immigration intake

	1984 May–June (%) (1)	1988 August (%) (2)	1988 (%) (3)	1990 (%) (4)	1991 November (%) (5)	1992 May (%) (6)	1996 (%) (7)
Intake too high/favour fewer	54–64	46	57–77	65	73	71	62–71

Sources: (1) Goot, Betts; (2) Morgan; (3)–(5) Saulwick; (6) Morgan; (7) Goot, *Sydney Morning Herald*, 25 November 1996

the southeast of Melbourne also points to consistency of attitudes over time. Two identical surveys were conducted, five years apart. Amongst Australian-born respondents in 1993, 86 per cent agreed with the proposition that 'so long as a person is committed to Australia it does not matter what ethnic background they are from'; in 1998 87 per cent agreed. When asked about the contribution of Asian immigrants to the 'Australian way of life', 60 per cent in 1993 and 61 per cent in 1998 agreed that they had 'a great deal to offer'; a minority of about 20 per cent disagreed.

Aboriginal issues

On the second of the indicators employed, opinion on Aboriginal policies, it is more difficult to form a view of long-term trends as pollsters have not employed a consistent measure of attitudes; further, policies since 1980 have shifted more markedly than in the immigration area, compounding the problem of attempting to compare attitudes over time—the polls measure responses to significantly changed circumstances. Bearing in mind these qualifications, there is some indication of a shift over a 30-year period, *but not of marked change over the last decade.*

In response to the question 'how much are governments doing for Aborigines', a marked change was recorded: those responding 'about right' and 'not enough' declined from around 75 per cent

Table 7.3 Attitude to Asian immigration

	1982/83 (1) %	1984 (2) %	1988 (3) %	1998 (4) %	1989 (5) %	1990 (6) %	1992 (7) %	1996 (8) %	1996 (9) %
Disapprove/ slow/too many/reduce	57	62	57	(77)	58	55	68	(<50)	53

Sources: (1), (3), (5–7) Morgan; (2) (APOP); (4) Newspoll, *Australian*, 9 August 1988; (8) AGB-McNair; (9) Goot, *Sydney Morning Herald*, 25 November 1996

between 1976–82 to 60–65 per cent in the period December 1983–October 1984, with one poll considerably lower (44 per cent). In 1990 one poll recorded that 37 per cent answered 'about right' and 'not enough'. In 1996, in response to the question of approval or disapproval of the government's cut in funding of $400 million in Aboriginal affairs, 34 per cent disapproved and 8 per cent neither approved nor disapproved. Later in that year a similar finding was obtained in response to the proposition that 'Aborigines are being treated over generously by the federal government'. Early in 2000, on the direct instruction of the prime minister's department, in a survey undertaken for the Council for Aboriginal Reconciliation Newspoll included the question 'compared with other Australians, Aboriginal people get too much special assistance from the government': 31 per cent of respondents disagreed, indicating little shift in attitudes when allowance is made for the change in wording—from 'are being treated over generously' to 'get too much special assistance'. (see Table 7.4)

Polls show consistently strong support for the view that Aborigines should receive the same benefits available to all Australians. As has been noted, the strength of this 'same deal' thinking was early recognised by the mining industry, which in 1984 made the slogan 'land rights should be equal rights' the centrepiece of its campaign against proposed land rights legislation. On four occasions between 1979

Table 7.4 **'How much are federal and state governments doing for Aborigines?'**

	1976 (1)	1978 (2)	1981 (3)	1982 (4)	1983 Dec. (5)	1984 Sept. (6)	1984 Oct. (7)	1990 (8)	1996 (9)	1996 (10)	2000 (11)
'About right; 'not enough'	75	72	75	74	65	(44)	63	37	(34+)	(34+)	(31?)

Sources: (1)–(3), (5)–(7) APOP; (4)–(6) Morgan; (8) Cited Goot; (9) 'Aborigines being treated over generously by the Federal government'—'Disagree'; a further 8 per cent neither agree nor disagree'—AGB-McNair; (10) AGB-McNair; (11) Newspoll

and 1988, the question 'because of their special problems Aborigines should receive more social benefits that whites' elicited large majorities opposed to special benefits for Aborigines (from 66 per cent to 93 per cent). In 2000, in response to the Newspoll question 'Do you personally think that Aboriginal people should, or should not have special rights such as ... native title [and] special seats in Parliament', 58 per cent responded that they should not, 35 per cent that they should.

On the general principle of Aborigines being accorded special rights to land there was again a strong majority against special rights, although difference in the wording of questions might explain the shift between 1993 and 1994 (see Table 7.5).

In contrast with such findings, when respondents were asked a specific question concerning land rights significantly different responses were obtained, highlighting the contradictory nature of views held on some issues of public significance. Consistency on the grounds of 'same rights for all' would lead to the expectation of a clear majority opposing the High Court's Mabo decision, which was depicted in most public discussions as conferring special benefits on Aboriginal people, yet this was not the finding of all polls. Thus, for example, Morgan polls twelve months apart found that a majority of respondents approved (see Table 7.6).

Table 7.5 **'Should Aborigines have different land rights to other Australians?'**

	1983 (%) (1)	1984 (%) (2)	1993 (%) (3)	1994 (%) (4)
More	13	12	19	10
Same	78	72	70	80
Less	5	10	5	6

Source: (1)–(4) (Morgan). (1) and (2) worded 'Should Aborigines have more, the same, or less land rights than other Australians?'; (3) worded 'Should Aborigines have different land rights to other Australians?', responses as 'more rights', 'same rights', 'less rights'; (4) 'Should Aborigines have more, the same or fewer rights than other Australians making claims over the same land?', responses as 'more rights', 'the same rights', fewer rights'.

Given 'equal rights' attitudes and the vehement opposition in the media to the Mabo decision, the extent of support in these polls for the High Court's decision is surprising. Other polls, using differently worded questions and providing a different range of possible responses produced varying results, but the trend was in favour of Mabo: an AGB-McNair poll in October 1993 found 53 per cent in favour of the Mabo decision, 24 per cent against. While a Morgan poll in January 1994 found that a majority disapproved of the Native Title legislation (40 per cent to 32 per cent, with 28 per cent undecided), a Saulwick poll in September 1994 found that 50 per cent considered the legislation to be fair, 8 per cent thought that it did not go far enough, and 33 per cent that it went too far.

Polls on Aboriginal issues thus reveal a complex picture, with changes in wording and context of questions producing markedly different results. It is plausible to argue that there has been a shift in support for government measures since the 1970s, but the change occurred in the 1980s, not over the last ten years. There has been a consistently high level of support for 'equal rights', generally above 70 per cent, but a majority in a number of polls

Table 7.6 'Do you approve of the Mabo case decision?'

	January 1993 (%)	January 1994 (%)
Approve	38	45
Disapprove	32	38
Can't say	30	17

Source: Morgan (*Time Australia*, 14 February 1994)

also hold the apparently contradictory view that the High Court's Mabo decision and the federal government's land rights legislation were fair and reasonable.

Ranking of issues

One further measure of attitudes over time is available, on the important question of how electors rank the issues with which they are confronted. Has the ranking of issues changed over time, and what are the prospects that opposition of the order of 60 per cent to 80 per cent to specific government policies can be turned into votes at elections? For a number of years the *Australian*'s Newspoll has asked electors to rank fourteen issues in terms of significance. These polls indicate that issues relating to immigration and Aboriginal policy rank at the bottom or near the bottom of electors' concerns and that there has been little shift in the ranking over the years of the surveys, 1993–99: these two issues have ranked between eleven and fourteen (out of a possible fourteen), with the most common rank of thirteen and fourteen. The surveys also indicate that in the context of the politicisation of racial issues in 1996 and 1997 (particularly after Hanson's maiden speech in September 1996) the significance attached to immigration and Aboriginal issues rose, but the highest rank achieved was eleven for immigration in January 1997 (see Table 7.7 and Figure 7.1). Such evidence indicates that while polling of attitudes on immigration and Aboriginal issues produces some results strongly critical

Table 7.7 Ranking of issues—respondents indicating that the issue is 'very important'

Issue	November 1993	June 1994	January 1996	September 1996.	January 1997	September 1997	January 1998	September 1998	May 1999	September 1999	January 2000
Education	*	*	*	*	*	*	*	*	78	74	77
Unemployment	79	77	69	71	75	79	77	76	71	69	69
Health/Medicare	70	74	72	73	77	76	76	74	78	75	75
Taxation	58	57	53	58	64	67	63	71	70	63	68
Leadership	61	60	56	57	61	64	63	61	62	57	60
Family issues	*	*	58	61	64	64	62	60	64	62	61
Welfare and social	60	60	55	59	62	65	63	60	63	59	60
The environment	64	62	58	61	63	64	64	57	60	61	66
Interest rates	50	57	55	53	56	52	52	52	52	48	49
Inflation	54	56	50	51	53	45	49	49	46	40	44
Balance of payments	*	49	48	43	48	45	45	41	*	*	
Industrial relations	39	41	41	41	44	49	43	39	38	35	41
Women's issues	37	41	35	36	39	41	42	39	43	37	41
Aboriginal issues	33	27	20	27	33	36	37	31	30	28	30
Immigration	32	32	32	34	45	43	37	29	32	28	37

Source: Newspoll (Australian, 16 November 1993; 2–3 July 1994, 24 January 1997, 9 September 1998, 31 January 2000)

Figure 7.1 Ranking of issues

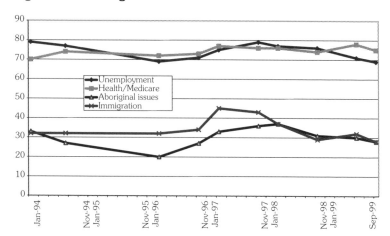

of government policy, in respondents' minds they are not issues of first rank importance. Such a finding is in keeping with the low vote obtained by single issue parties such as Australians Against Further Immigration in general elections.

Support for third party politics

The evidence considered above has shown little indication of a marked shift in attitudes in the 1990s. And yet arguments for a massive shift in voter opinion have been presented by a number of commentators. There is some quantitative data to support some of these viewpoints. Thus, for example, there is support for the view that over the last 20 years the number of swinging voters, those not tied to the one party, has grown substantially: from around 5 per cent to 30 per cent. Other data points to heightened disillusionment with the political system. Over 21 years from 1976 to 1997 a Morgan poll has rated fourteen occupations in terms of ethics and honesty. While attitudes to doctors, dentists, university lecturers and schoolteachers have remained unchanged or become more favourable, the rating of most of those in the financial and political fields declined sharply. Thus since 1976 bank managers have fallen from 66 per cent to 32 per cent, lawyers from 43 per cent to 29 per cent, and federal members of parliament from 19 per cent to 9 per cent, little above the respect accorded car salespersons.

It can be argued, however, that a widespread shift in attitudes to politicians and in levels of concern about the future are not necessary to explain the emergence of populist politics in which racial issues figure prominently—that support for this form of politics has existed over the last 20 years and has been tapped by some politicians, notably Sir Joh Bjelke-Petersen. In this interpretation, Hanson tapped into a constituency long present, not one brought into being over the last five or so years. Even the regional distribution of this constituency seems to have been long present, with its strongest appeal in rural Australia and the states of Queensland, Western Australia, South Australia and New South Wales.

An opinion poll on government assistance to Aboriginal people taken in September 1981, at a low point for the politicisation of Aboriginal issues and hence identifying the core constituency opposed to such programs, closely replicates the One Nation vote in 1998 with a correlation of over 0.9, on a scale in which 1.0 indicates a perfect correlation and 0 the complete absence of correlation (see Table 7.8).

Further indicators from the 1980s provide support for this argument. In 1984, in response to the request of a Melbourne talk-back radio host, listeners voted on the question 'should immigration be banned for two years so Australians could get the jobs available'; 23 580 (89 per cent) voted yes, 2940 no. In 1988, in response to a national telephone poll sponsored by a television station, 173 601 (82.4 per cent) agreed that 'Asian immigration should be restricted'. These polls were not scientifically valid samples but furnished clear evidence of the potential to galvanise opinion on the subject of immigration.

Table 7.8 Polls compared—views on government assistance to Aborigines, 1981 and One Nation Senate vote, 1998

	Total	NSW	VIC	QLD	SA	WA	TAS
1981 September: 'too much' being done by Federal government for Aborigines	11.2	9.8	4.8	22.2	11.4	18.1	6.6
Rank 1981		**4**	**6**	**1**	**3**	**2**	**5**
Rank 1998		**4**	**5**	**1**	**3**	**2**	**6**
1998 October: One Nation senate vote	8.7	9.3	4	14.4	9.4	10.1	3.7

Sources: Roy Morgan Research, 5–6 September 1981 (unpublished) and Australian Electoral Commission

In February and March of 1987 Joh Bjelke-Petersen tested the level of nationwide support for his prime ministerial ambitions. At this time Bjelke-Petersen was the first choice as prime minister of between 15 and 18 per cent of respondents. Between 24 and 27 per cent answered that they would support a party led by Joh. A Morgan poll established party affiliation of those who would vote for Joh: 75 per cent were National voters, 33 per cent Liberal, 13 per cent Democrat, and 8 per cent Labor. These levels of support are higher (but not by a large margin) than those obtained in polls by Hanson, perhaps not a surprise given the higher national profile and perceived level of achievement of Bjelke-Petersen.

A close link between the constituency of Bjelke-Petersen and Hanson can be further demonstrated by analysis of Queensland election results. The results for the 1986 Queensland election, when support for Bjelke-Petersen was at its height, provides indication of such a link. As indicated by Table 7.9, if the National and One Nation vote is combined for the 1998 election the result almost replicates the 1986 election outcome.

Table 7.9 Queensland elections, 1986 and 1998

Party	1986 election	1998 election
National (+ON, 1998)	39.64	37.9 (15.2 + 22.7)
Liberal	16.50	16.1
Labor	41.35	38.9
Independent + minor	2.51	7.3

Source: Queensland Electoral Commission. Pearson correlation (2-tailed) = 0.997, significant at the 0.01 level (2-tailed)

It can thus be argued that the novelty of the 1998 Queensland result has been exaggerated, through failure to see it in the appropriate context. The volatility of the National Party vote in Queensland also needs to be considered. Following the departure of Bjelke-Petersen, the National Party lost over 40 per cent of its vote between the 1986 and 1989 elections, as it did between 1995 and 1998 (see Table 7.10).

Thus on a broad range of polling and electoral data, there is strong support for the proposition that there has been no marked shift of opinion on racial issues over the last decade and that the potential for politicians to win public attention and significant support through a form of race based populism has been a constant element of Australian politics over the last 20 years. The evidence that exists of a shift of opinion points more to its occurrence in the 1980s than the 1990s. Pauline Hanson's One Nation did not so much bring into being as tap into an existing constituency, one characterised by its support for strong rhetoric, simplistic solutions, and a yearning for return to Australia's supposed golden age of equal rights and opportunity, often associated with the Menzies era.

Table 7.10   Queensland state elections—vote for major parties

Election	ALP	NAT	Variation in NAT vote	LIB	ON
1986	41.35	39.64		16.5	
1989	50.32	24.09	−39.2	21.05	
1992	48.73	23.71	−1.6	20.44	
1995	42.89	26.25	+10.7	22.74	
1998	38.86	15.17	−42.2	16.09	22.68

Source: Queensland Electoral Commission

Is the concept of 'two nations' a useful one to describe Australia at the end of the twentieth century?

Probably not. The danger with this way of describing contemporary Australia is that it over-dramatises and distorts the extent and significance of division. It is true that there are extreme positions fiercely held by a small number of 'true believers'—for example, on the issues of reconciliation, the 'stolen generations', apology and treaty—and that the number of adherents of these opposed positions may have grown, but analysis of opinion polls does not support the view of widespread recent polarisation within the community, at least on issues brought to prominence by Pauline Hanson's One Nation.

Would a change of policy by the Hawke and Keating governments, as demanded by the New Right, have lessened the potential for racial politics?

It is argued by conservative critics such as Padraic McGuinness, among others, that had the Hawke and Keating governments pursued policies less objectionable to large sections of the electorate in areas of immigration, multiculturalism and Aboriginal rights there would have been less scope for the emergence of One Nation. There is a two-fold problem with this type of argument: first, as noted above, the analysis of polls does not support the view that the policies of Hawke and Keating in these areas significantly changed public opinion. Second, such an argument runs the risk of blaming the victim for the incidence of racial animosity.

The history of a number of countries establishes that there is no simple correlation between government policy towards minorities and the incidence of bigotry. Studies of European anti-semitism in the 1920s and 1930s, for example, have established that in the eyes of the anti-semite it made no difference whether Jews accepted the injunction to assimilate and place loyalty to country above religion or chose to remain isolated, speaking their own language, living in separate communities, and placing their faith in the coming of the Messiah. It is instructive that one of the most highly assimilated and educated of peoples were the Jews of Germany.

A policy to reduce immigration from certain regions, the targeting by government of specific ethnic or racial groups, can do as much (or in all likelihood more) to legitimise bigotry than to lessen its incidence. Similarly, a reluctance by government to pursue Aboriginal rights can encourage animosity in those sections of the community vehemently opposed to significant change in the position of indigenous people.

To what extent did the New Right and John Howard facilitate the success of Pauline Hanson?

The logic of evidence considered leads to rejection of the simplistic argument which seeks to blame an individual for establishing the basis for the politics of race. Evidence has been presented to show that the basis for racial politics, appealing to an 'old Australian' constituency, has been present for fifteen or more years. The constituency for racial politics is, however, extremely volatile—as demonstrated by swings in One Nation's vote of over 50 per cent in the period of six months. The extent of the constituency is difficult to quantify, but in terms of national vote is probably in the range of 5 to 20 per cent.

The issue thus becomes one not of creating but of maximising the potential for racial politics and for facilitating its entry into the highest levels of government. It is in this context that the role of conservative propagandists and politicians warrant consideration.

On the interpretation presented here, the role of conservative critics, notably Hugh Morgan and Geoffrey Blainey, was significant for fashioning an Australian way of thinking and speaking about racial issues in the 1980s and 1990s. The promulgation of such modes of thought in the mainstream media facilitated the transition of Hanson from the status of Queensland populist to national political figure. John Howard's positioning of the Liberal Party within this mode of thought and his legitimising of key elements of Hanson's political message worked further to maximise the potential for racial politics, as did coalition preference decisions at the time of the Queensland election.

What was the significance of John Howard in the development of racial politics?

To a greater extent than to be expected from other potential leaders of his party, Howard led the assault on bipartisan policies which broke down the process of reconciliation, alienated moderate Aboriginal leadership, and led to a downgrading of multicultural policies and changes to immigration and settlement programs.

Paul Kelly, discussing the dilemma of Australian Liberalism writes: 'how did the coalition sell free market economics to the voters? . . . The Liberals had a new philosophy which nobody wanted to buy and which they couldn't sell'. Howard was in the forefront, unlike his rivals for leadership, of those who grasped the need to marry the party's policies based on 'dry' economics with a marketable social agenda, even though it involved adopting a contradictory stance. In so doing he built on the fashioning of racial issues by the conservative critics of the New Right.

Gerard Henderson has observed: 'it is one of the contemporary ironies that many political conservatives who are in the forefront of arguing for free markets in everything from cars to sugar recoil at the prospect of a free, or relatively free, market in migration'. Howard understood the problems of selling his free market agenda and succeeded in straddling the contradictory positions of economic internationalism and chauvinist nationalism. That he did so was central to his party's electoral success.

Howard's precise motivation is, according to some leading political commentators, difficult to fathom. Seeking to explain his approach to Hanson, Michelle Grattan writes that 'it is impossible to weigh precisely the relative contribution of political expediency, poor judgement, personal ideology and sheer stubbornness in Howard's litany of miscalculations on Hanson since 1996. All had their part'. Howard's colleague Tony Abbott suggests that 'one reason he has never sneered at Hanson is because he feels that her supporters (however misguided and misled) are the kind of people he grew up with—decent Australians, by and large, with no less right than anyone else to their place in the Australian sun'.

Whether he assumed his contradictory position on the basis of a pragmatic, cold-headed appraisal of the electorate or because it was congruent with his personal outlook, or both, the relative significance of the two factors varying over time is not an issue of major significance. What mattered was not his motivation, but the end product of his actions, the maximisation of the potential for racial politics.

8

The role of chance in national life

The history of Australia over the last half century has been characterised by relative stability: there have been serious problems—associated with urban planning and economic restructuring, to take but two examples—but no major wars, no great economic depression, no breakdown of the political system. It is generally assumed that this pattern will continue into the distant future. The history of Pauline Hanson's One Nation shows, however, the scope for chance, the combination of almost random events, to disrupt the pattern of national life.

From the early 1980s racial issues assumed greater significance in politics, leading to legitimisation in the mainstream of ways of thinking and speaking unfavourable to the according of distinctive rights and privileges to ethnic and racial minorities. The prospect of significant new directions in politics have beckoned, to a significant extent taken up by John Howard's Liberal Party.

For a time the impact of random events maximised the potential of racial politics. First, the likelihood that Pauline Hanson would win election to the national parliament was extremely remote, a thousand-to-one chance. It was dependent on gaining preselection in a seat by definition in the category 'unwinnable', the only type available to a political novice. Second, Hanson's loss of party endorsement in a blare of publicity was more effective than could have been planned: it allowed her to win both the conservative and the disaffected Labor vote, unusually large in the seat she contested given the lacklustre record of the incumbent.

The second magnitude of chance events relate to the nature of the politician who was elected in these circumstances and to the ability of advisers who flocked to her camp. Hanson's personal qualities fitted her like no other to assume the status of anti-politician and capture media attention. While others with a similar approach to contemporary issues, such as Graeme Campbell, floundered in the political half-light, Hanson became, next to the prime minister, the most talked about politician in the land. For a period of over two years the marketing of this 'product' was handled with great skill by John Pasquarelli and David Oldfield; that Hanson found herself in their company was again an unlikely outcome given the wealth of political ineptitude on the far right.

The third concerns national leadership in the crucial period of Hanson's emergence as a political figure. Previous Labor and Liberal prime ministers over three decades—Whitlam, Fraser, Hawke, and Keating—could have been expected to attack her simplistic and bigoted public statements (as they did after her maiden speech in newspaper articles and media interviews). Other potential Liberal leaders in the 1990s—Hewson, Downer, Costello—would, on the basis of their records, have taken an unambiguous line. Prime Minister Howard, however, acted in large part not to oppose or neutralise, but positively to reinforce Hanson's attack on the orthodoxies of the past and to rejoice that freedom of speech had been re-established in Australia.

The consequence of this conjunction of random events was not to provide the basis for racial politics, the potential for which, it has been argued, was there since the 1980s, but to maximise its influence. The consequence was that a political unknown launched a national movement with the potential to capture the balance of power in both houses of parliament. In a double-dissolution election fought by the major parties on their divergent native title policies not only would the focus have been placed on racial issues but the quota for a Senate seat would have been halved, presenting One Nation with the prospect of winning ten or more seats. Possibly no far right group has had the potential for such power in the country's history. This eventuality was inconceivable two years earlier. The danger to the democratic system that beckoned came from the potential for extremists from far right groups to secure parliamentary representation through the One Nation system of candidate preselection and from their ability to exercise a decisive influence in policy formation, as illustrated by the party's immigration and taxation policies.

But just as the compounding of chance factors saw One Nation on the brink of a major political role, so, following the Queensland election, the tide of political fortune turned.

The first and most significant random event was the timing of the Queensland election, which gave the conservative forces such a fright that there was a re-evaluation of the strategy of placing One Nation above Labor in the allocation of preferences. It was as a result of this preference decision that Pauline Hanson and a number of other candidates were unsuccessful in the federal poll. That the Queensland election was held immediately before the federal election was entirely the result of chance, the consequence of the timing of elections at state and federal levels over decades. Had the federal election been held first it is likely that preferences in most seats would have favoured One Nation above Labor, as they did in the Queensland state election.

Second, the balance of power in the Senate was held by independents, not a major party tied to fixed policy; there was thus a degree of flexibility and room for negotiation. The key vote was that of Senator Brian Harradine, who decided that the prospect of a double-dissolution election fought on the government's Wik legislation would cause great harm to the country; as a consequence, Harradine (and to a much lesser extent Prime Minister

Howard) compromised, allowing the Wik legislation to pass.

Pauline Hanson and her party, facing heightened pressure following the recognition of One Nation's potential, made a series of mistakes, further lessening electoral prospects. These mistakes (which may not have been made or been of such significance in more favourable circumstances) were a consequence less of chance than inherent weakness: based in part on the party's authoritarian structure, the extremist policies and background of some of its candidates and office holders, the personal ambitions and weaknesses of Hanson and her leadership group, and failure of will and/or confusion over the nature of One Nation's political role which led to the attempt to announce detailed policies. That the party began to unravel in this context was not so much a function of chance as of probability, but a probability that in different circumstances may not have been realised until after the bitterest of federal elections.

This episode in racial politics leaves the country facing a grave 'what if'. 'What if' a double-dissolution election had been fought on the Wik issue, before the Queensland state election showed the electoral potential of One Nation, enabling One Nation to win the balance of power in the Senate, possibly for a period of six years? How much disruption and damage would have been caused to relations with Aboriginal people, how much damage to the fabric of democracy? Perhaps little in the long term, to judge by the ineptitude of the Queensland One Nation parliamentarians. But at least some of the One Nation senators—of the calibre of David Oldfield in New South Wales, Robyn Spencer in Victoria and Len Spencer in South Australia—would have been more experienced and skilled in the art of politics and all would have been buoyed by the party's electoral success and the continuing presence of Hanson in the House of Representatives. What if a major crisis in world trade had developed in this period, devastating rural producers, creating massive unemployment and pushing interest rates beyond the capacity of home mortgagees to pay? What if . . .?

Appendix 1

IMMIGRATION INTAKE

A1.1 Permanent arrivals—Asian region and total

Year	Total settlers	Asian region	Asian as per cent of total
1950	132 650		
1951	100 732		
1952	97 146		
1953	56 935		
1954	79 051		
1955	99 404		
1956	94 105		
1957	90 208		
1958	83 491		
1959	97 777		
1960	110 079		
1961	95 407		
1962	90 464		
1963	108 150		
1964	134 464		
1965	147 507		
1966	141 033		
1967	135 019		
1968	159 270		
1969	183 416		
1970	185 325		
1971	155 525		
1972	112 468	10 511	9
1973	105 003	11 690	11
1974	121 324	11 010	9
1975	54 118	8741	16
1976	58 318	9181	16

Year	Total settlers	Asian region	Asian as per cent of total
1977	75 640	14 474	19
1978	68 419	20 079	29
1979	72 236	23 563	33
1980	94 503	26 303	28
1981	118 735	29 186	25
1982	107 170	25 770	24
1983	78 390	28 380	36
1984	73 110	31 570	43
1985	82 000	31 410	38
1986	103 330	35 860	35
1987	128 280	47 750	37
1988	151 550	56 540	37
1989	131 060	54 170	41
1990	121 560	59 340	49
1991	116 650	59 320	51
1992	94 250	44 600	47
1993	65 680	26 860	41
1994	77 940	29 760	38
1995	96 970	37 290	38
1996	92 500	36 320	39
1997	78 229	27 308	35

Source: Tables A1.3 and A1.4 in K. Betts, *The Great Divide*, Duffy & Snellgrove, Sydney, 1999.

Between 1950 and 1958 statistics do not differentiate between long-term and permanent arrivals—for these years, permanent arrivals here given are an estimate, extrapolated from the pro-portion of permanent arrivals within the total arrival figure for the years 1959–65. There are no reliable data on Asian immigrants prior to 1972. Until 1991 the Australian Bureau of Statistics included Middle Eastern countries in the Asian category. Where possible, Betts has removed named Middle Eastern countries from Asia, but it is not possible to do this for several countries, including Cyprus and Turkey for some of these years.

Appendix 2

CONFEDERATE ACTION PARTY AND
ONE NATION POLICIES COMPARED

Table A2.1 Comparison of selected Confederate Action Party and One Nation policies

Confederate Action Party	*One Nation*
Federalise the first degree crimes of murder, rape, arson and terrorism and reintroduce the death penalty.	Referendum on capital punishment.
Enact laws to guarantee the right of individuals to protect their families, their property and themselves; the right of citizens to own firearms.	Australians have the right to defend themselves and their families in their own homes. Firearms legislation should provide for safe and responsible ownership and use of firearms.
Remove government interference and over regulation from commerce and industry whilst working towards a flat tax situation. Abolish capital gains tax, F.B.T., and company take over tax deductions.	Introduce a 2 per cent flat tax applied at sale to each change of ownership of property, goods and services. Abolish direct tax, F.B.T., company tax, withholding tax, superannuation tax, payroll tax, sales tax.
Cancel the refugee program, and in future draw immigrants from traditional and Christian countries, overall immigration to be reduced at present and to be in accord with national sensitivities and requirements.	Temporary entry for refugees, until the danger in the refugee's country is resolved. Our immigration program will be non-discriminatory on condition that the numbers do not significantly alter the ethnic and cultural make up of the country. Immigration intake will be restricted to zero net migration.

When possible, deport foreign criminals.	Non-citizens will be deported for criminal offences where they are subject to being gaoled.
Introduce a two-tier youth national service policy.	Introduce twelve months national service for males and females upon completion of Year 12 or reaching eighteen years of age.
Create a strong and effective military defence with priority on self-sufficiency.	Increase defence capacity. Threat to Australia from the Asian region.
Abolish the *Family Law Act* and return the country to true family standards with strong support for the legal family unit.	Repeal *Family Law Act*.
Abolish the Aboriginal Affairs Department. We are one Australia— one nation.	Abolish ATSIC. No special benefits on the basis of race.
Cancel foreign aid until our national debt is eliminated.	Cease foreign aid immediately and apply savings to generate employment at home.
Rescind any legislation which removes total Australian Sovereignty over the nation's land and resources—including World Heritage areas. Review, towards rescision, all foreign originated conventions whose adoption overrules the Australian Constitution. Support the Constitution by denying 'interpretation' of external affairs clauses so as to usurp state rights.	'I am going to find out how many treaties we have signed with the UN, have them exposed and then call for their repudiation'.
Implement a national road and rail building program using at least 75 per cent of fuel taxes plus convict labour.	Government to build Alice Springs to Darwin railway, new roads and ports.
Hold a referendum to include Citizen Initiated Referendum and Recall into the Australian Constitution, so that the people can say 'No' to laws that the majority do not want.	Introduce Community Based Referendum to give the ordinary people of Australia the opportunity to directly address the issues of real concern.

Appendix 3

THE ELECTORAL FORTUNES OF ONE NATION

This appendix evaluates the electoral appeal of populist race-based nationalism. It first considers the fortunes over the last decade of three minor parties, Australians Against Further Immigration (AAFI) (which had its greatest influence in Victoria and New South Wales) and the Queensland based Citizens Electoral Councils (CEC) and Confederate Action Party (CAP). These parties struggled to make an electoral impact, although fringe candidates in Queensland had the capacity to win over 10 per cent of the vote in some electorates.

Australians Against Further Immigration contested three federal elections, 1990, 1993 and 1996, and a number of by-elections. It won much publicity with relatively strong votes at by-elections in the years 1994–96: its average vote was 8 per cent, with over 13 per cent on two occasions. These votes need, however, to be placed into context. At both by-elections when it won over 10 per cent the seat was safely held and only one of the major parties stood a candidate; in the contest for Blaxland the candidate for a second anti-immigration party, Reclaim Australia: Reduce Immigration, won 9 per cent of the vote, giving the anti-immigration parties a combined vote of 22 per cent, but the two-party preferred Labor vote increased from 63 per cent to 69 per cent. By comparison, in the 1995 by-election for the safe Liberal seat of Wentworth, in the absence of a Labor candidate the Greens won 26 per cent of the vote and a high profile independent won nearly 19 per cent (see Table A3.1).

When AAFI contested seats at a general election it won a

**Table A3.1 By-election results, 1994–97—vote for major parties
and AAFI**

Seat	State	Date	ALP (% of vote)	LIB (% of vote)	AAFI (% of vote)	AAFI Candidate
Werriwa	NSW	January 1994	50.13	33.82	7.24	R. Spencer
Bonython	SA	March 1994	45.92	32.19	6.82	D. McCormack
Mackellar	NSW	March 1994	no candidate	52.25	8.16	J. Phillips
Warringah	NSW	March 1994	no candidate	55.21	13.54	R. Spencer
Kooyong	VIC	November 1994	no candidate	56.86	7.91	A. Walker
Canberra	ACT	March 1995	30.48	46.29	4.17	R. Spencer
Blaxland	NSW	June 1996	58.83	no candidate	13.63	P. Krumins
Lindsay	NSW	October 1996	33.56	49.21	5.97	V. Townsend
Fraser	ACT	February 1997	49.1	no candidate	3.55	A. Walker
Average					7.89	
Median					7.24	
					GREEN	INDEP
Wentworth	NSW	April 1995	no candidate	52.84	26.04	18.85

Source: Australian Electoral Commission

minuscule vote, although one which grew at the aggregated state level as more candidates were fielded. In 1996 its Senate candidates won approximately 1.5 per cent of the vote in Victoria and New South Wales; at the same election its House of Representatives candidates won an average 1.74 per cent of the vote in Victoria in the thirteen seats it contested and a significantly higher 3.37 per cent in 21 New South Wales seats, with a peak of 5.63 per cent in the seat of Werriwa. The party made no impact in other states, struggling to average 1 per cent in the Senate (see Tables A3.2 and A3.3).

Fringe parties had much greater success in Queensland, the best result being victory in a highly publicised by-election. At the 1988

Table A3.2 Senate—AAFI vote, 1990–96

	Victoria	New South Wales	South Australia	Queensland	Western Australia
1990	0.75				
1993	0.69	0.67	0.38		
1996	1.47	1.68	1.01	0.68	1.26

Source: Australian Electoral Commission

Table A3.3 House of Representatives—average AAFI vote in seats contested, 1990–96

	Victoria	New South Wales	South Australia	Queensland	Western Australia
1990	1.24 (1)				
1993	1.29 (2)	1.25 (2)			
1996	1.74 (13)	3.37 (21)	2.24 (1)	0.85 (2)	1.11 (1)

Source: Australian Electoral Commission. Number of seats contested appears in brackets.

by-election for the seat of Barambah to fill the vacancy caused by the resignation of the former premier, Sir Joh Bjelke-Petersen, the Citizens Electoral Councils' T.J. Perrett won 32 per cent of the primary vote, defeating the National Party candidate on Labor preferences. Perrett defected to the Nationals before the next election and held the seat until defeated by One Nation in 1998.

In the 1989 state election the CEC candidates contested seven seats, winning over 10 per cent in two, with an average vote of 5.7 per cent. At the next state election in 1992 the newly formed CAP recorded a higher vote. The party contested twelve seats and won an average vote of 9.6 per cent, with over 10 per cent in five seats: Tony Pitt and Tony May received 16 per cent respectively in Maryborough and Callide, Sandra Hill and Trevor Howland 14 per cent in Mackay and Mirani. Nineteen ninety-two was, however, to be the high point of the CAP's vote. At the 1993 federal election it contested 24 Queensland seats, winning 2.9 per cent of the state vote, with 10.2 per cent in Groom, 9.1 per cent in Dawson and 5.7 per cent in Wide Bay. Its Senate vote was 2.86 per cent. At the 1995 state election it contested only eight seats, averaging 5.7 per cent of the vote in these seats, with relatively high votes in Barambah (9.3 per cent), Mackay (8.5 per cent) and Lockyer (6.6 per cent). Four of the seats in which the CAP polled well, Maryborough, Callide, Barambah and Lockyer, were to be among the top ten One Nation results.

The CAP's vote was symptomatic of a nationwide trend for an increase in minor party and independent vote. In Queensland it had grown from 3.55 per cent in 1980 to 8.14 per cent in 1995 (see Table A3.4).

The strength of the One Nation vote in the Queensland election of June 1998 had, however, no precedents in terms of minor party vote. One Nation won 22.68 per cent of the state vote, although this understates its level of support as it did not contest ten of the 89 electorates: in the seats contested its average vote was 25.4 per cent. Labor won 38.9 per cent, the Liberals 16.1 per cent, and the National Party 15.2 per cent. One Nation's vote exceeded 25 per cent in 38 seats, as indicated in Table A3.5. Only in the two

**Table A3.4 Independent and minor party share of the vote—
Queensland state elections, 1980–95**

Year	Formal primary vote	Formal vote (%)	Candidates
1980	41 834	3.55	45
1983	29 069	2.21	30
1986	35 006	2.51	38
1989	71 476	4.54	54
1992	124 269	7.12	42
1995	146 978	8.14	111

Source: Electoral Commission of Queensland, *Queensland's Electoral History.*
Includes Greens and Democrats.

Table A3.5 Analysis of One Nation vote—Queensland (1998) and New South Wales (1999) state elections

Vote (%)	Queensland, no. of seats	New South Wales, no. of seats
40–45	3	0
35–40	7	0
30–35	9	0
25–30	19	0
20–25	20	1
15–20	12	4
10–15	7	18
5–10	2	40
0–5	0	25

Source: Electoral Commission of Queensland, State Electoral Office, New South Wales

central Brisbane seats did One Nation poll under 10 per cent (see Map 1). The strength of this vote is further highlighted by comparison with the One Nation vote in the New South Wales election of March 1999, to be considered later in this Appendix.

Compared with other minor parties One Nation was thus spectacularly successful in Queensland. However, while it polled well across the state it lacked the localised support possessed by the Labor and Liberal Parties to enable it to win a majority in its own right in a constituency. So strongly did One Nation eat into the National vote that the Nationals only obtained an outright majority in one seat, that of the premier. Of the eleven seats won by One Nation all were won on preferences following the decision of the conservative parties to allocate preferences to One Nation ahead of Labor. Five of the seats won were formerly held by the National Party (four classified 'safe'), six by Labor (one 'safe').

One Nation narrowly missed victory in six additional seats, winning between 47 per cent and 49.9 per cent of the vote after allocation of preferences. Of the 89 Queensland electorates it was

Map 1—1998 Queensland election, Brisbane electorates. One Nation vote.

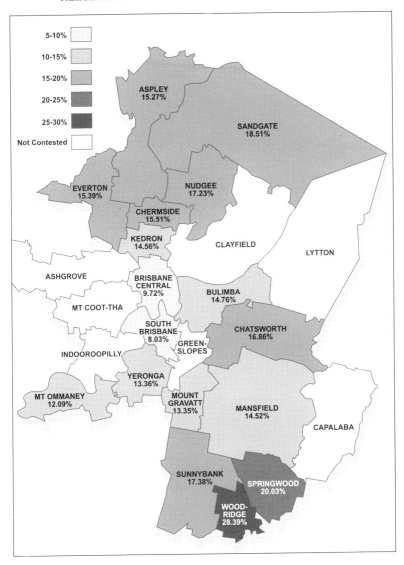

placed second in 23 after allocation of preferences, thus polling first or second in a total of 34 seats or 38 per cent of the total.

One Nation's vote was weakest in the Brisbane region: in inner metropolitan seats it averaged 12.6 per cent; in the outer metropolitan 21.5 per cent (see Map 1). It also polled relatively poorly in the five electorates largest in area in which it averaged 22.4 per cent of the vote. Of the 30 electorates ranked six to 35 in area, One Nation won ten; of the 25 smallest electorates (urban or fringe urban) One Nation won only Ipswich West, Pauline Hanson's base.

The party's areas of greatest strength were:

- the coastal strip north of Mackay where four seats were won—Whitsunday (30.71 per cent of the primary vote), Burdekin (33.07 per cent), Thuringowa (34.9 per cent) and Mulgrave (31.04 per cent). A fifth seat won, Tablelands (42.03 per cent), adjoins Mulgrave in the Cairns hinterland.
- the southeast corner of the state (with the exception of Brisbane and the Sunshine and Gold Coasts), which saw the strongest One Nation vote with seven contiguous seats recording over 38 per cent; these seats stretched from Maryborough (42.56 per cent of the primary vote) and Gympie (39.24 per cent) in the north to the hinterland seats of Barambah (43.54 per cent), Crows Nest (39.5 per cent), Ipswich West (38.63 per cent), Ipswich (39.53 per cent) and Lockyer (39.23 per cent) (see Map 2). One Nation won four of these seven seats, in addition to Hervey Bay (33.79 per cent), bordering Maryborough on the north.

The One Nation vote was at its peak in the June 1998 state election. A measure of its rapid decline was the by-election for the seat of Mulgrave following the resignation of the seat's One Nation representative in November 1998 which saw the party's vote halved from 31.04 per cent to 15.6 per cent. The October 1998

Map 2—1998 Queensland election, south-eastern electorates. One Nation vote.

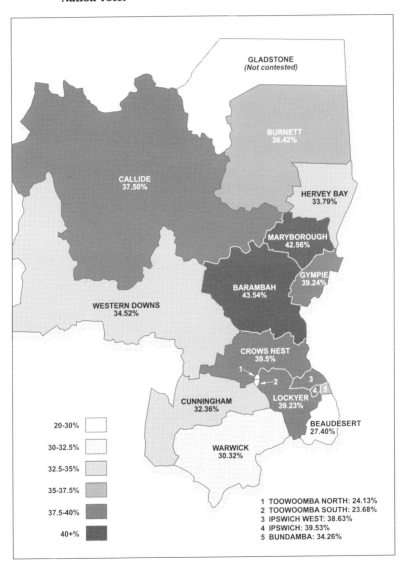

GLADSTONE
(Not contested)

BURNETT
36.42%

CALLIDE
37.50%

HERVEY BAY
33.79%

MARYBOROUGH
42.56%

GYMPIE
39.24%

BARAMBAH
43.54%

WESTERN DOWNS
34.52%

CROWS NEST
39.5%

1
2
3
4 5

CUNNINGHAM
32.36%

LOCKYER
39.23%

BEAUDESERT
27.40%

WARWICK
30.32%

20-30%

30-32.5%

32.5-35%

35-37.5%

37.5-40%

40+%

1 TOOWOOMBA NORTH: 24.13%
2 TOOWOOMBA SOUTH: 23.68%
3 IPSWICH WEST: 38.63%
4 IPSWICH: 39.53%
5 BUNDAMBA: 34.26%

federal election vote in Queensland seats also saw its state vote decline, by nearly 40 per cent, from close to 25 per cent to 14 per cent (see Table A3.6).

At the federal election the party's national vote was 8.43 per cent, although there was significant difference between the states: the peak was in Queensland with 14 per cent, a second level in New South Wales, Western Australia and South Australia around 9 per cent, and the lowest in Victoria and Tasmania, under 4 per cent. Although the level of support differed, there was a consistent pattern across the country: in the inner metropolitan areas the party's vote was lowest, rising in the outer and fringe areas of major cities, and reaching a peak in rural areas, although not in the most remote rural constituencies (see Table A3.7).

Close analysis of voting establishes that both the level of support and pattern of voting for One Nation in metropolitan areas is similar in four of the five mainland states. In the seat of Brisbane, One Nation polled 4.84 per cent, compared with an average of 7.6 per cent for the other Brisbane seats; for Adelaide the respective figures are 5.18 per cent and 7.7 per cent, for Perth 3.72 per cent for the inner urban seat of Curtin, for the other Perth seats 7.7 per cent. In Sydney nine inner urban seats averaged 3.67 per cent, the outer urban seats 8.09 per cent (see Map 3). In Melbourne, while there is a similar pattern, the level of support was much lower (see

Table A3.6   One Nation vote, 1998–99—lower houses of parliament

Election	Queensland	New South Wales	Western Australia	South Australia	Victoria	Tasmania	Australia
June 1998	22.68						
October 1998	14.35	8.96	9.27	9.8	3.72	2.46	8.43
March 1999		7.35					

Source: Electoral Commission of Queensland, Australian Electoral Commission, State Electoral Office, New South Wales

Table A3.7   One Nation House of Representatives vote, 1998—regional summary by state

	Queensland	New South Wales	South Australia	Western Australia	Victoria
Inner metrop.	4.84	3.67	5.18	3.72	2.07
Outer metrop.	7.6	8.09	7.7	7.7	2.93
Metropolitan (inner & outer)	6.55	6.28	7.31	7.15	2.75
Hinterland	15.35	10.1	10.45	10.76	4.66
Rest of state	18.07	12.07	14.09	12.01	7.88

Source: Calculations based on Australian Electoral Commission data.

Table A3.8   One Nation House of Representatives vote, 1998—index of One Nation vote, regional summary by state

	Queensland	New South Wales	South Australia	Western Australia
Metropolitan (inner and outer)	100	100	100	100
Hinterland	234	161	143	150
Rest of state	276	192	193	168

Source: Calculations based on Australian Electoral Commission data.

Table A3.7). The differentiation in the level of support between the states is to be found outside the metropolitan areas. As Table A3.8 shows, the strength of One Nation's Queensland hinterland and rural vote was not matched in other states.

In marked contrast with the Queensland state election, in the federal poll One Nation won over 20 per cent in only four seats and its vote exceed 30 per cent only in the seat of Blair, contested by Pauline Hanson (see Table A3.9). As in the Queensland election, its strongest level of support was in the southeast of the state, extending in the federal poll across the border to the New South

Map 3—1998 federal election, Sydney electorates. One Nation vote.

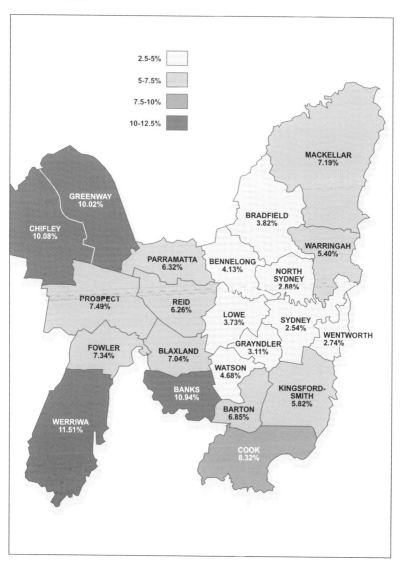

Table A3.9   Federal election, October 1998—One Nation vote greater than 15 per cent

Seat	State	Classification	(%)
Blair	Queensland	Hinterland	35.97
Wide Bay	Queensland	Rural	26.33
Maranoa	Queensland	Rural	22.4
Gwydir	New South Wales	Rural	20.77
Hinkler	Queensland	Rural	18.99
Kennedy	Queensland	Rural	18.84
Longman	Queensland	Hinterland	18.15
Groom	Queensland	Hinterland	17.97
Fairfax	Queensland	Hinterland	17.75
Oxley	Queensland	Hinterland	17.66
Forde	Queensland	Hinterland	17.1
Wakefield	South Australia	Rural	16.67
Newcastle	New South Wales	Hinterland	16.05
Dawson	Queensland	Rural	15.91
Cowper	New South Wales	Rural	15.32

Source: Australian Electoral Commission

Wales seat of Gwydir, but the level of support was considerably below that gained in the state election (see Map 4).

During 1999 there were two further tests of the party's electoral strength: the New South Wales election in March, at which One Nation contested 88 of the lower house seats and ran a ticket headed by David Oldfield for the upper house. It won 7.35 per cent of the lower and 6.3 per cent of the New South Wales upper house vote. In the Victorian election held in May One Nation only contested four rural seats, its vote ranging from 5.1 per cent to 10.8 per cent.

In the New South Wales poll One Nation's vote exceeded 15 per cent only in five seats, with its best vote of 20.5 per cent in the far northern seat of Barwon, part of the federal seat of Gwydir where One Nation had polled 20.77 per cent. There was no simple

Map 4—1998 federal election, rural electorates, Queensland, New South Wales and Victoria, and Brisbane hinterland seat of Blair. One Nation vote.

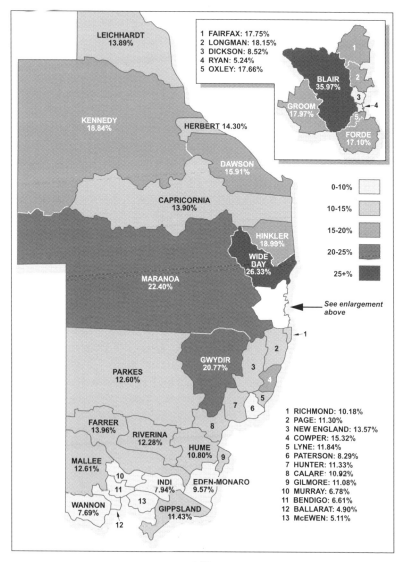

LEICHHARDT
13.89%

1 FAIRFAX: 17.75%
2 LONGMAN: 18.15%
3 DICKSON: 8.52%
4 RYAN: 5.24%
5 OXLEY: 17.66%

BLAIR
35.97%

GROOM
17.97%

FORDE
17.10%

KENNEDY
18.84%

HERBERT 14.30%

DAWSON
15.91%

CAPRICORNIA
13.90%

HINKLER
18.99%

WIDE
BAY
26.33%

MARANOA
22.40%

0-10%
10-15%
15-20%
20-25%
25+%

See enlargement
above

GWYDIR
20.77%

PARKES
12.60%

FARRER
13.96%

RIVERINA
12.28%

HUME
10.80%

MALLEE
12.61%

INDI
7.94%

EDEN-MONARO
9.57%

WANNON
7.69%

GIPPSLAND
11.43%

1 RICHMOND: 10.18%
2 PAGE: 11.30%
3 NEW ENGLAND: 13.57%
4 COWPER: 15.32%
5 LYNE: 11.84%
6 PATERSON: 8.29%
7 HUNTER: 11.33%
8 CALARE: 10.92%
9 GILMORE: 11.08%
10 MURRAY: 6.78%
11 BENDIGO: 6.61%
12 BALLARAT: 4.90%
13 McEWEN: 5.11%

pattern to the One Nation vote in New South Wales, with significant variation between neighbouring electorates. In addition to Barwon, other strong seats for One Nation were Oxley, a north coast hinterland seat (18.8 per cent), the Newcastle hinterland seat of Cessnock (16.1 per cent), the central-western seat of Dubbo (18.1 per cent) and the far-western seat of Murray-Darling (16.4 per cent), the largest seat in the state which recorded a relatively stronger vote than the most remote Queensland seats (see Table A3.10). In other rural seats One Nation polled relatively poorly, particularly in the central and southern regions—thus Upper Hunter 12.8 per cent, Orange 12.6 per cent, Lachlan 13 per cent, Burrinjuck 11.4 per cent, Wagga Wagga 8.0 per cent and Murrumbidgee 8.4 per cent.

Support in the Sydney region showed the same pattern observed in earlier elections, with the strongest urban vote in the outer suburbs, particularly the western fringe. The inner ring of electorates recorded a vote of 2 to 4 per cent, with the lowest vote in the harbourside electorates (North Shore 2.2 per cent, Vaucluse 2.1 per cent); a further ring of electorates to the north and south were typically around 4 per cent (Davison 3.8 per cent, Marrickville 4.2 per cent); the inner west around 7 per cent, with some seats recording votes of up to 10 per cent (Granville 9.1 per cent, East Hills 10.7 per cent), the far west mostly in the range 8 to 9

Table A3.10   New South Wales election, March 1999—One Nation vote greater than 15 per cent

Seat	Classification	(%)
Barwon	Rural	20.5
Oxley	Rural	18.8
Dubbo	Rural	18.1
Murray-Darling	Rural	16.4
Cessnock	Rural	16.1

Source: State Electoral Commission, New South Wales

per cent, with a peak of 11 per cent (Liverpool 8.9 per cent, Penrith 8.7 per cent).

WHO VOTES FOR ONE NATION?

The above analysis has established that the One Nation vote was strongest in the hinterland of capital cities, some coastal hinterland areas, and rural constituencies, particularly in Queensland and northern New South Wales. Its appeal was lowest in Tasmania and Victoria.

Consistent with this pattern, the One Nation vote was strongest in seats held by the National Party, where its vote averaged 14.9 per cent at the 1998 federal election. In Liberal held seats it averaged 8.4 per cent and in Labor seats 6.1 per cent. One Nation preferences were of sufficient size to potentially determine the electoral outcome in marginal seats (see Table A3.11).

It is not possible to establish with precision the vote taken by One Nation from each of the major parties. In the public view of Prime Minister Howard, 'the great bulk of One Nation voters are former coalition voters'. Grahame Morris, former Howard chief of staff, stated that approximately 80 per cent of One Nation voters had formerly supported the coalition. The Australian Election Study found that 54 per cent of One Nation voters had previously supported the coalition, 23 per cent Labor and the remainder either supported minor parties or had not previously voted.

Table A3.11   Federal election, 1998—One Nation vote correlated with winning party

	Average	Safe seat	Fair safe seat	Marginal seat
ALP	6.1	3.8	9.1	6.9
LIB	8.4	9.2	8.3	7.5
NAT	14.9	15.8	13.8	12.0

Source: Calculations based on Australian Electoral Commission data.

In Queensland the coalition vote fell 14.3 per cent, One Nation's vote was 14.3 per cent; in New South Wales the coalition fell 6.5 per cent, One Nation gained 8.8 per cent; and in Victoria the coalition fell 4.5 per cent; and One Nation gained 3.7 per cent. These close correlations, especially for Queensland and Victoria, do not by themselves establish the case for minimal loss of Labor votes. The data is also consistent with the interpretation that the presence of One Nation candidates led to some loss of Labor votes to One Nation, particularly in some outer urban electorates, but that loss was almost equally or largely compensated by Labor gains from the coalition parties, evident at the aggregated state level.

Further analysis below seeks to determine the demographic and socioeconomic character of One Nation support, commencing with the vote in the Queensland state election. The statistical data presented is also designed to illustrate, using a range of variables, the character of the constituencies recording One Nation support.

Using the statistical technique of multiple regression the One Nation vote in the federal election was measured against eleven variables covering population density of the electorate, age distribution, residential stability, birthplace and ethnicity, educational attainment, level of unemployment, workforce participation and median family income. The strength of Pauline Hanson's vote in Blair was found to skew the results for Queensland so for the purposes of this analysis it has been excluded. A second electorate, the New South Wales seat of Newcastle where the poll was held after the date of the general election due to the death of one of the candidates, also skewed results although not to the same extent as Blair and it has been included. The variables specified account for approximately 80 per cent of the One Nation vote (see Table A3.12).

As indicated by Table A3.12, there was some variation between the states. The strongest predictor of the One Nation vote was found to be lack of qualifications, applicable to all states studied except Victoria; next of significance was relatively high proportion of indigenous residents, a strong predictor in the case of Victoria

Table A3.12 Predicting the One Nation vote—eleven variables analysed utilising stepwise multiple regression

Variable	Queensland (excluding Blair)	Western Australia & South Australia	New South Wales	Victoria
No qualifications	1. high	1. high	2. high	
Aboriginal and Torres Strait Islander population			1. high	1. high
Non-English speaking background population		2. low	3. low	
Median income	3. low			2. low
Level of unemployment				3. high
Population density	2. low			
Change of address in the last five years			4. low	
R^2	0.781	0.795	0.809 (0.858 excl. Newcastle)	0.786

Numbers reflect the step at which the independent variable was entered into the stepwise regression model. Stepwise regression identifies the independent variable not currently included in the model that best fits the observed variance in the dependant variable. Therefore the step in which the independent variable is entered into the model is related to how much of the observed variance is explained by the independent variable. The order of steps can be considered a ranking of the influence of the independent variable on the dependant.

and New South Wales; other variables of relevance to at least two of the states are low proportion of non-English speaking background (NESB) residents and low median income.

While lack of formal qualifications was the strongest predictor, this variable should not be considered in isolation, for it is closely correlated with other variables, notably low median family income

(−0.85), high number of children under the age of five (0.66), high unemployment (0.6) and low population density (−0.54). To put this finding in other words, there is a close correlation between the One Nation vote and relative poverty, relatively large family size and residence outside the main centres of population. The relatively high number of indigenous residents is an important distinguishing characteristic for New South Wales and Victoria. The significance of the range of variables considered is more closely examined in the following discussion using data for specific states and electorates.

Examination of the fifteen seats which recorded the highest One Nation vote in the Queensland state election highlights the relatively low number of NESB immigrants and the key variable discussed above, the low proportion with formal qualifications. Thus the number of residents who speak a language other than English in their homes averages 3.77 per cent for the fifteen seats, compared with 7.16 per cent for Queensland and 16 per cent for Australia. The number without formal qualifications averages 81.26 per cent for the fifteen seats, compared with 76.3 per cent for Queensland and 58 per cent for Australia. Conversely, the number with a degree or diploma level qualification is 7.85 per cent, compared with 12.01 per cent for Queensland and 22.2 per cent for Australia. Consistent with the federal results for Queensland noted above (see Table A3.12), the proportion of Aboriginal and Torres Strait Islanders does not seem to be of major importance, with only four of the fifteen seats having an Aboriginal population significantly higher than the average for the state. With regard to the level of unemployment, again only four of the fifteen (different from the four seats with high indigenous population) are significantly above the average for the state, with the average for the fifteen seats at 10.63 per cent compared with 9.65 per cent for the state.

Table A3.13 contrasts the four seats which recorded the highest and lowest One Nation vote in the state election. As expected, there is strong differentiation on grounds of qualifications,

Table A3.13 Queensland state election, 1998—selected socioeconomic variables—seats with highest and lowest One Nation vote

	Barambah (%)	Maryborough (%)	Brisbane Central (%)	South Brisbane (%)
One Nation vote	43.54	42.56	9.72	8.03
Classification	rural	rural	urban	urban
Electors per sq. km	1.56	4.35	991.52	1326.32
Age				
0–4	7.63	7.3	4.14	4.81
5–16	20.52	18.91	7.22	8.82
17	1.29	1.34	1.01	1.16
18–59	53.16	53.28	68.79	67.38
60	17.4	19.17	18.83	17.83
total 18+	70.56	72.45	87.63	85.21
Population mobility (address 1991)				
same	53.42	54.11	39.57	38.64
different: Queensland	40.13	37.55	40.35	39.44
different: other	6.28	8.34	20.08	21.92
Aboriginal and Torres Strait Islander	5.45	1.88	1.79	2.26
Birthplace				
Australia	91.22	91.76	74.88	67.38
Overseas: Main English speaking countries	5.82	5.34	11.28	10.6
Overseas: other	2.97	2.9	13.84	22.02
Language spoken in home: other than English	1.86	1.8	13.48	24.53
Qualification (highest)				
Degree/diploma	7.07	7.48	28.25	25.41
Vocational	9.18	11.48	9.87	9.34
No qualification	83.75	81.04	61.88	65.25
Employment				
Unemployed	11.91	14.52	9.11	12.39
In labour force	56.64	53.63	63.66	60.72
Not in labour force	43.36	46.37	36.34	39.28

Source: Electoral Commission of Queensland

numbers of dependent children, ethnicity, rural location and work-force participation. There is also lower population mobility in the rural electorates.

To investigate further the significance of socioeconomic status, a comparison was made using federal election results between 30 seats with a high One Nation vote and 33 seats with the lowest vote. The One Nation vote was correlated with census information on income, unemployment and indexes of relative socioeconomic disadvantage, economic resources, and a combined index of educational attainment and occupational status. Differentiation was evident across all variables, with the most marked differences on the indexes of educational attainment—occupational status and level of unemployment (see Table A3.14).

Examination of relatively affluent electorates, mainly located in urban areas, reveals a consistently low One Nation vote. The least

Table A3.14 Federal election, 1998—high and low One Nation vote and selected socioeconomic variables

	Seats	One Nation vote (%)	Income $	Unemployed (%)	Socio-economic disadvantage (index)	Economic resources (index)	Education & occupation (index)
Australia/high	30	16.3	617	10.4	966	970	943
Australia/low	**33**	**3.42**	**877**	**8**	**1045**	**1044**	**1365**
Queensland/high	11	20.63	621	10.5	959	969	930
Queensland/low	**1**	**4.84**	**1023**	**6.6**	**1069**	**996**	**1106**
New South Wales/high	8	14.57	606	10.9	972	961	970
New South Wales/low	**8**	**3.45**	**1023**	**6.6**	**1069**	**1068**	**1115**

Source: Calculations based on Australian Electoral Commission data.

affluent electorates, on the other hand, recorded a stronger One Nation vote, but there were two distinct patterns: seven of the electorates recorded votes above 12.5 per cent (five above 15 per cent), whilst nine were below 12.5 per cent (five below 7.5 per cent). One differentiating factor was location of the electorate, with all votes above 12.5 per cent in hinterland or rural areas (see Tables A3.15 and A3.16).

The character of the socioeconomically disadvantaged seats was further explored by examining eight electorates taken from the above, three rural seats recording high One Nation votes and four urban and one hinterland Sydney electorates which recorded low to medium votes (see Table A3.17).

This analysis indicates that the disadvantaged seats recording the highest One Nation vote were distinguished by rural location, numbers employed in agriculture, higher number born in Australia and correspondingly lower number of non-English speaking background residents (very few from Asian countries), and fewer

Table A3.15   Federal election, 1998—One Nation vote and top ten electorates ranked on index of relative socioeconomic advantage

Division	Classification	One Nation vote	Index advantage	Unemployed (%)
Bradfield (NSW)	Urban	3.82	1261	3.5
Mitchell (NSW)	Hinterland	6.65	1176	3.6
Kooyong (Vic.)	Urban	2.09	1168	5.5
Ryan (Qld)	Urban	5.24	1151	6.6
Berowra (NSW)	Hinterland	6.03	1149	3.9
North Sydney (NSW)	Urban	2.88	1146	3.9
Menzies (Vic.)	Urban	1.83	1145	6.2
Curtin (WA)	Urban	3.72	1143	6.9
Higgins (Vic.)	Urban	1.56	1124	6.8
Warringah (NSW)	Urban	5.40	1120	3.8
Average		**3.92**	**1158**	**5.1**

Source: Australian Electoral Commission

Table A3.16 Federal election, 1998—One Nation vote and fifteen lowest scoring electorates ranked on index of relative socioeconomic disadvantage

Division	Classification	One Nation vote	Index disadvantage	Unemployed (%)
Above 12.5 per cent				
Bonython (SA)	Hinterland	14.81	878	16.2
Wide Bay (Qld)	Rural	26.33	924	14.1
Oxley (Qld)	Hinterland	17.66	934	10.7
Grey (SA)	Rural	12.6	941	11.9
Cowper (NSW)	Rural	15.32	943	17.9
Gwydir (NSW)	Rural	20.77	944	11.0
Hinkler (Qld)	Rural	18.99	944	12.9
Average		18.07	929.71	13.53
Below 12.5 per cent				
Fowler (NSW)	Urban	7.34	878	17.9
Gellibrand (Vic.)	Urban	3.46	914	16.1
Pt Adelaide (SA)	Urban	9.06	916	13.3
Chifley (NSW)	Urban	10.08	932	10.5
Throsby (NSW)	Hinterland	11.39	936	13.6
Reid (NSW)	Urban	6.26	939	12.9
Blaxland (NSW)	Urban	7.04	942	11.9
Braddon (Tas.)	Rural	4.21	944	12.5
Average		7.36	925.13	13.59

Source: Australian Electoral Commission

residents living in rented accommodation. The low levels of income may be disregarded: all the seats here considered had relatively low levels of income (compare the average income of $1158 for advantaged seats) and the higher cost of living in urban areas may cancel out the differences observed between the rural and urban seats.

Comparison of the five disadvantaged seats in the Sydney region indicates that Chifley and Throsby, which recorded a higher than average One Nation vote, were distinguished by outer urban or hinterland location, higher proportion born in Australia, fewer

Table A3.17 Federal election, 1998—One Nation vote and eight socioeconomically disadvantaged electorates

Seat	Wide Bay (Qld)	Gwydir (NSW)	Hinkler (Qld)	Fowler (NSW)	Blaxland (NSW)	Reid (NSW)	Chifley (NSW)	Throsby (NSW)
One Nation vote	26.33	20.77	18.99	7.34	7.04	6.26	10.08	11.39
Classification	rural	rural	rural	urban	urban	urban	urban	hinterland
Area (sq. km)	53 826	114 463	36 570	53	50	66	123	392
Aboriginal and Torres Straight Islander origin	3.3	8.9	2.5	1.3	0.6	0.9	3.1	1.8
Birthplace								
Australia	85.4	90.1	85.6	44.9	54.2	52.1	65.7	71
Southern Europe	0.4	0.5	0.8	8.9	7.4	4.9	4.2	9.8
South-east Asia	0.5	0.2	0.6	22.2	9.5	7.5	6.5	0.9
Languages spoken in home other than English	2.3	2	2.7	60.2	53.4	52.0	27.0	19.3
Median age	37	35	34	30	32	32	28	32
Employed	44.3	50.6	49.9	44.5	46.4	46.0	54.5	48.9
Unemployed	14.1	11.0	12.9	17.9	11.9	12.9	10 5	13.6
Employment								
Government	18.6	18.6	16.4	12.7	14.9	16.1	15.7	16
Agriculture	15.6	27.1	9.5	0.4	0.2	0.3	0.7	0.6
Manufacturing	9.7	6.1	14.2	26				
						13.9	9.7	9
Trade	13.1	12.5	15.1	10.6	12	10.9	13	16.8
None	66.8	65	65.3	67.2	62.8	60.6	64.7	62.6
Accommodation								
Rented dwelling	24.4	25.9	26.8	37.8	31	36.6	31	27.2
Dwelling owned	19.5	15.9	23.3	22.3	16.2	15.9	26	42.3
Dwelling being purchased	47.7	46.9	42.9	33.1	45.6	40	37.3	25.1
Median family income	493	532	606	617	665	645	728	678

Source: Australian Electoral Commission

who spoke a language other than English in the home, higher income and higher levels of home ownership.

Lastly, selected regions within the seat of Blair, the seat contested by Pauline Hanson and which recorded the highest One Nation vote, were examined (see Table A3.18). At the 1996 election One Nation's primary vote in Blair ranged from a high of 58.65 per cent at the small Maidenwell polling booth to 18.01 per cent in the north Ipswich booth of Karana Downs. Correlation of these booths with census data indicates a marked differentiation for six of the variables: in the booths recording the highest One Nation vote there was a much higher proportion of the population aged 55 and over, without formal qualifications, unemployed, and with family incomes below $300 per week; lower numbers had tertiary educational qualifications and there was a lower workforce participation rate.

These findings serve to reinforce the results of the multiple regression analysis, while highlighting the level of poverty to be found in parts of Australia: thus in Maidenwell, where 27 per cent of the population was over the age of 55, nearly two-thirds of the residents had no formal qualification, unemployment was nearly 20 per cent, and nearly three-quarters of families had an income below $300 per week. This contrasts with Karana Downs, which recorded a relatively low One Nation vote, where unemployment was 4.7 per cent, 23 per cent had some form of tertiary qualification and over 60 per cent had incomes over $300.

OVERVIEW

This analysis has demonstrated that the One Nation vote during 1998–99 was strongest in the hinterland of capital cities, some coastal hinterland areas, and rural constituencies, particularly in Queensland and northern New South Wales. Consistent with this pattern, the One Nation vote was strongest in seats held by the National Party. One Nation also polled relatively strongly in some outer urban electorates.

Table A3.18   Federal election, 1998—Blair electorate, selected regions and socioeconomic variables

	Maidenwell	*Rosewood*	*Nanango*	*Karalee*	*Karana Downs*
	2 census collector districts	*Urban Centre*	*Urban Centre*	*Urban Centre*	*Urban Centre*
ON primary vote	58.65	39.94	39.91	27.65	18.01
ON two part pref. vote	65.87	50.53	52.19	35.00	22.55
Total persons	708	2010	2711	1989	4434
Aged under 15	18.08	27.31	26.37	28.21	31.19
Aged 15 and over	81.92	72.69	73.63	71.79	68.81
Aged 55 and over	27.3	23.4	21.00	9.6	8.7
Aboriginal/Torres Strait Islander	0.42	3.18	2.47	0.4	0.61
Birthplace					
Australia	86.37	91.65	88.55	83.69	79.22
Overseas—main English speaking countries	8.73	6.72	8.02	11.21	15.34
Overseas—non-English speaking countries	4.9	1.63	3.43	5.09	5.44
Not fluent in English (aged over 5)	3.25	0.9	2.14	2.46	3.18
With qualifications	35.52	30.53	33.77	45.1	50.28
No qualifications	64.48	69.47	66.23	54.9	49.72
Diploma or higher qualifications	7.59	3.56	7.36	12.61	22.94
Unemployed	19.8	9.7	14.4	5.4	4.7
In labour force	58.46	52.65	51.72	76.93	74.83
Not in labour force	41.54	47.35	48.28	23.07	25.17
Income $0–299	74.85	58.92	65.08	43.55	38.75
Income $300–699	21.58	33.43	23.97	37.58	35.53
Income $700–1499	3.56	7.22	9.74	18.12	22.39
Income $1500+	0	0.43	1.22	0.75	3.33
Same address in 1991	56.27	49.37	48.71	64.93	51.65
Different Address in 1991	43.73	50.63	51.29	35.07	48.35

Source: Australian Electoral Commission, Census of Australia, 1996.

One Nation scored its lowest vote in the most affluent electorates. In the most socioeconomically disadvantaged electorates One Nation polled strongly in rural and hinterland locations, and recorded an above average vote in outer urban seats, with the exception of Victoria and Tasmania. The relatively strong outer urban votes were in areas in which recent immigration had made less impact and where there were, in the measurement of economic disadvantage, marginally higher levels of workforce participation and higher rates of home ownership.

Lack of formal qualifications was found to be the strongest predictor of the One Nation vote, a variable closely correlated with low median family income, high number of children under the age of five, high unemployment, and location outside the main urban areas. In New South Wales and Victoria a relatively high number of indigenous residents was an important distinguishing characteristic of seats recording a high vote. Seats with a high One Nation vote were also characterised by the small number of immigrants from a non-English speaking background, especially a low number of residents born in Asian countries.

Sources

Note: All sources listed below can be found in the 'Select bibliography' on page 263.

INTRODUCTION

For an introduction to the concept of minority group rights see Will Kymlicka.

CHAPTER 1   THE RACIAL IMAGINATION

There is an extensive literature on the development of racial thought. Kenan Malik and Stephen Castles provide useful introductions. Etienne Balibar discusses the concept of 'racism without races'. Martin Barker produced one of the first analyses of the 'new racism' in which he discussed the ideas of Enoch Powell and other British politicians, as well as pseudo-scientific writings. The linguist Tuen van Dijk has written a number of works on contemporary nationalist rhetoric.

CHAPTER 2   CHANGE IN POST-WAR AUSTRALIA

There are a number of studies of post-war immigration and Aboriginal politics. For a general introduction see Andrew Markus' *Australian Race Relations*, as well as the works of David Hollingsworth and James Jupp. Robert Birrell has written extensively on immigration policy.

Statistical information is provided in publications of the Department of Immigration (which underwent a number of name changes in the period covered) and the Australian Bureau of Statistics. The Office of Multicultural Affairs published annual reports on access and equity policy. For the cost of multicultural programs, see the article by Neil Edwards. The most recent costing was provided by the National Multicultural Advisory Council in 1999 (http://www.immi.gov.au/nmac/append-h.htm, accessed 26 January 2000).

The Aboriginal and Torres Strait Islander Commission Website (http://www.atsic.gov.au/) includes a number of issues papers. See also the site of the Minister for Aboriginal and Torres Strait Islander Affairs (http://www.atsia.gov.au/) and the Council for Aboriginal Reconciliation (http:/www.austlii.edu.au/au/orgs/car/). For the 1980s' campaign against land rights, see Ronald Libby.

Paul Keating's leadership style is discussed by Michael Gordon. The source of the quotation dealing with the 'inability of whites to stop talking about blacks' is Colin Tatz (1979: p. 1). Jupp's characterisation of multiculturalism is from his article 'Tacking into the wind . . .', p. 31.

CHAPTER 3   THE NEW CONSERVATISM AND THE
NATURALNESS OF BIGOTRY

The periodical *Quadrant* is an important source for research into the origins of the New Right in Australia. See also the *IPA Review*. Published works include the volume edited by Ken Coghill and Paul Kelly's *End of Certainty*. Important newspaper and magazine articles were published in the *Bulletin*, 2 July 1985 (Tim Duncan), 10 December 1985 (Tim Duncan and Anthony McAdam); *National Times*, 19–25 August 1983 (Patricia Angly), 3–9 February 1984 (Alan Ramsey), 13–19 September 1985 (Marianne Carey and Tina Povis); *Sydney Morning Herald*, 2 March 1985 (Paul Sheehan), 23 November 1993 (Gerard Henderson); *Rydges*, July 1985 (Paul Coombes); *Australian*, 11–12 October 1986 (Charles DeLisle), 31 May 1993 (Frank Devine), 31 July–1 August 1993 (Gideon Haigh), 11–12 December 1993 (Matthew Ricketson).

The speeches and occasional writings of Morgan and Blainey can be difficult to source, especially as much of their activism predates the availability of newspaper files in searchable electronic format. The major sources for material utilised in the chapter are: Hugh Morgan, p. 50, *Journal of the Melbourne Chamber of Commerce*, April 1986, p. 13; p. 52, unpublished transcript of talk, 'Othello and the Duke: The nature of citizenship', *Australian Institute for Public Policy*, 27 May 1988; p. 58, *National Times*, 19–25 August 1983; p. 61, Ken Barker (ed.); p. 61 elaboration is taken from *Church and Nation*, 25 July 1984, p. 17; p. 66, 'Othello and the Duke'—a similar perspective on immigration was developed in his Earle Page Memorial Lecture, 28 November 1991, entitled 'Australia and the World: Immigration and its Consequences', in *Verbatim Report*, June 1992; p. 69, *IPA Review*, May–July 1988, p. 18; p. 70, *IPA Review*, May–July 1988, p. 17, *The Age*, 26 and 28 January 1985; p. 71, 'Othello and the Duke'; p. 72, 'Othello and the Duke', *Sydney Morning Herald*, 13 and 14 October 1993, *The Age*, 3 and 14 April 1994; p. 77, *Sydney Morning Herald*, 1 July 1993; p. 77, *Quadrant*, December 1993; p. 79, *The Age*, 28 July 1993, 12 June 1993; p. 81, transcript of opening address, RSL Victorian Branch, 78th Annual State Conference, 30 June 1993, see also *Verbatim Report*, July 1993.

Geoffrey Blainey: p. 63, *The Age*, 20 March 1984, *Warrnambool Standard*, 19 March 1984; p. 64, *The Age*, 12 June 1993; p.67, *Australian*, 11–12 October 1984, *The Age*, 17 May 1994; p. 69, *Australian*, 25 September 1988, *IPA Review*, Summer 1985–86, p. 15; *Quadrant*, July–August 1993, p. 11; p. 72, *Australian*, 5 September 1986, *Canberra Times*, 8 October 1987, 1986 speech quoted in the *Australian*, 31 May 1993; p. 73, *The Age*, 13 May 1993; p. 76, *The Age*, 26 June 1993, *Australian*, 9 November 1993; p. 76, *Sydney Morning Herald*, 23 November 1993; *The Age*, 12 June 1993; p. 79, *IPA Review*, Summer 1985/86, p. 15.

Important published collections include Ken Barker's edited work and a collection of Blainey's journalism in *Eye on Australia*. His Latham Memorial Lecture is in *Quadrant*, August 1993. For the 1984 immigration controversy, see Markus and Ricklefs. Tracey Aubin discusses Peter Costello.

CHAPTER 4   JOHN HOWARD, LEADER OF THE OPPOSITION, PRIME MINISTER

A number of transcripts of John Howard's 1995–96 speeches and interviews were provided by the prime minister's office, those more recent were obtained from the prime minister's Website. In August 2000, transcripts of speeches and interviews covering the period 1997–2000 were available online at http://www.pm.gov.au/news/speeches/main00.htm.

The quotation depicting the 'Menzies era as a golden age . . .' is from Gerard Henderson, *Howard Government*, p. 31; the objection to multiculturalism is from the same source, p. 27. Paul Kelly deals with the 1988 immigration controversy; the 1995 comment (p. 91) is in *ABM*, April 1995, p. 70. The 1992 call for a cut in immigration can be found in David Barnett, p. 601; the 1994 comments are in John Howard, 'Some thoughts on Liberal Party policy in the 1990s', *Quadrant*, July–August 1994; and the 1993 comments in David Barnett, p. 609 and *ABM*, July 1993. Barnett's comment on Howard's strategy on immigration (p. 94) is on p. 676 of his book and the views of Michael Barnard are quoted on p. 719. The Liberal Party staffer (p. 95) is in Scott Prasser and Graeme Starr (eds), p. 35; Robert Manne (p. 101) is quoted in *Two Nations*, p. 25; Jackie Huggins' observation (p. 106) is in Mary Kalantzis and Bill Cope, p. 322.

For Howard's 1996 election undertakings and subsequent actions, see Kalantzis and Cope in Phillip Adams (1997). See also Cope and Kalantzis, *A Place in the Sun*; Gray and Winter, *The Resurgence of Racism*.

CHAPTER 5   THE POLITICS OF PARANOIA

This chapter is based on the publications of right-wing organisations held by the State Library of Victoria and the National

Library of Australia, supplemented by ephemera in private collections. Several scholars have written on the far right in Australia, notably David Greason.

The analysis of the League of Rights is based largely on the League's publications, particularly *On Target*. Senator Boswell's speech is in Hansard, 27 April 1988. AAFI published newsletters and election publicity material and received some coverage in major daily newspapers, as did Australia First. The 'Grand Plan' was tabled in the House of Representatives on 28 October 1996 and was subsequently reprinted by the Australian League of Rights. The links between Campbell and Drane were explored by 'Background Briefing' on 21 July 1996 (a transcript posted on the ABC Website was accessed on 17 May 1999). The CEC was studied through its ephemeral publications and the national press. Perrett's maiden speech is in the Queensland Hansard, 30 August 1988. Laurie Oakes' article appears in the *Bulletin*, 27 September 1988, David Gearson's is in the periodical *Without Prejudice*, November 1992. The discussion of the CAP and shooters groups draws on material in the periodicals *Lock, Stock and Barrel*, *Wake Up Australia*, *Fight* and *Strategy*.

Important articles on extremist groups were published in *The Age*, 23 March 1991 (Sheena MacLean), 29 May 1993 (Rosemary West), 22 June 1993 (Gerard Henderson), 5 and 19 May 1996 (Murray Mottram), 11 June 1996 (James Button), 30 August 1998 (Mark Forbes), 27 June 1998 (Farah Farouque); *Australian*, 26 July 1993 (Madonna King), 19 January 1996 (Colleen Egan and Jamie Walker), 3 May 1997 (Mike Steketee), 22–23 November 1993 (Matt Price); *Australian Financial Review*, 14 June 1996 (Geoffrey Barker); *Bulletin*, 22 May 1984 (Tim Duncan), 27 September 1988 (Laurie Oates), 4 April 1989 (Lyndall Crisp), 23 May 1995 (Greg Roberts); *Sunday Herald Sun*, 14 July 1996 (Gerard McManus); *Sydney Morning Herald*, 4 January 1992 (Mark Skulley), 12 September 1998 (Jon Casimir).

CHAPTER 6   PAULINE HANSON'S ONE NATION

On Queensland populism and politics, see Allan Patience, Hugh
Lunn and Henry Reynolds. Charles Porter wrote the 'Foreword'
to the book by 'Peter B. English'. See also articles in the *Sydney
Morning Herald*, 12 and 28 February 1987.

There have been several attempts to give an inside view of the
workings of One Nation. The two most significant to date are
Margo Kingston's excellent *Off the Rails* and John Pasquarelli's *The
Pauline Hanson Story*. The biography by Helen Dodd is of limited
use. There have also been accounts by one-time party faithful,
including Bruce Whiteside and Barbara Hazelton.

An excellent collection of political commentaries can be found
in *Two Nations*, edited by Nadine Davidoff. See also Geoffrey
Gray and Christine Winter (eds), *The Resurgence of Racism*.

The tracking of One Nation's history is made easier by the
availability of Melbourne's *Age*, the *Sydney Morning Herald* and
the *Australian Financial Review* on searchable CD-Rom for the
period 1996–99. The more important articles include: *The Age*,
30 November 1996 (David Leser), 6 June 1998 (Tony Wright),
4 July 1998 (Michael Gordon, Greg Roberts), 12 September 1998
(Marian Wilkinson), 13 September 1998 (Mark Forbes), 7 February 1999 (Alex Mitchell), 27 February 1999 (Greg Roberts), 18
December 1999 (Greg Roberts); *Australian*, 31 May–1 June 1997
(Brian Woodley), 1 July 1998 (Nicholas Rothwell, Leisa Scott,
Natasha Bita), 4–5 July 1998 (Leisa Scott, Nicholas Rothwell),
18–19 December 1999 (Leisa Scott), *Australian Financial Review*,
5 October 1998 (Geoffrey Barker); *Sydney Morning Herald*,
26 September 1997 (Greg Roberts), 15 December 1997 (Greg
Roberts), 12 February 1999 (Murray Mottram and Greg Roberts).

The secret manoeuvrings which preceded Ettridge and Oldfield
joining the party, and the structure of the party, are discussed in
The Age, 12 September 1998, see also Max Spry. For character-
isations of Oldfield, see *The Age*, 12 September 1998, *Australian*

Financial Review, 12 August 1998 (Peter Dawkins) and Margo Kingston. For a discussion of the party's links with the far right, see *The Age*, 21 June 1998 (David Greason and Michael Kapel), *Australian*, 7 September 1998 (Glenn Milne).

For much of the period 1997–99, One Nation had an excellent Website containing press releases, the full text of policy documents and coverage of party conferences. Bruce Whiteside's article 'The Pauline Hanson Support Movement' was accessed on this site on 25 May 1999 (http://www.gwb.com.au/gwb/news/onenation/phsup.htm), as was a report of Hanson's speech at the Queensland state conference in which she characterised democracy as mob rule (also reported in the *Courier Mail*, 30 November 1998). Part of this site, maintained by Global Web Builders, was still accessible in August 2000 (see http://www.gwb.com.au/gwb/hanson.html).

CHAPTER 7   INTERPRETATIONS

For an introduction to interpretations of the rise of racial politics and One Nation, see Nadine Davidoff (ed.), part three of the collection of the writings of Robert Manne, Geoffrey Gray and Christine Winter (eds) and Kenan Malik.

APPENDIX

The *Australian* Electoral Commission has electoral returns and a detailed atlas for each electoral division on its Website (http://www.aec.gov.au). Gerard Newman and Andrew Kopras of the Parliamentary Library's Statistics Group compiled 'Socio-economic Indexes for Electoral Divisions', Parliament of Australia, *Current Issues Briefs*, 4, 1998–99 (http://www.APH.GOV.AU/library/pubs/cib/1998-99cib04.htm). The Electoral Commission of Queensland published Statistical Profiles: *Queensland State Electoral Districts* (1998).

Select Bibliography

Aubin, Tracey (1999) *Peter Costello: A Biography*, Sydney: HarperCollins

Balibar, Etienne (1991) 'Is there neo-racism?', in E. Balibar and I. Wallerstein (eds) *Race, Nation Class: Ambiguous Identities*, trans. C. Turner, London: Verso, p. 21

Barker, Ken (ed.) (1985) *The Land Rights Debate: Selected Documents*: Institute of Public Affairs

Barker, Martin (1981) *The New Racism*, London: Junction Books

Barnett, David (with Pru Goward) (1997) *John Howard, Prime Minister*, Ringwood: Viking

Betts, Katharine (1999) *The Great Divide: Immigration Politics in Australia*, Sydney: Duffy & Snellgrove

Birrell, Robert (1984) 'The social origins of Australia's immigration debate. A comparison with Canada's immigration policy', *Overland*, no. 97

—— (1990) *The Chains that Bind: Family Reunion Migration to Australia in the 1980s*, Canberra: Australian Government Publishing Service

—— (1997) *Immigration Reform in Australia: Coalition Government Proposals and Outcomes since March 1996*, Clayton: Centre for Population and Urban Research, Monash University

Blainey, Geoffrey (1984) *All for Australia*, Sydney: Methuen Haynes

—— (c.1991) *Eye on Australia*, Melbourne: Schwarz and Wilkinson

Campbell, Graeme and Uhlmann, Mark (1995) *Australia Betrayed*, Carlisle, WA: Foundation Press

Castles, Stephen (1996) 'The racisms of globalisation' in Ellie Vasta and Stephen Castles (eds) *The Teeth are Smiling: The Persistence of Racism in Multicultural Australia*, Sydney: Allen & Unwin

Coghill, Ken (ed.) (1987) *The New Right's Australian Fantasy*, Melbourne: McPhee Gribble

Cope, Bill and Kalantzis, Mary (2000) *A Place in the Sun: Recreating the Australian Way of Life*, Sydney: HarperCollins

Davidoff, Nadine (ed.) (1998) *Two Nations: The Causes and Effects of the Rise of the One Nation Party in Australia*, Melbourne: Bookman Press

Dodd, Helen (1997) *Pauline: The Hanson Phenomenon*, Moorooka, Qld: Boolarong

Edwards, Neil (1992) 'The economics of multicultural Australia', *Australian Journal of Public Administration*, vol. 51, no. 2, June

English, Peter B. (1985) *Land Rights and Birth-Rights: The Great Australian Hoax*, Bullsbrook: Veritas

Goot, Murray and Rowse, Tim (1991) 'The backlash hypothesis and the land rights option', *Australian Aboriginal Studies*, no. 1

—— (eds) (1994) *Make a Better Offer: The Politics of Mabo*, Sydney: Pluto Press

Gordon, Michael (1993) *A Question of Leadership*, St Lucia: University of Queensland Press

Gott, Murray (1998) 'Hanson's heartland: who's for One Nation and why', in Nadine Davidoff (ed.)

Gray, Geoffrey and Winter, Christine (eds) (1997) *The Resurgence of Racism*, Clayton: Monash Publications in History

Greason, David (1992) 'Lyndon LaRouche down under', *Without Prejudice*, no. 5

—— (1997) 'Australia's racist far-Right', in Chris Cunneen et al. (eds) *Faces of Hate: Hate Crime in Australia*, Sydney: Federation Press

Hanson, Pauline (1997) *The Truth: On Asian Immigration, the Aboriginal Question, the Gun Debate and the Future of Australia*, Parkholme, SA: St George Publications

Henderson, Gerard (1994) *Menzies' Child: The Liberal Party of Australia*, 1944–1994, Sydney: Allen & Unwin

—— (1995) *A Howard Government? Inside the Coalition*, Sydney: HarperCollins

Hofstadter, Richard (1965) *The Paranoid Style in American Politics*, Cambridge, Mass.: Harvard University Press

Hollingsworth, David (1998) *Race and Racism in Australia*, second edn, Katoomba: Social Science Press

Jupp, James (1992) 'Immigrant settlement policy in Australia', in Gary Freeman and James Jupp (eds), *Nations of Immigrants*, Melbourne: ——

—— (1997) 'Tacking into the wind: immigration and multicultural policy in the 1990s', *Journal of Australian Studies*, no. 53

—— (1998) *Immigration*, second edn, Melbourne: Oxford University Press

Kalantzis, Mary and Cope, Bill (1997) 'An opportunity to change the culture', in Phillip Adams (ed.) *The Retreat from Tolerance: A Snapshot of Australian Society*, Sydney: ABC Books, p. 68

Kelly, Paul (1992) *The End of Certainty*, Sydney: Allen & Unwin

Kymlicka, Will (1995) *Multicultural Citizenship: A Liberal Theory of Minority Rights*, New York: Oxford University Press

Libby, Ronald (1989) *Hawke's Law: The Politics of Mining and Aboriginal Land Rights in Australia*, Nedlands, WA: University of Western Australia Press

Lunn, Hugh (1984) *Johannes Bjelke-Petersen: A Political Biography*, second edn, St Lucia: University of Queensland Press

Kingston, Margo (1999) *Off the Rails: The Pauline Hanson Trip*, Sydney: Allen & Unwin

Malik, Kenan (1996) *The Meaning of Race: Race, History and Culture in Western Society*, New York: New York University Press

Manne, Robert (1998) *The Way We Live Now: The Controversies of the Nineties*, Melbourne: Text Publishing

Markus, Andrew and Ricklefs, Merle (eds) (1995) *Surrender Australia?*, Sydney: Allen & Unwin

Pasquarelli, John (1998) *The Pauline Hanson Story by the Man Who Knows*, Sydney: New Holland

Patience, Alan (ed.) (1985) *The Bjelke-Petersen Premiership*, Melbourne: Longman Cheshire

Prasser, Scott and Starr, Graeme (eds) (1997) *Policy and Change: The Howard Mandate*, Sydney: Hale & Iremonger

Reynolds, Henry (1989) 'More scandal in Queensland', *Australian Society*, February

Rossiter, Clinton (1955) *Conservatism in America*, New York: Knopf

Spry, Max (1999–2000) 'Two's company, three's One Nation?', *Current Affairs Brief 4*, Parliamentary Library, Parliament of Australia (posted on the Library's Website)

Tatz, Colin (1979) *Race Politics in Australia*, Armidale: University of New England

van Dijk, Teun (c.1993) *Elite Discourse and Racism*, Newbury Park, CA: Sage Publications

Index

Aboriginal Affairs, Department of   21, 36, 132

Aboriginal and Torres Strait Islanders, government policies   11–13, 18–20, 21–3, 33–6, 39, 41–4

Aboriginal and Torres Strait Islander Commission (ATSIC)   36, 41, 179, 230

Aboriginal children, removal of   36, 110, 136, 170

Aboriginal land rights   xi–xiii, 21–3, 34–6, 38–9, 42–4, 61, 67–8, 73–5, 105, 130, 141, 144, 170, 179, 210–12

Aboriginal Legal Service   21

Aboriginal Medical Service   21

Aboriginal society, depictions of   61–2, 71, 76–8, 80, 168

Aborigines and Torres Strait Islanders   11

Abbott, Tony   162, 221

Acton, Larry   43

Adult Migrant English Program   30, 41

AGB-McNair opinion poll   211

All for Australia   65–6, 70

American National Rifle Association   136

Anti-discrimination Board   171

Asia, immigration from Asian countries   16, 25, 28, 32, 33, 37, 39, 45, 63, 71, 88–91, 100–1, 105, 117–18, 122–3, 191, 207–9, 226–7

Asian Studies Association of Australia   123

assimilation   ix, 13–6, 19, 73, 145

Australia, betrayal of   71–2, 117–18, 121–3, 129, 133–6, 138, 140–2, 164, 166–7, 171

Australia Betrayed   121

Australia Council   27

Australia First Party   124–5

Australia, history, conceptions of   62, 69–71, 93, 95–6, 104, 107–8, 192 *see also* 'Black Armband' view of history

Australia, threat to unity   72, 79, 81, 122, 166–7 *see also* one nation, concept of

Australian Broadcasting Commission (ABC)   28, 69, 205

Australian Capital Territory   35, 127, 233

Australian Ethnic Affairs Council   26

Australian Heritage Society   120

Australian Institute for Public Policy   54

Australian Institute of Mining and Metallurgy   73

Australian Institute of Multicultural Affairs   27, 28

Australian League of Rights   116–20, 125, 127, 136, 173, 176, 185

Australian Lecture Foundation   54, 55, 57

Australian Mining Industry Council   34, 57, 60

Australian Reform Party   124

Australian Right to Bear Arms   137

'Australian way of life'   12, 14, 25, 69

Australians Against Further Immigration (AAFI)   116, 120–2, 124, 177, 214, 230–2

Australians United for Survival and Individual (AUSI) Freedom Scouts   139–40, 176

Austria   199

Babb, Jeff   176

Barker, Geoffrey   158

Barnard, Michael   68, 94

Barnett, David   83

Beazley, Kim   41, 101, 159, 174

Bendigo   127, 169

Betts, Katherine   207, 228

Bjelke-Petersen, Johannes   126, 144–6, 177, 215–17, 232

Black, Harry   189

'Black Armband' view of history   70, 93

Blainey, Geoffrey   49, 57, 62–73, 76, 79, 80, 82, 86–7, 93, 103, 105, 147, 220

Blainey: Eye on Australia   66

Bogle, Brendan   176

Borbidge Government   128

Bosch, Henry   78

Boswell, Ron   119–20, 125

Brennan, Justice   76

Brett, Judith   200

Briggs, Ted   176

Brisbane   128, 145, 148, 172

Bryant, Martin   138

Bureau of Immigration, Multicultural and Population Research   29, 40, 98

Burke Labor Government   34

Butler, Eric   117, 119, 124–5, 127, 176

Butler, Jacqui   128, 150

Calwell, Arthur   17, 146
Campbell, Graeme   ix, 68, 116–17, 120–2, 124–5, 136, 147, 153–4, 160, 199, 223
Campbell, Michelle   154
Canada   16, 38, 74
Canberra   64, 129, 138, 145, 155, 162, 174, 205
Caribbean   8
Carr, Bob   159
Casey, Ron   68
Centre 2000   54
Centre for Independent Studies   54, 57
Centre for Policy Studies   54
Chamber of Mines, Western Australia   59, 73
Chifley, Ben   84
Christian Institute for Individual Freedom   120
Christianity, beliefs, theology   61, 69, 117–18
Citizens Electoral Councils   125–30, 185, 234
citizens initiated referendum   118, 124–31, 142, 185, 231, 234
City–Country Alliance   184–5
Cobar   139
Cold War   ix, 7, 97, 202–3
Coleman, Peter   56, 68
Collingwood, Bevan   189
Committee on the Elimination of Racial Discrimination   109
Commonwealth Arbitration Court   12, 20
communism   117–18, 135, 139, 203
Confederate Action Party   130–6, 176, 193, 229–31, 234–5
Conservative Speakers Clubs   120–21
Costello, Peter   75, 159, 173, 223
Council for a Free Australia   120
Council for Aboriginal Reconciliation   36, 106, 108, 111–12, 209
Court, Richard   75
Crossroads Conference   57, 75
Czechoslovakia   33

Dalgleish, David   189
Devine, Frank   65, 68
Dodd, Helen   188
Doring, Bob   137–8
Douglas, C.H.   116
Downer, Alexander   82, 90, 94, 111, 116, 223
Drane, Ted   124, 136, 147
Duncan, Tim   117
Dunstan, Don   17

elections: federal (1996) 64–8, 150–2, 240–57 *passim*; federal (1998) 173, 175, 184; New South Wales (1999) 241–5, 246; Queensland (to 1998) 131–2, 217–18, 231–2; Queensland (1998)   147, 169–73, 184, 193,
217–18, 224, 233–8, 248; Victoria (1999) 242
End of Certainty   84
equality, equal rights, conceptions of   x–xiii, 80, 151–3, 156, 180, 191, 194–5, 209–11
Ethnic Affairs Commissions   31
Ettridge, David   162–3, 168–9, 173–4, 186–90
Europe, southern   14, 17
Evans, Ray   57, 58, 60

Fabian Society   117, 126, 139
Federation of Ethnic Communities' Councils   31
Feldman, Bill   189
Feulner, Edwin J.   55
Fightback   95
Firearm Owners Association of Australia   137–9
Fischer, Tim   60, 76
Fitzgerald, Dr Stephen   33
Fitzgerald Royal Commission   144
France   199
Fraser, Malcolm, Fraser government   22, 31, 54, 82–3, 223
Furphy, Joseph ('Tom Collins')   123

Galbally Report   26–8
Germany   199, 219
Goebbels, Joseph   163
Gorton, John   17, 77
Grace, Peter   55
Grassby, Al   20, 25, 72
Grattan, Michelle   54, 101, 174, 201, 221
Grearson, David   129–30
Greek community   31, 153
Greens, the (party)   233
Guilt, 'guilt industry'   69–70, 73, 77, 86, 170
gun control   132, 134, 136–40, 166, 171, 229
Gympie   137–8

Hanson, Pauline   ix, 60, 65, 82, 99–101, 104, 113, 124–5, 131, 145–95 *passim*, 199, 204–6, 212, 215–16, 219–22, 225, 239, 245, 253
Hansonism   xv, 83, 199
Harradine, Senator Brian   43, 44, 224
Hassell, Bill   75
Hawke, Bob, Hawke government,   28, 37, 84, 89, 218–19, 223
Hazelton, Barbara   155, 187
Henderson, Gerard   85, 91, 99–100, 168, 221
Heritage Foundation of the United States   55
Herron, John   110

Hewson, John 82, 90–1, 95, 102, 223
High Court of Australia 22, 38–9, 42, 44, 63, 73–6, 108, 135–6, 194
Hill, Heather 187, 189
Hitler, Adolf 9, 117, 134
Hobbes, Thomas 77
Hofstadter, Richard 114–15
Holding, Clyde 34, 60
Holt, Harold 15, 17
Howard, Colin 74
Howard, John, Howard government, ix, xv, 39–45, 54, 82–112 *passim*, 137, 159, 168, 170, 173, 179, 199, 200, 204, 219, 220–5, 244
H.R. Nicholls Society 54, 57
Huggins, Jackie 106
Human Rights and Equal Opportunity Commission 36
Hurford, Chris 33
Hyde, John 54

immigration policy 11–18, 23–7, 28, 31–3, 40–1, 45, 105
Indonesia 129, 135, 139
Institute for Economic Democracy 120
Institute of Legislative Action 136
Institute of Public Affairs 54–5, 57
International Jew 117
International Year of Indigenous People 37
Internet 115–16
Inverell forum 121
Ipswich 148, 150, 187
Ireland 12
Israel 11
Italian community 31, 153

Japan 134
James, Peter 187
Jewish community 31
Jones, Alan 68, 101
Jupp, James 29

Kaiser, Mike 147
Keating, Paul, Keating government 37–8, 44, 73–4, 81–2, 84, 92–5, 97, 99–102, 121, 159, 200, 202, 204, 218–19, 223
Kelly, Paul 84–5, 112, 168, 173, 220
Kennedy, John F. 138
Kennett, Jeff 159
Kerr, Duncan 102
Keynes, John Maynard 55
Kingston, John 189
Kingston, Margo 161, 172, 174–5, 179, 181
Kissinger, Henry 130

Knuth, Jeff 138, 189
Koehler, John 126
Kosovo 109
Ku Klux Klan 10

La Rouche 129–30, 176
Ladies in Line Against Communism (Lilac League) 120
Lang, Jack 144
Langton, Marcia 108
Latham Memorial Lecture 55
Lawson, Henry 123
Lee, Jeremy 118, 133
Legislation (Cwth): *Family Law Act* (1975) 157; *Immigration Restriction Act* (1901) 18, 39; *Land Fund and Indigenous Land Corporation Act* (1995) 39; *Native Title Act* (1993) 39, 109; *Native Title Amendment Act* (1998) 43, 108, 179, 180, 225; *Racial Discrimination Act* (1975) ix, 22, 73
Leviathan 77
Logos Foundation 118
Longreach 43, 179, 195

Mabo decision xii, 38, 43–4, 63, 72–81, 166, 207, 210, 212
Mackay 176
Mackay, Hugh 200, 202
Mackellar, Michael 26, 90
Malaysia 134
Manly 162, 187, 189
Manne, Robert 101, 168, 199, 202
Mansell, Michael 108
Maralinga 34
Maryborough 132, 189
Marx, Karl 179
McAdam, Anthony 54, 57–8, 85
McCarthyism 92, 97, 102
McCormack, Denis 121–5, 154, 165, 231
McDonald, Geoff 118, 135
McGuinness, Padraic 68, 218
McKell, William 15
McLachlan, Ian 79
McNiven, Ian 137, 139
McPhee, Ian 90
Melbourne 45, 54, 94, 110, 121, 129, 145, 208, 215
Menzies, Robert xv, 17–18, 20, 83–4, 96–8, 146, 217
Middle East 17, 32, 39
Migrant Access Project Scheme 30
Migrant Resource Centres 27
Morgan, Hugh 38, 49–50, 52, 57–62, 66–77 *passim*, 79, 81–2, 86, 103, 170, 220
Morgan Gallup Poll 210–11, 214, 216

Morris, Desmond 8
Morris, Grahame 246
Multicultural Education Program 28
multiculturalism ix, x, 26–30, 40–1, 72, 87, 100, 104, 121–2, 141, 147, 157, 166, 171, 177, 182–3, 193–4
Multilateral Agreement on Investment 170
Murphy, Ian 139
Muslim religion 18

Naked Ape, The 8
National Aboriginal Consultative Council 22
National Action 156
National Farmers Federation 55
National Front, France 191
National Native Title Tribunal 39
native title *see* Aboriginal land rights
Nazi era 6, 7, 67, 134, 141, 156, 164, 166
Nelson, Shaun 189
new class 53, 56–7, 97, 166–7
New Right xiv, 49–54, 56, 58, 67, 70, 83, 92, 154–5, 218–20
New South Wales 20, 22–3, 29, 34–5, 45, 128, 139, 144–5, 159, 180, 184, 188, 215, 230–3, 234, 238–46, 247, 250–2, 255
'New World Order' *see* 'One World Government'
New Zealand 16, 38
newspapers, magazines, mainstream 63, 66, 68;
    The Age 98; *Australian* 152, 173, 212; *Australian Financial Review* 77, 98, 147; *Bulletin* 54, 89; *Toowoomba Chronicle* 181; *Quadrant* 56, 68; *Queensland Times* 150, 181; *Sydney Morning Herald* 57, 74, 77, 98, 161; *Time Australia* 207; *Washington Post* 97–8;
fringe;
    Exposure 138; *Fight* 133, 193; *Heritage* 120; *Intelligence Survey* 120; *Lock, Stock and Barrel* 138, 176; *On Target* 120, 125; *National Interest* 133; *New Citizen* 120; *New Times* 120; *Strategy* 138, 169, 206; *Wake Up, Australia* 133, 206
Newspoll 209, 210, 212
Northern Territory 21–2, 34–5, 77, 109–11
Nossal, Gustav 112

Oakes, Laurie 89, 112, 128–9, 181
Office of Multicultural Affairs 29, 30, 40, 98
Oldfield, David 60, 161–4, 169–71, 173–5, 179–81, 186–90, 195, 205, 223, 225, 241
One Australia Movement 120
one nation, concept of, 80–1, 86–7, 104, 156

One Nation Party *see* Pauline Hanson's One Nation Party
'One World Government' 118–19, 126, 133, 138–9, 141, 166–7, 169, 171, 205
Organisation of Petroleum Producing Countries (OPEC), 23
Owen, Rod 137, 176
Owen, Ron 138

Paff, Jack 189
Pakistan 8
Papua New Guinea 153
Paranoid Style in American Politics, The 114–15
Pasquarelli, John 147, 153–60, 162, 187, 191, 223
Paterson, Andrew 'Banjo' 123
Pauline Hanson Support Movement 166, 188
Pauline Hanson: The Truth 165–9, 191, 193
Pauline Hanson's One Nation Party 113, 133, 138; budget statement181–3; constitution 188–9; electoral support 172–3, 184–5, 204–6, 215–16, 218–19, 224, 230–55 *passim*; far right influence within 176, 188; governance of 162, 185–9; leadership 172, 174–6, 178, 180, 185–6, 225; members of parliament 185, 188–9; policies 165, 170–1, 175–9, 182–4, 195, 229–31; party registration 186; preferencing, by other parties 172–3, 224; relations with media 180–2; resignations from 176, 187–90
Peacock, Andrew 54, 82, 85, 90
Pearson, Noel 44
Perkins, Charles 108
Perrett, Trevor 126, 128, 234
Perron, Marshall 77
Perth x, 54, 180
Pitjantjatjara 34
Pitt, Tony 131–6, 193, 234
Podhoretz, Norman 55
political correctness 97–9, 100–3, 154, 166
populism xv, 143–5, 215, 217
Port Arthur 137–8
Porter, Charles 144
Powell, Enoch 8
Pratt, Dorothy 189
Prenzler, Peter 189
Protocols of the Elders of Zion, The 117
Provis, Ross 139
public opinion polls xviii, 17, 201, 206–18

Queensland ix, 20–3, 35, 43–5, 100, 104–5, 120, 126, 128–30, 137–8, 144–8, 150–2, 161, 164, 169–73, 175–6, 181, 184, 188–9, 205, 215–18, 220, 228–9, 231–9, 239–55 *passim*

Queensland Immigration Control
  Association   135

race   xiv, 4, 122, 169
racial discrimination   xi, xiii, 12, 19, 23, 37,
  72, 100, 153, 156
racism, racist   3–10, 91, 100, 102, 104, 122,
  157, 164, 166, 190–5
Reagan, Ronald   51, 55
Reclaim Australia, Reduce Immigration   232
reconciliation   36–7, 106–8, 111–12, 124, 170
Red Over Black   118, 135
referendum (1967)   20–1
refugee program   109–10, 132, 177, 229
refugees, Indo-Chinese   24
Rehame   158–9
Returned Servicemen's League   31, 68, 79
Reynolds, Henry   145, 205
Rossiter, Clinton   53
Royal Commissions into Aboriginal Deaths in
  Custody   36
Ruddock, Philip   90, 109–10
Ruxton, Bruce   68, 147–54

Saulwick opinion poll   211
Sawyer, Peter   128–9
Scruton, Roger   55, 58, 70
Shakespeare, William   67
Sheehan, Paul   57
Sinclair, Ian   89
Snedden, Bill   17
South Africa   7, 10, 17, 89
South Australia   20, 22, 34–5, 45, 165, 180,
  215, 231–2, 239, 246, 254
Soviet Union   7, 33, 202–3
Special Broadcasting Service   27–30, 41
Spencer, Len   225
Spencer, Robyn   121, 177, 225, 233
Sporting Shooters Association of Australia   136
Stanbrook, Ivor   8
Stevenson, Dennis   127
'Stolen Generation' *see* Aboriginal children,
  removal of
Stone, John   57, 68, 75, 89–90, 147, 153–4
Strong, James   57, 59
Sydney   x, 31, 36, 45, 54, 84, 112, 145, 180,
  182

Tasmania   23, 34–5, 43, 137, 180, 238, 251,
  255

Ted Drane's Australian Reform party
Thatcher, Margaret   51
Tickner, Robert   151
Tingle, John   137
Thomas, David   164, 187
Toowoomba   120–1
Trewartha, Paul   187
Turkey   18
Turner, Jeff   189
Tyranny of Distance, The   66

United Graziers Association   43
United Kingdom   ix, 7–8, 12, 14–15, 17, 31,
  37, 51, 54–5, 78, 199
United Nations   6, 16, 55, 108–11, 117–18,
  132, 158, 166, 169–71
United Nations Educational, Scientific and
  Cultural Organisation (UNESCO)   6, 56
United States of America   7, 16, 38, 51, 54–5,
  89, 122, 130, 136, 138–9

Veliz, Claudio   58
Victoria   20, 23, 29, 34–5, 45, 116, 118, 121,
  145, 153, 180, 205, 233–4, 240–1, 245,
  248, 253–4, 257
Voters Veto campaign   126–7

Wake Up Australia   128, 150, 158
Walsh, Peter   147
Waik, McKenzie   115
Weishaupt, Adam   139
Western Australia   ix, 20, 22, 34–5, 45, 54,
  59, 60, 75, 109, 180, 215, 234, 238–9, 241,
  245–7
Western Australian Mining Industry
  Council   34
'White Australia' Policy   ix, 18, 24, 31, 89,
  157
Whiteside, Bruce   131, 188
Whitlam, Gough   17, 20, 21, 37, 68, 82, 223
Whitlam Government   21–3, 26
Wik decision   xii, 42–4, 108, 166
Wilkinson, Marian   164
Williams, Daryl   111
Women Who Want To Be Women   150

Yugoslav community   31
Yugoslavia   31

Zemanek, Stan   68, 105